# 388th Anthology Vol. I

# 388th Anthology Vol. I
## Tales of the 388th Bombardment Group (H) 1942–45

*Compiled and Edited by*
*Janet Pack and Richard Singer*

Writers Club Press
San Jose New York Lincoln Shanghai

388th Anthology Vol. I
Tales of the 388th Bombardment Group (H) 1942–45

Writers Club Press
an imprint of iUniverse, Inc.

For information address:
iUniverse, Inc.
5220 S. 16th St., Suite 200
Lincoln, NE 68512
www.iuniverse.com

ISBN: 0-595-19551-2

Printed in the United States of America

*For Our Dads*

# CONTENTS

# FOREWORD

We were a fortunate group of young men, hardly dry behind the ears, to have as our Commander and leader Col. Bill David. Bill has passed on now, but still lives in my memory along with other men—many of whom made the ultimate sacrifice.

Lt. Col. Ben McLaughlin, our first Ground Executive, was mainly responsible for making the base one of the best in the European Theater of Operations. We had our own dry cleaning plant with 24-hour service, an Officers' Club, an NCO club, an Airmen's Club, a movie theater and a fully-equipped gym. Lt. Col. Charley Lohnes, Ben's successor, carried on traditions that had been established.

Col. Gil Goodman deserves special mention. He held several key positions and was outstanding in each one, in addition to flying 33 war missions.

Lt. Col. Andy Chaffin of Group Ops flew 29 missions and sometimes described the recognition flares as "Yaller, Yaller" in the pre-mission briefings.

I regret that space does on allow me to mention the many officers and airmen who will always live in my memory. Suffice it to say, "They came, they saw—and they conquered."

Chester C. Cox  
Brig. Gen., USAF (Ret)

# INTRODUCTION

It was in February, 1943, that the newly-activated 388th Bombardment Group (H) was assigned to the 8th Air Force, and its home for the next two years would be Station 136, located at Knettishall in East Anglia, England.

On June 23, 28-year-old Col. William B. David took official command of Station 136, built originally for the RAF. That same day, 17 Flying Fortresses touched down. They would be the first of many. The whole of the ground echelon did not arrive until July 8, and for months they lived in tents while housing was constructed.

On July 17, with Col. David in the lead plane, the 388th departed for its first mission—Amsterdam. It was the first of 306 combat missions the group would carry out.

Over the next two years, 6,000 men saw duty at Station 136. They were commanders, clerks, doctors and firefighters. They were armorers and mechanics; men who could return heavily-damaged planes to combat status within 24 hours. They were cooks and anti-aircraft gunners.

And they were the combat crews; the fliers of the 560th, 561st, 562nd and 563rd Squadrons. Among these, 538 died in action; 742 were taken prisoner. Today, two men are still listed as missing.

In all, the 388th dropped 36,974,200 pounds of bombs onto enemy targets—ports, marshalling yards, oil refineries and weapons factories. Its planes hammered Berlin and its crews participated in three missions carrying 2,000 former POWs home to their native lands of France and Belgium.

Its job in England accomplished, the 388th packed up shop. On June 9, 1945, the first Fortresses left for the States. The last plane departed on July 5, carrying Lt. Col. Chester Cox, Col. David's successor. Ground echelon stayed behind awhile longer, and went home by ship.

Back in the States, crewmen of the 388th were given personal leave before reporting to Sioux Falls, South Dakota, the marshalling point for redeployment to the Pacific. But when Japan surrendered on August 14, the group stood down. At the close of war, some men of the 388th continued their military careers, but most returned to civilian life.

Today, the 388th BG (H) Association—formed in 1950 by the veterans themselves—is still an active group. In July, 1992, more than 225 veterans, together with their wives, their children and their grandchildren, traveled to the 388th Memorial at Knettishall to commemorate the efforts of the 8th Air Force and pay tribute to their fallen comrades. Veterans and their families still return every year to walk the grounds where Station 136 once stood, and to visit the museum and memorial that honor their memory.

These are their stories, in their words.

# Prologue: An Historic Perspective

By Oreste Leto, Jr., navigator
Sears' crew, 560th Squadron

*In recent years, Oreste Leto and members of his former crew have often spoken to groups of high school students, explaining the role of the Army Air Corps in World War II, and their individual roles within the Corps, flying a B-17 with the 388th Bombardment Group (H) from Knettishall Air Base in England. The following narration is excerpted from his presentation.*

First, let me put all of this into perspective. What you see here are a bunch of old men. In the era of which we are speaking, we were all young boys out to do all we could do to help our country in time of need. Here's a picture of me back in 1945. You wonder how a fellow can deteriorate in just 55 years! The world then was in a lot worse shape than today. Few, including most of our leaders, knew what was happening inside Japan and Germany; neither were we aware of their exploiting their neighbors such as Poland, Russia, the Low Countries, China and France, or what was happening in the horrible concentration camps within. Therefore, we started in 1939 to slowly get ready, first manufacturing arms and then starting to draft men to use these arms—first to protect ourselves and then help the free world. Of course, on Dec. 7, 1941, we were plunged into total war with the Japanese attack on Pearl Harbor and, a few days later, when the Germans declared war on us. Let me tell you about my part in this.

I volunteered for the Air Force in July 1942, at the age of 20. I had graduated from West Chester University with a degree in math. Although wishing to be a fighter pilot, as did most young boys of that era, I ended up as a navigator in a B-17 Flying Fortress after a year and half of rigorous and intense training in mathematics, map drawing and reading, Morse Code, flying, aircraft recognition, much physical training, use of all types

1

of instruments including celestial navigation and, of course, much gunnery with the .50-caliber machine gun. I was then (with a lot rope-pulling) assigned to a crew with my first cousin, Louis Leto, who, like me, was raised and educated in Kennett Square, Pennsylvania. We picked up our new B-17G, # 43338-398, at Savannah, with maps and a bunch of other stuff, and were told to go to England via Goose Bay, Labrador.

When we were over the Atlantic opposite Norfolk, Virginia on the way to Goose Bay, I got the bright idea that it would be nice to buzz the old town and drop a note to my folks on the farm and tell them where we were headed. We started our let-down through the clouds from 10,000 feet and broke the clouds at 1,000 feet at Plankinton's Quarry, less than a quarter-mile from the farm. Of course, we had to buzz the town clock a couple of times and I did drop a note to my folks, who by this time were quite aroused. In fact, on the last pass over the old farm house, we were so low that the vibration from the engines knocked some plates off of the mantle in the living room.

After staying at Goose Bay for a couple of days waiting for the weather to clear over England, the Army decided to send us to Iceland to wait for the weather to break. This we did, flying over the ice caps of Greenland. After supper, they gave us a half of tank of gas and sent us on to Prestwick, Scotland. The weather over Prestwick was horrible and, not being used to such bad weather, we were informed that it was too bad to land; so they sent us down to Valley, Wales. When we got there they said the weather was worse in Wales, so they sent us back to Prestwick!

Prestwick told us to climb to 10,000 feet above the clouds and wait our turn as there were 10 planes ahead of us and they would let us use the radio beam and radar and they would assist us in finding the field. At this time we started to worry about our gas supply. I got another bright idea; this time to drop down over the Irish Sea where there were no hills and get under the 300-foot ceiling, then go between the hills around the airport up the Ayr River, which my maps showed went right by the Prestwick Airport.

No sooner had we broken out of the clouds at 300 feet than we passed over a British cargo ship which opened fire at us with 20mm guns. What we did not know was that we were now in a war zone and that any plane under 2,000 feet was considered hostile. We at once went back into the clouds and got away from there in a hurry, followed the river to the airport and finally landed after much fuss due to the bad weather.

Here, they took our nice new bomber away from us put us on a train to a bomber base in East Anglia. There, we were put in decent barracks to live; and then were put through some of the most intense training you could imagine to get us used to their weather and their strict ways of doing things.

For the most part we bombed factories, oil refineries, railroads; and a couple of times we tried to help the ground troops. In the latter, we were not very effective.

When I flew in combat we had escorts on most of our missions. Often, the German fighters would slip through and cause some damage, but our biggest trouble was anti-aircraft fire around most of our targets. I know of no one who didn't show fear at this stage of a mission. It was cold and very uncomfortable, with temperatures dropping as low as 70 degrees below zero, especially in the winter of 1944-45. Of course, when we got home to the base, we had barracks which kept out most of the cold and all of the wind. When I did not fly combat with my crew, I took new navigators up for their first training flights using the different instruments and trying to get them used to the different weather condition of the European Theater of Operations.

Would you like to hear how a typical day started for me?

If we were in any kind of lead position, the navigators and the bombardiers would go to pre-briefing, which was always six hours before take-off (that could be anywhere between 4 a.m. and noon). In this case, let's say take-off is 6 a.m.; therefore I would get up at midnight for pre-briefing. Here, the intelligence officer gives us the target to memorize, with pictures and routes in and out. This takes about two hours. Then we have breakfast and meet all of the officers who are going to fly. This takes, at a maximum, half-an-hour, and then we are loaded into trucks and taken to the briefing room. This is the room where they pull the curtain up and everybody either moans or cheers. Here are the targets, number of planes that are going, the formation, where we will assemble, what to expect in the way of enemy action and, last, the predicted weather. This takes about 45 minutes, after which the pilots and the engineers go out to the planes to check for gas and all mechanical things and go over the planes with the crew chiefs. The gunners go to gun shops and pick up all of the .50-caliber machine guns which, in the B-17G, numbered 12.

My two nose guns were always put in place by my tail gunner, while the bombardier's was put in by a waist gunner. The lower ball turret gunner always installed his own guns and the top turret guns were taken care of by the engineer. While they were doing all of this I would go to the navigators' briefing room and take Mercator projection maps and plot the course using the latest weather forecast. By this time, five hours had passed and we hustled to pick up our parachutes, Mae Wests, put on our heavy clothes and catch a truck out to our ships, which were scattered all over the field. It was by this time, about 15 minutes before start engines, that you met your full crew.

What determines whether you go or scrub the mission is the weather over the target and not the weather over the base.

You line up on the runway, take off at 20 to 30 second intervals and fly out in a straight line for a given time, then all climb to a given altitude and place and try to form up in our usual group of 39 planes. And, if any of you don't think that is not time consuming and hairy, think again—especially when you know that there are at least 1,200 other bombers up there with you, all circling, trying to form up. From here on *everything* is to be done with precision.

"Friendly coast out" is usually Control Point #1, and this point has to be met by 15 seconds either way to keep your proper spacing in the bomber stream. In other words, this is the place the groups of 39 airplanes merge into a line that is usually three minutes apart.

The next critical point is Control Point #2, which is usually the enemy coast, where the whole force assembles on its way to various targets. Be aware, the enemy is—with his radar—watching every move from the take-off, to assembly, to the joining points. And your route.

The next critical point is Control Point #3, where you are to meet your fighter escort. It is important to be at the right place at the right time, for the Germans with their radar can quickly direct their fighters to any unescorted group. Even late in the war, it was impossible to keep all of the bombers covered all the time; but remember we could, unless it was a massive attack, defend ourselves fairly well.

We tried to fly to the target in corridors that missed flak or anti-aircraft batteries even if it meant flying other than a direct route; but of course when you go into your target it is necessary to fly right through it and take your punishment in order to do your job of delivering your bombs where you are supposed to. That was my greatest fear in all of the flying, for you can't dig any fox holes up there and the metal on that airplane is so thin that you can drive a pencil through it. The bomb run is where everybody concentrates and tries his most—especially the bombardiers and the navigators.

After you drop your bombs, you are working for yourself and your buddies and not for Uncle Sam. This is the point enemy fighters like to pick up cripples from the flak; and we were instructed never to leave formation to help our buddies regardless, as that weakens the integrity of the formation, which could result in greater loss.

Now you are ready for the long ride home. You have to be on your feet for 12 to 14 hours and, at this altitude, it can be very tiring. If your ship has escaped damage and the weather is good, the last hour is especially pleasing and gratifying if you have hit your target and the losses were not too great.

On landing you take your airplane back to its hardstand, bring the log up to date, take your machine guns out, truck them to the gun shop, clean and oil them for the morrow. Then you go to debriefing where the Red Cross girls give you a cup of coffee and a doughnut—which you wolf down, for it is at least 15 hours since you had breakfast. The Flight Surgeon comes around while you are being debriefed and gives everybody two ounces of whisky to calm the boys' nerves. Being a non-drinker, I always passed mine to my buddies. From there to supper, and then to bed. For me it has been 18-plus hours since I was awakened—and tomorrow is another day.

I was home on leave on V-E Day.

In those days everyone was most gracious to all service men and women for their efforts in helping our nation in time of need. I'm very proud that I was able to help. Those were the roughest and most brutal years of my life.

But the most satisfying.

*The Sears' Crew: From left, top row, Robert E. Howe, bombardier; Bill Rohner, engineer; Charles Iffland, co-pilot; middle row, Robert Walters, tail gunner; Sidney W. Gearlloch, ball gunner; Charles F. Mahone, radio operator; bottom row, Lewis, waist gunner; Louis Leto, waist gunner; Rolland Sears, pilot; Oreste Leto, navigator.*

# And So It Was...

By Bob Seney, crew chief, 563rd Squadron

The date was December 7, 1941.

I woke up that Sunday morning thinking how lucky I was, reflecting back on my short time on this earth. I had the start of a good-looking future.

I was born March 28, 1921 in Modesto, California. Our small family seemed wonderful. Mom and Dad, Mammy (Mom's mother), and her husband "Dad" Johnson lived in a nice rented home. Dad worked on the M. & E. T. which was a short line railroad running between Modesto and Empire. When I was nine, we all moved to Tracy where Dad acquired a job with the Southern Pacific Railroad as a switchman. The town of Tracy was a railroad center and, as in every other town in the 1930s, we were just another family facing unemployment due to the Depression. We had nothing as Dad became unemployed when the railroad had to lay off many of its workers. I went through grade school and started into high school. My years in school were not really happy years, as we see with the young students of today. Never went to a dance, never dated a girl; sure as hell didn't make the honor roll.

In my senior year, Dad became very ill and was sent to the Southern Pacific Hospital in San Francisco, where he passed away April 29, 1939. I graduated from high school in June of 1939 with no plans for the future and frightened of what I was to do. Mom moved us to Stockton and entered me in a business college. A good friend of the family, Tom Hill, who also worked for the S.P., stayed with us as a roomer. After about six months, Mom returned to Tracy and I went into a room-and-board house in Stockton. Mom married Tom Hill shortly after returning to Tracy.

Mom was in the local Bank of America one day and Mr. Selma, an officer of the bank, asked how I was doing. She told him I was going to business college in Stockton. He suggested that the bank was interested in hiring young men and I should make an application for a job at their headquarters in San Francisco. This I did, and they hired me on April 19th, 1940 and sent me to a town called Lincoln. Six weeks later, I was transferred to Yreka.

I liked my work, and having received a $10 per month raise after finishing my first year with the bank, I was now making a salary of $80 a month. I was living in a boarding house with a wonderful couple, Mr. & Mrs. McCormick. She treated me like her son. They had three daughters; two lived at home. It was a good life. I had also found the girl of my dreams, Marietta Riffel.

Yes, on Dec. 7, I woke up to a bright future.

I got dressed and went downstairs to breakfast. Mrs. Mac did not like for the roomers to use her telephone unless it was an emergency. Since I had been out with Marietta the previous night to Collin's Tavern, a hangout for the young crowd, I wanted to call her up. I went down to the bank to call Marietta, and it was she who broke the news to me about Pearl Harbor.

Oh, sure, we knew about the war "over there" and how bad it was, but that was far away. Also, here I was in Yreka, 20 years old, madly in love, miles from the big cities and living my life with my future ahead of me. I went over to her place where we listened to the radio trying to get all the news we could. The local paper went to press that day with an "extra." You never hear that word anymore. The papers were sold to motorists traveling through Yreka who knew nothing of the attack.

You must think back to this era. There was no radio station in our area and news was hard to acquire. I well remember that night when Marietta and I drove in my little beat-up Plymouth coupe to the top of the Scott Valley summit so we could pick up a distant radio station for updated news. I knew my life was going to change and my future would be uncertain. It was a feeling I was not used to.

I continued my job as usual. There was a retired major by the name of White who lived in Yreka. He always dressed in his military uniform for every parade in town and walked proudly down the street, straight as an arrow. All the small towns held parades every chance they had in those days.

Major White was put in charge of forming a state military unit that would guard the bridges that spanned the canyons and rivers on Highway 99 which was the north-south route through the state into Oregon. I, along with many other young men, joined the unit and received training in military procedure. We went out and stood guard on the bridges—didn't have a gun and wouldn't know what to do if I did. But we were at least doing something.

It was a strange time, as people did not know what to expect next. Our country was supposed to be immune to such actions as being bombed. Would the Japanese invade California? Would they launch planes from carriers off our coast? You had to live through that period before you criticize what action we took. I remember our little town had blackout regulations. It was amazing how many people were so upset at such an idea. Who the hell would want to destroy Yreka?

Life continued, and on March 28, 1942, I reached the age of 21. After much thought and discussions with Marietta, I knew it was my patriotic duty to enter the service of our country. I notified Mr. Harmon, the manager of the Yreka Branch, that I would be leaving to join the Army. Mr. Harmon was a typical banker of the '30s. A true gentleman and well-liked by everyone. He was kind enough to write a letter that I could give to the Army informing them of the work I had been doing at the bank, and it was quite a good recommendation. I said my good-byes to all my friends and a special farewell to Marietta, then headed down to Tracy where I spent a couple of days with my mother. I left my old car with her in Tracy.

On April 22, 1942, I reported to the Army Recruiters office in Stockton to enlist. I, along with about 15 other young men, was put aboard a bus for a trip to San Francisco where we were unloaded to take a physical before being sworn into the Army.

I must take a moment to inform you about myself. I was not what you could call lean; I was not what you could call slim. I was skinny. I was about 5' 9" tall when I graduated from high school. Since then I had grown to 6' 2", but had not gained a pound. My weight was around 130 pounds. I was a very private person and well aware of my physical appearance. We were taken off the bus and sent upstairs where we, along with multitudes of other young men, were to take a physical examination. First order: "Take off everything except your shorts and join the line." Looking down the line I could see stations where doctors were checking every body part a man had. It was a slow and thorough examination, and the doctors didn't waste time. "Bend over and spread your cheeks. Damn it! Look the *other* way and spread your *other* cheeks!" Well, I was doing fine until a sergeant took my height measurement and my weight. He told me that I was underweight and would not qualify for the service. I was 4F.

I couldn't go home and back to work after all the good-byes. The sergeant told me that he had an idea he had used before that would put some quick weight on me. "I'll give you a chit so you can spend the night at the YMCA. You go out and buy yourself a bunch of bananas, eat them and drink lots of water and come back tomorrow morning." This, like a nut, I did. I ate bananas, drank water, ate bananas, drank water. The next morning I returned to my good old friend the sergeant. He put me on the scales and weighed me. Still not enough. He told me he was going to fudge my height a little, and told me to slouch down when I arrived at the induction base. Thus, on April 23, 1942, I was sworn into the service of the United States Army.

And so it was.

We boarded a train from San Francisco and traveled to the Presidio at Monterey. There was quite a bunch of us in the group. We were met by a sergeant, herded into trucks and taken to the base. I received my introduction to a barracks. It was a two-story building with many beds alongside each other against each wall with space down the center. At the end on each floor was the latrine. I knew my days of privacy were over. They immediately had us fall out as we had to visit more doctors. I could see we were going to be well taken care of. Again, the long lines formed and it wound up we were going to get shots for every sickness there was. At one spot there was a man on each side of you and each one gave you a shot to cure what you didn't have. Others took blood pressure and God only knows what else they did. I do have good memories of the "taking of blood" for the Wassermann Test. I swear they took at least a pint.

Well, I had started feeling woozy after all the excitement of the day. The bananas were rolling around in the water mixing with other food I had eaten. Also, this new life was going to take some time to get used to. I was sitting down while this "expert" was taking my pint of blood. I kind of whispered to him, "I'm getting sick and I think …" That's as far as I got. They sat me in the corner and some poor soldier had to come in and clean up the area. It was at least 25 years before I could eat another banana.

And so I ended my first night in the service of Uncle Sam. We all slept pretty good that night and were up bright and early the next morning. First order of the day was to acquire our new clothes for the duration. Through another line. Picked up everything from shorts to shirts to pants to shoes to overcoat. We were told to ship our civilian clothes home because we wouldn't need them. Got ourselves dolled up in our new finery. What a change. We no longer had a special personality. We were all the same; identical people. We next were sent to take aptitude tests. At this point I proudly submitted my letter from the bank to an officer. He thanked me, and I have an idea that my letter joined many others at the bottom of the waste basket.

The tests were not bad. We fell in that evening for our first retreat at an Army base. It was the lowering of the flag for the day while standing at attention and the bugler sounds retreat. It was an impressive time and to this day I get a lump in my throat when standing at retreat while visiting a base.

In April of 1942 the Air Force was a part of the Army and was designated the USAAC, or the United States Army Air Corps. So when I enlisted, I was also a part of the Air Corps. We were indoctrinated in Army life while we were at Monterey. Didn't spend much time there, as new men were arriving all the time. Some said we were on our way to the

Hawaiian Islands to fight the Japs. Others had heard we were going East. We packed our belongings in duffel bags and boarded trucks that took us to the train station where a troop train was on the siding. The Army band was there to greet us, and they were proudly playing that old familiar song, *The Eyes of Texas Are Upon You*. The secret was out. We were bound for the great state of Texas. So much for Army secrecy.

This life was going to take some getting used to, as I have said before. The train ride was sure different from the ones I used to take. We were served meals from the baggage car where the cook had set up his stove and other necessities. The meal, if you want to call it that, was brought through the cars of the train and placed gently (?) in your mess kit. After finishing the meal it was required that the mess kit and knife and fork be cleaned. Well, maybe. We traveled this way through different towns and I must say the people of America sure noticed the troop train and would wave and greet us as we passed through. For a bunch of lonely and lost young men, it helped our spirits.

We wound up at Shepherd Field in Wichita Falls, Texas for six hard weeks of the well-known Basic Training. Here was a group of young men from many different walks of life brought together under adverse circumstances with the realization we would have to work together as a unit, counting on the people running the show to find our niche in doing what we could to keep our country free. Basic Training is defined as a place where the drill sergeant attempts to take civilians and mold them into a group that will work together, talk together, stick together and respect authority without question. It was not easy, but was required if we were to succeed in the job ahead. We were up at the crack of dawn. Learned how to make a bed; not nearly as easy as the way I made it at home.

We would have to stand inspection by the commander of our squad, and had better pass or the drill sergeant would raise holy hell with us. We marched and marched, learning how to keep in step, how to follow commands. We marched to chow, marched to the parade grounds where we practiced marching. It sure was true that the young men taking Basic

Training here were from all walks of life. This was brought out in our attempting to march together in unison. The drill sergeant was always teaching us to stay in step by counting cadence "Hut two three four…" The only name I remember at that base was a fellow named Villavoso. This poor guy was straight off the farm. He did not walk, he took a stride as if crossing a field. He drove the drill sergeant nuts. All heads were going up and down together except Villavoso. With his stride, he would be going up and down with us once in awhile. The reason I remember his name is because all we heard when we were marching was the sergeant saying in a loud voice, "Get in step, Villavoso!" His name is well-remembered by all in that squad, I'm sure.

We found out what KP was as we all had duties there. KP is, of course, Kitchen Police. I don't know why, but I usually wound up on the pots and pans. I swear that was the dirtiest job there was. This tour lasted for about six weeks, then we were again up in the air because no one knew what was next.

One of the highlights of my stay at Shepherd Field was the visit by Bob Hope and his crew putting on a show for us. Jerry Colona, Frances Langford, Les Brown and his Band, along with others, put on a wonderful show in one of the big hangars. It was really something and helped our morale. One thing I will always remember about basic training in Texas was the marching—marching every day, no matter how hot it got. This area in June was blistering hot, and a rain storm could come up in no time at all. Made no difference; we continued to march. This was the only place you could march in the rain and get dust blown in your face at the same time.

The day came when my name appeared on the ship-out list. I was being sent to Love Field, Dallas, Texas to attend Aircraft and Engine School. I could hardly change a tire on a car, but you soon learn that the Army is never wrong and I was to become what the Army thought I was best suited for. In looking back, at that time our country was in need of mechanics for the future Air Force they had in the works. So, like a true soldier, I went to Dallas, Texas.

There was quite a group of men that arrived to attend this school. The school was civilian-run and we were housed in a very nice building. Bunk beds, but only one story. We had civilian cooks and were served cafeteria-style with a choice of food at each meal. We had no KP duty while here. We were on a crash course.

That was the best camp I was ever in. This was not a base and the bus to downtown ran right by the door. Our teachers sure knew their business and we were expected to study each night and work hands-on during classes. Since I had always been interested in airplanes, this was a chance in a lifetime for me. We did have time off, and went into Big D often. The people of Dallas were wonderful to us. We all met girls, and they would invite us to their homes. The parents would welcome us and we got some good home-cooked meals. My mother came to visit me while I was there, and a family I visited with insisted my mother stay with them.

As we were still in the Army, bed check was conducted each night at 10. With the bus running by the barracks door the temptation to "go to town" and miss bed check did happen more than once. When the sergeant made bed check he was almost run over by fellows jumping from bed to bed so no one was found missing. We received a good foundation in basic A & E studies and everyone applied themselves for the job ahead. Each day an instructor would go through the school and bring us up to date with what was happening "over there." This was in June or July of 1942, and every-thing was going the wrong way. We did not hear much good news as islands in the Pacific were falling to the Japanese, and over in Europe, Hitler was advancing at his own pace. London was under siege and our men were in desperate trouble almost everywhere. It was frightening and we all wanted to get our training over so we could do our part. We all fin-ished our training and I, along with others from the school, again boarded a troop train. This one took us to Salt Lake City, Utah to a staging base.

At this spot we again returned to the Army barracks. Our stay here was short. From here the assignment was made to a base where each person would be assigned a specific type of aircraft. We would work on the base perfecting our knowledge from the school and applying it to that aircraft. My transfer came through, and I was sent to Gowen Field, Boise, Idaho.

I arrived at the base and was assigned to a barracks. It seemed to me that there was total confusion, as people were going everywhere. I was immediately sent out to the line where I was introduced to the B-17E, the Flying Fortress.

That plane was too large to fly!

Remember, this was 1942. The B-17 had four engines and carried 10 men—pilot, co-pilot, bombardier, navigator, flight engineer/top turret gunner, radioman, ball turret gunner, two waist gunners and tail gunner. This was to be my assignment in World War II, working on this monster to learn all I could as fast as I could and be certain I did everything right, as many lives depended on what I did. My time here was long hours doing every job on the plane, from fueling it to changing engines, running 25-hour inspections, 100-hour inspections and fixing problems reported by the pilots. We worked 12-hour shifts from 6 a.m. to 6 p.m. Then we would change shifts on Saturday. The day shift would work 24 hours, from 6 a.m. Saturday morning until 6 a.m. Sunday morning. This way, we changed shifts; one weekend we worked 24 hours and the next we had 24 hours off. One thing about it, we did not have a union to help us get a 40-hour week! Of course we never complained, as we knew we had a job to do and wanted to get it done.

I took my first ride in a B-17 there. It was a machine gun training mission where all the gunners were learning how to use their new toys. All assigned crews were in training for combat duty. We were also doing the same thing, knowing our time was coming. This was another place where it was necessary to put in time on KP for awhile. We also stood guard duty as it was necessary to guard the planes at night. I was there during the winter months, and I didn't think any place could get that cold. It was also hard working on the aircraft at night in that cold weather. If your hand slipped off a wrench and hit metal, the suffering was painful, to say the least. The men, both officers and enlisted at Gowen Field, were trained for the duty of forming a fighting group.

Thus, the 388th Bombardment Group was originated.

The cadre consisted of 42 officers and 226 enlisted men, and, on February 4, 1943, we departed Gowen Field for Wendover Field, Utah. The train left at 18:00 hours after a send-off by the post band. Although the trip by air was less than one hour, the trip by train took 22 hours. The coaches were the very oldest type with gas lights and no sleeping provisions or mess facilities. We arrived at Wendover Field tired, dirty and hungry.

Wendover is located on the Utah-Nevada border and the nearest city, Salt Lake, is located 120 miles east. We did have barracks, but they were made out of tar paper and were one story. The bathroom was a separate building from where we slept. We did not have running water.

Commanding Officer Col. William B. David insisted his men stay in shape. We were required to rise at 5 in the morning, fall out and do calisthenics for 30 or 45 minutes each day. This is a wonderful place to train flight crews because there are thousands of square miles of nothing but salt flats.

We were now ready to bring our group to a full complement of flight crews and ground personnel with the goal of forming a bombing group ready for combat duty. The 388th Bomb Group at this stage consisted of four squadrons, the 560th, 561st, 562nd and 563rd. I was in the 563rd, and our Commanding Officer was Captain Henggeler. I thought we had long hours of work at Gowen Field, but here we were on call 24 hours a day.

I had acquired the rank of staff sergeant and was assigned to be crew chief of one of the planes in our squadron. Flight crews started arriving, along with ground personnel to build our group into a combat-ready outfit. We spent long hours getting the group into shape. Our job on the line was to keep the aircraft in flying condition so the crews could practice working as a unit.

I remember the time spent trying to perfect formation flying. I flew as flight engineer once for Captain Henggeler while training in formation. It was not an easy task as these planes were big and there was no such thing as "fly by wire" as we have today. Tight formation was required to obtain the maximum efficiency of fire power from the gunners in the group. The pilot had his hands full attempting to keep his wingtip tucked next to the plane he was flying alongside. He also had other planes in the formation to be aware of. Each squadron at this point had nine crews and the group had a total of 36 B-17s. That is quite a group to put up in formation flying.

It was during the last days of training at Wendover that our Group lost its first crew. A crash landing near Pocatello, Idaho was made and seven men were killed. This article appeared in the Desert newspaper, May 6, 1943 regarding the 388th's first loss on May 5ᵗʰ—B-17 #42-29562 at Soda Springs, Idaho:

> "Three Army Air Force flyers were in the Soda Springs hospital this a.m. after a spectacular crash which wrecked their four-motored bomber and killed or fatally injured their seven flying companions, as scores of Soda Springs residents watched, helpless to aid the storm-tossed aviators.
>
> "The plane was on a routine training mission from Wendover Field, Utah, to Pocatello, Army officials said.
>
> "Civilians furnished the dramatic recital of the efforts of the plane and crew to escape the sleet, wind and snow which apparently threw them off course. Civilians lining their automobiles along the road outside Soda Springs watched the big bomber undershoot on an attempt to land and crash into the hillside after apparently striking some obstruction on their third try. The horrified citizens rushed to the crashed bomber and extracted four men and the bodies of five men who had been killed instantly. The body of the tenth flyer was found the next morning.
>
> "The civilian group which attempted to light the landing strip was organized by Sheriff McCrackin and his deputy, Williams. The crash occurred about 11:30 p.m."

We finished our training the 1st of May and started for Sioux City, Iowa. A long trip on the troop train. The base was wonderful, compared to Wendover. We had inside plumbing and were close to Sioux City. We knew that this was to be our last stateside base. Our next move would be into the combat zone. At this base the group was assigned brand-new planes direct from the factory. We continued to run flights, looking for problems prior to going overseas. We were allowed to go into Sioux City when not on duty. I had a relative living there, Miss Lillian Nalon. My father's mother was killed in an accident when my father was quite young, and this lady raised my dad. I called on Aunt Lil at her home and had a nice visit.

The last week of May, 35 planes departed the base for a flight to McChord Field, Washington, on a check-out to see if we were ready for combat. It was required that some ground personnel also fly this mission to be available if any mechanical problems developed. I was first in line and flew this mission. Up early that morning, I performed the preflight check-out of our aircraft and everything was fine. The pilot I was flying with had a habit of almost always finding some problem with the plane he had flown. I knew he would find some fault with my plane when he flew it. Not every time, but more than usual.

It was seldom when we could really find a problem, and when another crew flew the same plane, they would not have any problem. Other crew chiefs had the same reaction with him. The pilot was Lt. Marvin Karnholz.

He was flying my aircraft with me in it. It was quite a sight to see 35 B-17Fs take off at one-minute intervals and form into our combat formation. I rode in the waist with the two gunners. It was a long flight to McChord Field. I did not find out until later that the pilot had requested that when he landed at the base, he would require that all the spark plugs in engine Number 3 be changed, as the engine was running rough. He knew I was on board his plane, but he did not call me up into the cockpit to check out the engine. When we landed, I went with the crew to find where we were to sleep. I guess the mechanics at the base changed the plugs. He never said a word to me.

The planes flew three missions out over the Pacific Ocean and must have passed muster as we were declared combat ready. Going to dinner at the mess hall with a group of the fellows, I heard someone call out "Seney!" It was a young fellow I had graduated with from Tracy High School. His name was Ed Ferguson, and what a small world we live in. We got together and he took me out to show me the type of plane he was working on. It was a reconnaissance aircraft used for artillery spotting, a mighty small plane with room for just the pilot and spotter. He was quite impressed with our planes. I told him we were ready to go overseas after this trip. We did have a nice visit.

When the group was ready to depart, one of the planes blew an oil cooler on one of the engines and I stayed to change it. The rest of the group departed for Sioux City while I changed the cooler. It didn't take long and we were ready to depart. We had the pleasure of flying from west to east all by ourselves. I crawled back to the tail gunner's position and put on the earphones. The pilot had picked up a good radio station that played smooth music. He did have to change stations often as we would outdistance the station's range and have to pick up another. It was sure nice to be flying all by ourselves and not have to cuddle up to another plane for formation flying. We made it back to the base and we all waited our orders. They were not long in coming.

On June 8th, 1943, the first squadron flew to Salina, Kansas for final check. Approximately 400 officers and enlisted men were in the air echelon that went to Salina. On June12th, the rest of the group, including me, left for Camp Kilmer, New Jersey, where we spent three weeks listening to lectures and going to New York. I did get into New York one time; went to the Astor Hotel and to the top where Harry James and his band were playing. There were quite a few soldiers there, and I don't think any of them bought a drink—they were all furnished by the people there. The waiter would ask what you wanted and said it was already paid for. Not one soldier that I saw abused this kindness by making a fool of himself. I also went to the top of the Empire State Building while in town.

It must have been the first day of July when our group proceeded to the waterfront and I had my look at the biggest ocean liner I had ever seen. We boarded the *Queen Elizabeth* for our trip "over there." Both the *Queen Elizabeth* and the *Queen Mary* were converted to troop carriers for the duration of the war. Both the Queens traveled the Atlantic Ocean without an escort. We departed from New York and, as we passed the Statue of Liberty, we all bid her a farewell and said a little prayer that we would see her one more time if we were lucky enough to return.

Staterooms that in peace time were occupied by two people now held about 15 soldiers. Hanging bunk beds were stacked four-high with little room between them. We also were informed that we would spend one night in the stateroom and the next night we would have to sleep up on deck. I believe that liner carried 24,000 soldiers on each trip between America and England.

When we boarded the ship we were issued carbine rifles. Why, I'll never know, because when we docked they took them back. It was strange walking around on this ship. You could see just a part of her beauty—the still-beautiful stairways from deck to deck; spacious areas that must have been the ballroom.

We were fed twice a day. Breakfast started around 6 in the morning and ended around 11 and dinner started around 4 in the afternoon. We did spend a lot of time on deck and we had good weather. There was a detachment of MPs on board in case any serious problems were to develop. I remember I was sitting on the deck one day and one of the MPs noticed one of the soldiers leaning over the rail. He was not sick, but was trying to look at one of the lower decks. The MP said, "Sergeant!" and about 10 guys turned around. He pointed to the one and told him not to lean over the rail. He then turned to his companion and said, "I hate it when we have a group of Air Force men on board. You can't just say *sergeant* because damn near everyone *is.*"

One other day I was up on deck about half asleep leaning against a wall when just above me an anti-aircraft gun started shooting. I was at once wide awake. I remember it so well because it was the 4th of July and I thought the British might be celebrating. I knew better than that! Just practicing, I found out later.

Standing at the back of the ship you could watch its wake and see that we were always turning from side to side. This was in case a U-boat was trying to track us. As it was, we had no problem and the day before we pulled into Glasgow, Scotland, a British aircraft greeted us.

The *Queen Elizabeth* was unable to dock at Glasgow as it was too large. We had to be taken ashore by smaller boats. There we loaded onto troop trains and headed to our new base. English trains were nothing like our trains. They had compartments, and we were stuck in the compartment until we reached Thetford, the closest town to our new "home away from home."

We were picked up by trucks and transported to Knettishall, our home for the duration. As is usual, the base was not finished and we wound up in tents for the first week.

Just a little history as to what was going on at this stage of the operation. Our base was located in East Anglia, an area to become noted for being the largest airport area up to that time. Bases were being constructed in this section to support the aircraft of the 8th USAAF, and airfields were being built for B-17s, B-24s, fighters such as the P-47 (the first fighter to support the large bombers), P-38s, and, finally, the lifesaver, the P-51 Mustang. Bases were everywhere, and when we arrived construction was going strong.

For six months, from November 1942 until the following May, the American day bomber offensive from England was carried out largely by four B-17F Fortress groups. We arrived in July, and were considered one of the early groups of the 8th Air Force.

The flight crews and some of the headquarters personnel flew to England in our new B-17Fs by way of Gander. One plane and crew was lost and never reached England. It was one of the 563rd Squadron ships. As a matter of fact, it was the Karnholz crew I flew with from Sioux City to McChord Field.

We moved into our quarters, huts constructed of half-circle framing with corrugated metal roofs, called Quonset huts, or Nissens—no toilet facilities in them and a pot-bellied stove at one end. Our toilet facilities were located in another building that required us getting our exercise running back and forth. The quarters were located around the base by squadron, and were better than a mile from the flight line. This would not work for the ground crew, as we had to be located next to the planes. Back to the tents. The ground crews placed tents next to the revetments where the planes were parked. Since we were in a combat zone, the planes were dispursed around the field. A taxi ramp circled the field and the 563rd Squadron was located close to the control tower. Each ground crew had their individual tent that slept five people. We installed a "Chick Sales"—a latrine—a respectable distance from the tent. It was necessary to relocate the one-seater every so often.

This is where we lived for better than two years.

I must say, it did get cold in England in the winter. They furnished us coal for the stove, but it was too much work trying to get enough of it, so the American mind went to work. We mixed high octane gasoline with oil using a converted ammo can for a container, hooked up tubing running from the outside container to the stove, installed a faucet to control the flow and had ourselves a stove fired by a flammable liquid—and a warm tent. This system was used by all the line crews. We did see a few tents go up in flames, but our crew did fine. I don't think OSHA would approve today, but it served our purpose.

*Bob Seney, right, and crew (from left) Fred Bleuchamp, John Nemecek and Elton King, on the flight line.*

The 388th Bomb Group consisted of many units. Ours was made up of the 29th Station Complement, 214th Financial Detachment, 587th Postal Unit, 877th Chemical Company, 1211th Quartermaster, 1284th Military Police Company, 273rd Medical Dispensary, 1751st Ordnance Supply & Maintenance Co., 2019th Engineering & Fire Fighting Platoon, 452nd Sub Depot, 434th Air Service Group, and the 560th, 561st, 562nd and 563rd Squadrons. As you can see, we had a complete city of needed citizens to make our outfit a complete fighting unit.

Of the 41 planes flown over to England by the Group, not many lasted long. The Germans controlled the air space over all of the occupied countries. Our fighters at that time were the P-47 and were limited in flight time due to fuel capacity. Drop tanks were not in use at that time. This meant that our bombers were escorted as far as the French coast by the fighters, then, due to low fuel, the escorts had to return to England. The German fighters would pick up our bombers and attack them all the way to the target. The fighters would break off the attack as the bombers started their bomb run. When our planes started the bomb run, the pilot of the lead plane would set his controls on autopilot and the bombardier would fly the plane using the famous Norden bombsight. The bomb run was critical, and the aircraft would fly straight and level with all planes holding formation. This is when the German anti-aircraft guns would cover the sky with their deadly flak. On our bomb runs, the German fighters would return to base and refuel, then return to the battle as our bombers left the target area. Our losses were so bad at first that there was talk in the high command that we could not withstand the rate of loss. It was at this time that the P-38 and then the famous P-51 came on the scene. Modifications were made whereby drop tanks were installed, allowing the planes to escort our bombers all the way to the target.

Of the more than 450 combat crews to pass through the 388th Bomb Group, 138 were missing in action, more than 200 completed their tours, and more than 100 returned to the States at the end of the war in Europe. In the first 100 missions, the group lost 83 crews. On the remaining 206 missions, the group lost 58 crews. Remember a crew consisted of 10 young men, many in their teens.

The 388th flew its first mission July 17, 1943. Twenty aircraft were airborne by 06:26 hours. Two groups were involved, the 388th and the 385th, with the 388th as the Lead. The target was an aircraft factory in Amsterdam. All planes returned to base by 10:19 hours.

On September 6, 1943, 24 aircraft took off by 05:47 hours, not knowing that this would be the most disastrous mission in losses for the 388th Bomb Group of all the 306 missions flown. Eleven of our aircraft failed to return. That represents 110 young men.

The target that day was Stuttgart, Germany. Fighter opposition was the strongest encountered to date, with about 150 enemy planes attacking our formation—FW-190s, ME-109s, 110s and 210s, with a few JU-88s. A few spasmodic attacks were made on the formation on the route to Stuttgart, but the largest concentration was first met in the vicinity of the

IP (Initial Point). The attacks were very intense from this point to the target, decreased over Stuttgart, but regained intensity until the formation reached Bernay on the route out. The attacks centered on the Low Group (known by combat crews as Purple Heart Corner) and, as a result, one entire Low Squadron was missing—the 563rd. The Low Squadron was hit by flak after the IP; then, as the damaged planes would drop out of formation, they would be hit by fighters. It was a tragic day.

My duty while in the group was that of crew chief of a B-17. I was now a master sergeant and had a crew of five men. Also available to the ground crews were specialists such as radio men, armament crews and, when required—when the plane was so damaged we could not repair it at the revetments—it would go to the sub-depot. While stationed there, I think I had six or seven planes. When one was lost in combat, another was flown in within a day or two. Each squadron had nine aircraft when we started. This was increased, and I am sure we had at least 15 in each squadron within a year.

I mentioned before that we lived on the line. It was our job to have the aircraft ready for combat at all times. When we first arrived, the ground crew and flight crew were close, but it did not take us long to back off. We were all young then, and the flight crews would come out fresh from the USA and were eager to get into combat. These boys grew into men overnight. They would come back from a six or eight-hour flight into hell, and their attitude would change from "Let's give 'em hell" to "I've just seen hell."

It was my job to preflight the plane prior to the arrival of the flight crew. I would run up all the engines, check every part of the plane and make sure it was ready to fly. This would be about an hour prior to the crew arriving. Prior to that, the armament crew would bring the bomb load, which could be 500-pound bombs, incendiary bombs, armor piercing or cluster bombs. The flight crew would arrive with all their gear and we would visit either in the tent or, if the weather was nice, outside. Many of the missions called for early morning take-off as the Group would take off from the field and climb to altitude where they would then get into formation. We on the ground crew had to be on the line until the plane taxied out with the crew. I would always stand in front of the plane when the pilot started the engines and stayed until he was ready to taxi out. I would then stand where he could watch me as I waved him out of the revetments. The last thing I did was to stand at attention and salute him and the crew. The pilot would always return the salute.

Many times the CO of our squadron would fly my plane, and he, too, would return the salute. It was a trying time when the Group returned and the crew I had saluted that morning did not join their comrades in the barracks. They might have joined many of their comrades who never returned to their families; they might have jumped from their planes, landing in enemy territory to be taken as a prisoner of war. Some of the planes that were so badly damaged by enemy action that they could not return to England, headed to Switzerland or Sweden where they were interned for the duration of the war. Some who bailed out over occupied countries would be hidden by that country's underground and would work their way back to England with the help of those wonderful people. If caught in this dangerous task, these people were subject to execution by the German government. Many of our soldiers owe their lives to these people and will be forever indebted to them.

As I previously stated, the ground crews backed off getting too close to the flight crews. One exception to this was made by us early in our operation. We had lost our B-17F on the Stuttgart raid, so we were delivered a brand new aircraft direct from the factory. Many aircraft were named by someone and "nose art" was added to many of the planes. It happened that this plane we received had been named by someone, and we think it was done at the factory. In beautiful script, the name *Mary Ellen* covered the nose section. This aircraft was an F model and we immediately prepared it for combat. About this time, a new replacement crew had joined our squadron and was assigned to the *Mary Ellen*. Lt. Joe Gunn was the pilot, and he and his crew would fly our ship for most of their missions. They were all a wonderful bunch of fellows and our ground crew thought a lot of them. They were there during the time that enemy fighter opposition was so bad. I remember when they returned from one mission, the tail gunner was telling us how he was firing at fighters attacking from the rear one after another. He said he had fired so many rounds that the barrels of the two .50-caliber machine guns had heated up and expanded to a point that, when he fired, the tracer shells made an expanding pattern and the shells seemed to just circle around the attacking plane so that he could not hit it.

The crew would always arrive early and we would sit around and talk. This was during the winter and I must say it can get cold in England. We did have snow at times. Our ground crew would work nights before a mission to fill the tanks full of gas and check out any final work that had to be done. We would have the armament crews out loading the bombs and inserting the fuses. We would try to get a little sleep before it was time to pre-flight the plane. Doyle Galbraith, the flight engineer of the crew, would at times come into the tent while we were still sleeping and start a fire in our stove to get the tent a little warm for us. It sure made a difference, because that tent did not have any insulation!

The ground crews knew about what time the mission would return to base and it was always with anticipation that we counted the returning ships. They would fly over the base in formation and break off one by one to make their landing. Any aircraft with injured onboard would shoot off red flares and immediately make the landing approach. Ambulances were always standing by during the arrival with doctors and attendants. After landing, the aircraft would be waived to the closest revetment so the wounded could be treated immediately and be transferred to the base hospital. This was standard procedure and many crews would need this service.

I well remember one such incident when we were waiting for the planes to arrive and, as the formation approached the field, three aircraft in close formation were approaching by themselves low and at full power. As they crossed the field, red flares were being fired from the lead plane, the *Mary Ellen*. The two wingmen pulled out and Lt. Gunn made a fast landing, pulling into a revetment near us. The radioman was injured and was bleeding badly. The plane had been hit by flak over the target. You did not call 911 and get to the hospital in a hurry. It took four hours from the time he was hit until they could get him to a doctor. Remember too, he was in an aircraft that was not pressurized and had to have an oxygen mask on until they could drop to a lower altitude. When they were able to get out of enemy territory, Lt. Gunn and his two wingmen left the formation and hightailed it for the base.

The flight engineer, Doyle, gave us a rundown as to what occurred during the mission. It is the radioman's job to open the door into the bomb bay where the bombs are located and notify the pilot when the bombs have cleared. Once in awhile, a bomb may fail to fall or may hang up and this could cause a problem When the pilot is notified the bombs are away, he can then close the bomb bay doors. Well, it seems the radioman always placed an extra radio on the floor and straddled it while waiting for the bombs to be released. While sitting there, a large piece of flak came through the bottom of the fuselage and hit the radio, sending fragments into his thighs and seriously injuring him. The waist gunners heard him scream and notified the pilot. He had to hold formation, so he instructed the co-pilot to go back and check on the injured crewman. By this time they had cleared the target and were heading for home. Lt. Gunn asked Doyle to take over the co-pilot's seat. The co-pilot was tied up working on the wounded radioman, and with the help of other crew members gave him morphine to relieve some of the suffering.

While the co-pilot was treating the wounded man, the pilot had to relieve his bladder. Since the engineer was in the co-pilot's seat, Lt. Gunn told him to keep it straight and steady while he used the relief tube in the bomb bay. The co-pilot had done all he could with the radio man and started forward to the cockpit. What a surprise when he entered the bomb bay and saw the pilot! He asked who was flying the plane. He was informed by the pilot that Doyle was doing the flying. Doyle told me that the co-pilot was quite upset, but Doyle got a big kick out of it. The radio man was in the hospital for quite some time. This meant that another radio man would fly with the Gunn crew. It also would mean that the first man would not finish his 25 missions with his crew. If he missed five missions with them it would mean he would have 20 missions in when the crew flew their 25th. He would then become a replacement crew member with some other crew for his last five missions. The Gunn crew did finish their 25 missions and returned to the States. The pilot, now Captain Gunn, returned to the 388th and flew additional missions as a Command Pilot.

As the war progressed, the power of the USAAF increased as more fighters were added and extended penetration of support for the bombers allowed us to gain control of the air. The bomber crews' required missions were increased from 25 to 30 and later to 35 before they could return to the USA.

I well remember the first Christmas, Dec. 25, 1943. We had been at the base almost six months. In this short period our spirits were not too high. We had lost many planes and many young men. It was not easy for us on the ground to wait for our crews to return only to realize it would not happen. For the flight crews it would be much harder, returning from a mission to the same barracks shared by friends who were now gone; they knew that tomorrow they would return to the sky and face the possibility that their beds might be the ones unoccupied tomorrow night.

Christmas Eve was a stand-down as weather was bad.

The base had a Tannoy public address system which allowed the central area to communicate with everyone. Speakers were located by each revetment around the base and in the squadron centers. It had been snowing that day, and in the evening a light coating of snow covered the base. It was a beautiful sight. Our ground crew was in the tent and we were having our own personal thoughts about where we would rather be at this time of year. Someone thought it would be a nice idea to play Christmas songs over the Tannoy system. They were beautiful, but I really don't think it cheered us up. I had never heard it so quiet. Not one plane was running up their engines. I think the CO realized what our feelings were, and the carols were shortly stopped. It did make an impression on everyone on the base, I think. So much for our first Christmas in England.

England is at the same latitude as central Canada and the weather can be miserable much of the time. Since the 8th Air Force was there for strategic bombing of specific targets, accuracy was required. To deliver the bombs on the target accurately, the Norden Bombsight was used. But the weather would not always comply. The 8th was proud of the fact that a mission was never aborted because of enemy action. Not true as far as weather was concerned. Many missions were recalled due to bad weather over the target area. It was determined by the powers to be that it was going to be necessary to find some way to "see through the clouds" if we were to do our job. Thus, the brainy people developed the Pathfinder. Certain modifications were made to a B-17F. The ball turret was removed and a radar unit was installed. When the plane was airborne, the radar unit was extended through the turret opening. A radar operator with a scope sitting in the radio room would be able to see the outline of the land through the clouds. He would pick out reference spots, such as rivers, towns and other areas; and, by using a map, could lead the group to its target. Definitely not precision bombing, but they did the job required. The Pathfinders, or Lead ships, were at this time all located at one base and a ship would be sent to the Group just prior to the mission.

One night, my ship was grounded due to battle damage and was on stand-down for the morning mission. We had been working on it all day and quit work about 22:00. George Taylor, another crew chief, shared the revetment with me and was getting his plane ready to fly. The ordnance crews were loading his plane with 500-pound bombs. The bomb bay was busy with all lights on. George had his workers filling the plane with fuel. The whole field was busy getting ready for the mission. The tower turned on the runway lights as the PFF was approaching to lead the mission. Unbeknownst to us, a German fighter had crossed the Channel undetected and was following the PFF; and, as the B-17 touched down, the fighter fired. The PFF continued its roll-out and all hell broke loose at the field. You never saw a field get blacked-out so fast!

The landing PFF shot off red flares as they had injured on board. No one on board was killed, but many things happened on the base. Everyone on the line was up waiting for another pass from the fighter who was well on his way back to the Fatherland. When the plane fired, some of the ordnance crews were taking bombs to ships for loading. All traffic came to a halt with the attack. It was a dark night with no moon and you could not see your hand in front of your face. When the red flares went off, personnel were dispatched to the PFF. One Jeep ran into a loaded trailer carrying bombs. They could not explode, but caused much damage to the Jeep and a couple more fellows were injured. After that, the ground crews were a little more concerned about the amount of light we had around the planes we were working on after dark. The mission departed in the morning with the PFF leading, but no one will ever forget that night.

Whenever we changed an engine on our plane, it was necessary for it to be slow-timed. This means that the plane would take off and cruise for two or three hours over England running the new engine at different RPM settings, allowing us to check the gauges to make sure all was well. As crew chief, I usually flew on these trips. I never found anything wrong with the engines, but I did have some strange rides. One time, while cruising at about 10,000 feet, the pilot thought it would be a good time for me to learn how to fly a B-17. This was fine with me. He had the co-pilot give up his seat and I climbed in and had a ball. The pilot turned it over to me and had me make turns, climb and descend. It was lots of fun for me as the pilot could take over if necessary. I was at the controls for 15 or 20 minutes and didn't do any damage.

On another slow-time run, a British bomber came alongside us. It had a Canadian insignia on the tail indicating it was being flown by the boys from Canada. We had heard stories about these guys. Their elevator did not reach the top floor. We were flying straight and level as they came alongside and we waived to each other. The pilot of the other ship then moved in so his wingtip was over the top of ours and proceeded to very gingerly drop his wing until it gently touched ours. He then made a sharp bank away from us as our pilot made a few interesting comments. I, like the pilot, did not care to fool around at 10,000 feet in a four-engine aircraft.

We did have fun at times when flying over England. The farmers were always complaining to the Group COs about "those damn Yankees flying so low when we are tilling our fields." Well, I found out what they were talking about. It was lots of fun, too. On one slow-time, the pilot suggested we do some hedge hopping. Sounded good to me. We dropped down just off the ground sailing along about 150 mph. As it happened, we were below the trees that lined the roadway. No problem. We just pulled up to go over them in fine shape, but to our amazement there was another B-17 flying parallel to the trees on the other side. We passed darn near over the top of him.

We did have some accidents at the base when planes were departing or landing.

On October 14, 1943, the target for the day was Schweinfurt and the planes taxied out for take-off. Lt. Swift of the 561st Squadron was flying a replacement aircraft, the *Hard Luck*, as his, *Virgin on the Verge*, was grounded by previous battle damage. He started his take-off roll and was almost airborne when the co-pilot, Lt. Tipper, called out that the oil pressure on Number 3 engine was zero. The ship began to pull to the right and he saw flames coming from the dying engine. Observers reported that smoke came from the tires as the brakes were applied. With a rough field ahead of him, followed by a solid wall of trees, Lt. Swift ordered wheels up. The take-off became a belly landing. The ship stopped with her nose crushed in by a tree. All of the crew escaped unharmed. The entire neighborhood was evacuated of personnel; departing planes were sent to a different runway, and preparations were made for the explosion as the plane, fully loaded with fuel and bombs, began to burn. Two of the ambulances that were dispatched stopped at our revetment to watch the spectacular fire. When the explosion came, I was standing between the ambulances talking to the drivers. We were across the field from the accident, but the concussion from the exploding bombs bounced me against the ambulances as both rocked back and forth.

All other planes were launched before the explosion, and the mission was successful.

Another time, one of the planes was up on a test flight when it developed problems. The wind direction made it necessary for the plane to use one of the shorter runways. A group of us saw the plane as it was on the downwind leg of the landing pattern and we realized it was in trouble. We saw the propeller of Number 1 engine fall off. This was caused by the engine having a runaway propeller. A runaway propeller is usually the result of a malfunction in the governor that controls the pitch of the prop, making it impossible for the pilot to change the pitch; he should immediately feather the engine so the prop will not windmill. The feathering of the prop is controlled by oil pressure. Here we had a case where there was zero oil pressure and feathering could not be accomplished. When the engine has no oil, a runaway propeller will build up an uncontrollable speed. This results in the engine freezing up and the propeller burns off the engine.

The pilot made a short approach to the field at an excessive speed. He had to set it down as he could not go around for another approach. We watched as he attempted his landing and the plane left the runway and started across the field. In a revetment of the 562nd squadron, a crew chief was up in the nacelle working on the landing gear. The uncontrolled plane crashed into this plane, killing the crew chief. All the crew escaped but we sure had another big fire on the base.

Planes returning from missions with battle damage were always a problem when trying to get the Group down. More than once a plane that seemed okay would have a landing gear fold up on landing. I remember one plane returning to the base lowered its landing gear and the green light on the control panel would not come on to confirm the gear was locked down. The pilot made a low pass over the tower so it could be checked by one of the engineering officers. It's hard to get a good look when the plane is going by at 100 miles per hour. The tower said it looked good and the pilot made a perfect landing with no problem. Once in awhile a plane would return to the base and could not lower its landing gear. Whenever this happened, the plane would be diverted to another field that had facilities we did not have. Also, we did not want him to attempt a landing and close our field.

We did get time off while stationed at Knettishall. Three-day passes were issued, giving us a short break from the base, and we also received a week off a couple of times. Three-day passes were used for trips to London. Whenever I went to London I always stayed at the Red Cross billet at Picadilly Circus. The Circus is a roundabout where about five streets meet and traffic circles the area. They have many of these in England. In the middle of this circle was a large covering of what appeared to be heavy plywood. The plywood had been placed over the famous statue of Eros.

On one visit to London I met a young girl whose name was Betty. I escorted her home that evening and she introduced me to her family. Her father was a greengrocer. Her mother also worked, but I forget where. She also had a nine-year-old sister. They invited me to visit them anytime I had a chance. The English were in the same position as the people in America, as food and other items were unavailable due to the war. I visited with them many times and spent the night with them. It was wonderful to have a real bed to sleep in as well as a bathtub. I would always bring the family items from the mess hall, such as sugar or butter. They were very nice people and we would go down to the local pub in the evening. This was a family affair and the young daughter was always with the family.

Another thing I remember about London is the fog. You have not been in fog until you have visited London. To make it worse, the city was blacked out. Between the two it was almost impossible to get around. They have the famous Underground in London, and you can travel almost anywhere in the city with the system they have. It's not bad traveling from station to station. It's when you come up from the Underground. Can't see your hand in front of your face. I mean that literally. Get off the Underground in Picadilly Circus and when you hit the street—nothing. The Red Cross was less than a block away and it would take 30 minutes to find it.

Another experience I had while visiting London will always be remembered. After the Normandy invasion, the Germans started using another of their secret inventions that was going to win the war for them. They started launching the famous V-1 flying bomb. A jet engine was made to which a bomb could be attached. The contraptions would be launched from a slanted ramp and they were bound for London. They would fly until the fuel ran out, then head for whatever was under them. There was no control after launch. The first V-1 was launched on June 12, 1944. They made a sound that I'll never forget. These were the first jet sounds and were something unusual. They would fly very low. You could watch them coming, realizing that whenever the engine cut out, they would fall and explode. On June 15th, 144 V-1s were launched toward London. That night I had escorted a young lady home and it was so late that the Underground had stopped running. This required that I try to find my way back to the Red Cross billet at Picadilly. While walking along I came to a building that had been taken over by the U.S. Army stationed in London. I stopped to talk to some of the guys. They were outside the building watching the V-1s that were arriving over the city. We would watch as they came into view and wait for the engine to cut out. When they did, about five seconds later you would hear the explosion, and know more casualties had been added to the ever-rising total of dead and injured. One of the fellows suggested I spend the night with them as they had extra beds. Sounded good to me, so I was taken upstairs and given a bunk for the night. Well, I must have been asleep about an hour when I was awakened and found myself about three feet above the bed coming back down amidst all kinds of noise. A V-1 had fallen less than a block from where we were. All was fine with us, but it was sure a learning experience to actually be close to the receiving end of one of those things.

London was a city I had wanted to return to after the war. I told Marietta many times that I would love to see London at night when the lights were on. When I was there they were never on. The only light you saw in London at night was from the burning buildings.

I married Marietta after the war. And we did return to London.

On Jan. 9, 1944, the mission was Frankfurt, Germany. This was always a tough target. Lt. Hennessey and his crew were assigned to the *Mary Ellen*. A Pathfinder led this mission as there was complete cloud coverage. The flak over the target was heavy as usual. The *Mary Ellen* was disabled by flak over the target deep in enemy territory. The plane had to drop out of formation and head for the deck. It crashed in Germany. Lts. Hennessey and Richardson returned to England on March 22, 1944. Some time later a sergeant from the photo section came out to my tent with a picture of what was left of the *Mary Ellen*. The picture showed the tail section with the aircraft number and the call letter "Q" on the rudder. (When calling the tower, the pilot used the "Q, Queenie" to let them know which plane it was in the squadron.) This picture was sent through the French Underground to England and on to our group. I still have that picture.

It did not take long before we had another new ship in the revetment.

The 1st of March, 1944, we started a campaign to hit Hitler where the German people were told it would never happen. By this time, we had the fighters that could accompany the bombers deep into Germany. Our target was Berlin.

We attempted two or three raids, but due to the weather they had to be recalled. On March 8, 1944, the 8th Air Force delivered thousands of pounds of bombs on the City of Berlin in the first daylight raid.

*"The following TWX is quoted for the information of all concerned from Gen. Le May, Commanding General, 3rd Bombardment Division: The crew of the 45th Combat Wing delivered a punishing blow today to the morale of all Germany. In successfully putting bombs on the enemy's capital and his vital plants, they furthered the war effort more than any of us can adequately evaluate at the present writing. The major part of the hurt to the 3rd Division forces fell on the gallant crews of the 96th, the 388th and the 452nd bomb groups. The spirit and fight these units displayed today made it easier on the other two wings who wanted to share the brunt of the battle with them. Convey to the officers and the men who participated my deepest admiration for the courage and determination with which they pushed the air attack in the heart of the enemy's territory and blasted Berlin. Signed, Le May."*

Fighter attack by the Germans was intense, with many of our planes lost. Our support fighters could not cover all the bomber groups, but they did a superb job when in combat with the enemy. Our planes departed from Knettishall at 07:40, returning at 16:30; flight time, almost nine hours from take-off to landing. This included assembly time, flight into the target with fighter contact, flak, which was heavy over Berlin, then fighting your way back. These were long and tiring missions on all the crew, but the pilot and co-pilot had to fly the aircraft and could do nothing to protect themselves. They just sat there and fought the controls, attempting to keep the plane in formation and get it back home.

The missions were now concentrated on strategic targets, such as steel ball bearing plants, railroad yards, all manufacturing plants (including those building aircraft) and other specialized targets. Our fighter aircraft were also strafing airfields as they returned from air cover for the heavy bombers.

Unknown to us peons, plans were well underway for the invasion of Normandy. No one knew where the invasion would be, but plans were building. In April, many missions were concentrated on the coastal areas, from Holland south. We knew that something big was coming as we started attacking the railroad marshalling yards near Paris, hitting coastal positions and flying in weather where the PFF ship was used because of full cloud cover. This started late in May. On June 6, 1944, D-Day, orders were received as follows: "Guns will be manned, but not test-fired at any time. Gunners will not fire at any airplane unless being attacked."

All available heavy bombers of the 8th Air Force were dispatched in waves to attack coastal defenses between Le Havre and Cherbourg in France. The attacks were in direct support of the Allied Invasion Force which landed immediately after the bombing of the beach area was completed. Our first mission that day took off at 02:48 hours. The targets were attacked by PFF methods due to complete overcast. Bombing was done by groups with squadrons flying abreast. With Lt. Col. Chet Cox in the lead aircraft, we were the first to drop bombs in support of the invasion. Bombs were away at 06:56 hours from 15,500 feet from the A Group and 07:03 hours from 13,850 feet from B Group. The aircraft returned to base by 10:43 hours. A second formation from our base departed at 06:19 hours, consisting of six aircraft that joined up with the 96th Group to hit tactical targets just inside the French Coast. The cloud coverage was 10/10, so again the PFF was used. The planes returned at 12:34 hours. Sgt. Cadena of Lt. Hayden's crew stated, "The most spectacular sight I've ever seen was on D-Day; for as far as the eye could see, there were planes in the sky." A third mission consisting of 11 aircraft of A Group with a PFF, took off at 17:44 hours and another 11 aircraft of B Group, also with a PFF, took off at 17:44 hours. Railroad yards were bombed by both groups with A Group bombs away at 20:58 from 20,500 feet and B Group bombs away at 20:22 from 22,000 feet. Weather conditions were extremely bad when the groups returned to England, and nine aircraft landed at other bases. Those returning to Knettishall landed at 00:10—that's 10 minutes after midnight.

It had been quite a day and everyone was thinking about the young men who landed in France with our prayers going out to them.

We were also concentrating our raids on the site in France where the V-1 rockets were being launched. The Germans tried a new launch procedure. They would attach one of the V-1 flying bombs to an aircraft, send it over the North Sea and launch it toward London. These were not bound for any military target, as they could not be controlled. Their purpose was to destroy as much of London as possible and break the morale of the British. I can tell you for a fact they did not break the British morale. The British survived the horrible Battle of Britain and, seeing what destruction that caused, Mr. Hitler should just as well have given up.

About the launching of the V-1 from an aircraft: The route those damn things took was sending them over East Anglia, including our base. We could stand outside our tent and see them approaching. The jet engine emitted a flame that could be seen for miles. When they reached overhead, and they were not too high, the sound could be heard. It was an unusual sound and I have never forgotten it. We could hear it for a long time. When they approached, we all prayed that the launcher put sufficient gasoline to clear our base. We never had one fall on us, but once in awhile, after passing over the base, you would hear the engine cut out, followed a few seconds later by an explosion. We had an older fellow (he must have been 40) who didn't like those things. One time one went over and we couldn't find him. Later he showed up and we asked him where he had been. He answered, "When I saw that one coming, it was so low, I climbed that tree and held it down so it would get over." You know, I believed him.

The next super weapon launched by the Germans was the V-2, a large rocket with a powerful warhead, and a trajectory that would carry it to

London. This was a devastating weapon, as there was no warning of its approach. The damage was so bad that the British Government at first claimed the destruction was caused by a gas buildup. From our base we could see the contrails of these rockets as they left their launching pads in France. We did not know what we were seeing for some time, but it didn't take long before the BBC released the dreadful news. This became a priority target for our bombers for awhile. As the Allied advance continued through France, the launch site was overrun.

Another project the 388th Group was involved in that has seldom been talked about was Operation Aphrodite. Some members of the 560th Squadron were assigned to this project. This was an experimental project undertaken by both the British and the USAF to take war-weary aircraft (planes that were no longer capable of flying combat, but could still fly) and turn them into flying bombs. The 560th was working with the B-17. What they would do is completely strip the plane of all unnecessary equipment, making it as light as possible. It would then be turned into a bomb by loading it with explosives. A pilot and radio operator would then take the plane up and head toward France. Another B-17 (called the mother ship) was following from the rear and above. The mother ship had equipment that allowed it to control the flying bomb. Prior to reaching the coast of England, the pilot and radio operator would bail out and the mother ship would then control the flight of the flying bomb, known now as a drone. The idea was to have the mother ship control the drone, flying it directly into a target. From what I heard, this was not very successful. It seems the mother ship would miss the target by miles. It did not work out as planned.

We continued our missions, now hitting deep into the heartland of Germany. The Germans were running short of fuel and their pilots were overworked as our fighters were taking over control of the airspace. When our group started out, a crew was required to complete 25 missions before returning stateside; it had since been increased to 30 and, finally, to 35.

When I lost the *Mary Ellen* on the Frankfurt raid, January 29, 1944, the replacement ship went by the name *Mary's Sister*. Our chance of keeping a plane increased with the new fighter protection. This is the ship on which I flew a mission.

Now, I'll tell you a little story about what the combat crews went through. On July 24, 1944, Lt. Noyce was assigned to fly our ship. The crew reported to the ship and take-off time was delayed because of bad weather over the target. We were all sitting around the tent talking and I am not quite sure how the subject came up, but I made the remark I would like to fly a mission. The bombardier said to me that this would be a good mission as it was a "milk run." I said, "Fine." The bombardier said he would have to get the pilot to agree. He came back and said it would be okay, but I had to get a parachute. I went tearing down to the parachute shop and picked one up. It had to be hooked up three or four different ways; but this was a milk run, so I just threw it in the plane. I did not have any flying gear, so they fixed up an oxygen mask for me. I wore my sheepskin pants and jacket. They had an extra flak suit for me. That thing weighed at least 25 pounds and you wore it like a vest. I put it next to my parachute. The pilot said I was to fly in the waist, which was fine with me. We loaded up and taxied out for take-off. The skies were covered with clouds.

We were airborne around 09:30 and immediately entered the clouds in a climb. We broke out on top of the clouds at around 10,000 feet. The pilot ordered the crew to put on our oxygen masks. The waist gunners helped me get mine adjusted. The sight after breaking out above the clouds was breathtaking. In every direction you looked there were aircraft. Lead planes were shooting off colored flares so pilots could join the correct Groups. Planes kept breaking through the clouds and forming with their Group Leader. It was amazing—all the Groups forming over England to be in the proper place at the proper time. It takes quite some time getting everybody in their correct position. It seemed as far as I could see, Groups were following other Groups. At a certain point each Group, or a Wing, would head for its specific target. The weather cleared as we approached

France, and the ground looked a long way down. (This mission was support for ground troops west of St. Lo. The whole 8th Air Force was dispatched for saturation bombing to aid a break-through of our ground forces in that area.) I was looking out the waist window as we started our bomb run. As I looked up above I could see bursts of flak. It was way above us, so no sweat. The Lead plane did not release its bombs, and the Group made a large circle to make another run on the target. We also dropped from 20,000 feet to around 18,000. Run Number Two was over the target. We saw flak again but this time well below us. The Lead plane again failed to release the bombs. This was close support and the release had to be on target as our troops were down there.

Pass Number Three. As we approached the drop zone, I did not see any flak above or below, but I sure heard it. For this run, the pilot was down to 16,000 feet. The enemy had our range. (The report on flak when we returned was "meager but accurate flak…as well as 10-12 rockets.") One of the waist gunners told me the pilot had ordered everyone to put on parachutes as Number 2 engine had been hit.

When the flak started hitting the plane, it reminded me of hail on a tin roof. I had positioned myself so I was sitting on top of my flak vest. When he told me to put on my parachute, I picked it up and tried to put it on. With the heavy wool pants and jacket there was no way I could get that thing on. I finally threw it down and said to myself, if it goes down, so do I. The engine continued to run fine and we unloaded our bombs and got out of there.

After clearing the target, the Group started losing altitude, so we could take our oxygen masks off. The waist gunner told me that the bombardier wanted me to come up front. I received all this information from the waist gunner because I did not have ear phones and could not hear the conversations. I got myself in gear and went up into the bombardier's compartment. He told me he was sorry he had said it would be a milk run. Then he held up a piece of flak that had come through the Plexiglas nose and hit his flak suit.

The trip home was duck soup. We landed and taxied to the revetment. The pilot could not stop the Number 2 engine and asked me to come to the cockpit. I pushed the mixture control into the off position as he had done, but the engine would not stop. I knew what was wrong the minute I pushed the mixture control. There was no pressure, indicating that the cable must be severed. I idled the throttle back so it was running at about 700 rpm and cut the magneto. The engine stopped with no problem. I got out of the plane from the rear and started around to the front and knew I was in trouble. The Line Chief, Pinky Bebernis, was waiting for me.

I got holy hell for my little escapade, but I didn't care. I had been on a mission.

The plane was out of commission for about a week. A piece of flak had cut the cable controlling the fuel mixture. When that happened, the mixture control went to full rich causing the Number 2 engine to release smoke from the exhaust. This is what the pilot saw when he ordered us to put on parachutes. The Plexiglas nose had to be replaced. A large piece of flak had punctured one of the main gasoline tanks and that was one big job, replacing it.

I not only got a ride, I also had to work day and night to get the plane back in flying condition. So much for my combat experience.

It only gave me even more respect for the crews that flew these missions day after day.

# STEPPING UP TO THE PLATE

By John P. "Jack" Gauthier, pilot, 562nd Squadron

Our start as a crew was a little different than most.

I had been ordered to Salt Lake City after completing B-17 transition training, to be assigned a crew. That happened as planned, but when the crew was formed and we were sent to Drew Field, Tampa, Florida, the assigned bombardier was taken off the crew because he outranked me. He was a first lieutenant, so his assignment to my crew was a violation of Air Corps policy which stated that the first pilot of a crew must be the senior officer.

Because of his reassignment, I and my remaining crew were in limbo for a week or more awaiting assignment of another bombardier. It never happened. Instead, the eight remaining members of my crew were reassigned. Once again I was in limbo, this time waiting for an entire crew.

There was a pool of potential co-pilots. These were newly graduated pilots who, through no fault of their own, became co-pilots to those of us who were lucky enough to get the additional training. I had been agitating to do some flying and finally got the attention of the Squadron Operations Officer who picked one of these newly graduated pilots to fly with me. Ralph Reese had never flown a B-17, but seemed eager to go flying with a flight engineer and me. On our first flight we stayed in the pattern while I made some practice landings, all of which that rugged old bird survived without damage. After demonstrating that I was master of the airplane, I asked Lt. Reese if he thought he could land that big bird. He said he didn't know, but would like to try. Well he greased it. Made a beautiful landing, much better than any I had made. Momentarily I hated him. Convinced that he had lucked-out, I said, "I'll bet you can't do that again." He tried, but the pressure was too great or he ran out of luck. His second landing was pretty bad. I felt better.

Nevertheless, on that first flight I was impressed with Ralph's assured steadiness and was convinced that with experience in the airplane he would become a competent B-17 pilot. So I asked him if he would like to crew up with me. He agreed, so I asked that he be assigned to my crew and he was. For a few days there were just the two of us, but soon we were joined by the other eight members which made us a complete crew. Our crew roster was then as follows :

| | | |
|---|---|---|
| John P. (Jack) Gauthier | 2nd Lt | Pilot |
| Ralph M. Reese | 2nd Lt | Co-pilot |
| Albert C. (Al) Weidenbusch | 2nd Lt | Navigator |
| Harry J. (Monty) Montevideo | 2nd Lt. | Bombardier |
| Seymore E. (Jack) Vann | Sgt. | Flight Engineer |
| Arthur Smith | Cpl. | Radio Operator |
| Basil E. Smith | Cpl. | Tail Gunner |
| Eugene Forti | Sgt. | Ball Turret Gunner |
| Raymond A. Rome | Pfc. | Waist Gunner |
| John W. (Dutch) Dorion | Pfc. | Waist Gunner |

Once our crew was formed, combat training started immediately. Like all other crews headed for the 8th Air Force, we did a lot of day-and-night, cross-country, high altitude, formation and "blue bombing." It was apparent from the start that we had a sharp navigator and a bombardier we should have called "Shack." Most of our training missions were accomplished without difficulty, but one night cross-country was a sweat for Al as there wasn't much visibility, and it became a sweat for me when we reached Tampa on our return.

We were on top of an overcast. I had been trained in basic instrument flying but had never made an actual instrument approach. I made what was probably the worst non-precision approach ever completed successfully, but we broke out with about a 500-foot ceiling and landed without incident. Pure Steve Canyon-like skill. Al told me he thought it was great, that he enjoyed flying down the streets of Tampa.

One mission we flew was not a part of the training syllabus. It was a search mission over the Gulf of Mexico in very questionable weather. We were searching for survivors of a MacDill Field B-26 ditching. Because of the ceiling, we flew very close to the water and I had a ball. I guess I was the only one having fun. Al was sweating out finding Tampa when we finished the search and most of the others were afraid I was going to put them in the drink. We found no sign of the missing airplane or its crew but navigationally the mission was a success. Doing dead reckoning with only a little help from a wobbly bird dog (radio compass), Al made a field goal on Tampa Bay.

After what seemed years, but was actually about four months, we finished our combat crew training and were shipped to Hunter Field, Savannah, Georgia. Arriving there on April 14th, I was issued a brand spanking new B-17G. Boy, was it nice! I use "I" here because I signed for it like it was mine "to have and to hold for as long as we both shall exist." Wow, was I naive.

We stayed at Hunter Field for only a few days while flying the airplane twice to check all systems. There were few discrepancies, so we were able to depart for Ft. Dix, New Jersey on 18 April. Arriving there in the late afternoon, we were immediately restricted to the base on the grounds that we had to be ready to leave at any time. I checked the weather and decided that an early departure was very unlikely, so we gambled. Ralph's home was in Philadelphia, so we officers went there. Ralph got to see his parents and I had the pleasure of meeting them. It was readily apparent why Ralph was so cool and steady. He came from that kind of environment.

Our next destination was Bangor, Maine. Our only purpose in stopping there was to get a new weather briefing and refuel. I wondered why we were directed to stop there when the following stop, Goose Bay, Labrador, was well within the fuel range of the airplane. I guess the big decision makers were worried about the competence of new crews. Our route to Bangor took us over Rhode Island where I had a brother stationed at the Quonset Point Naval Air Station. He wanted to show off his little brother B-17 pilot by having us buzz the field. He had cleared it with his buddies who worked in the tower, so we did a fair job of beating up the field. I later learned that they really did not expect us to fly below the height of the hangar roofs and that all hands involved got a chewing out for setting it up. All of our guys enjoyed it. Being Army, we got a kick out of buzzing a Navy field.

The stop at Bangor, Maine was short. We re-fueled, briefed and were on our way to Labrador. The flight was uneventful. There we delayed for two days due to marginal weather over the North Atlantic. With nothing to do but wait, we killed some time fishing. Being from Minnesota where the fishing is usually good, I expected it to be even better this far north. It wasn't. After chopping holes through the ice and freezing our butts for hours we had only a few very small fish.

At this time we had been together as a crew for four months. We four officers spent most of our time together, day and night. Today's popular word for what was happening among us is bonding. We had confidence in each other as members of the same crew and we cared about each other as people. We shared material things, loaned each other money and were completely at ease with each other. Yes, we bonded. My relationship with my own brother was never as close as I felt to these three men. My relationships with the enlisted men on the crew were not as close, nor should they have been. With one exception, I liked and respected all of the enlisted crew, but I did not deal with them to the same extent as I did the officers. Jack Vann was our crew engineer and senior NCO. I used the chain of command through him to deal with them in routine matters. We were friendly, but not to the extent that enlisted crew members called me or the other officers by our first names. There were lapses, but by and large we maintained the commissioned-enlisted relationships that were traditional, effective and expected.

As we neared the time when we would be entering combat together I knew that each member of the crew would do his job well and would do his utmost to keep me and the others from harm's way, just as I would do all in my power to take care of them. I'm sure that the camaraderie that existed among the officers and the discipline that existed in all crew members was a big factor in our later success as a Lead crew.

On the third morning after arrival at Goose Bay we were cleared for the most challenging leg of the trip. The weather forecast was not as good as we'd have liked, but with scattered to broken clouds at multiple levels and visibility varying from three to 10 miles, it was judged flyable by the weather guessers. We realized that this flight to Iceland was big-league flying and that in experience we were minor league flyers, so we prepared carefully. Our preflight inspection of the aircraft and flight planning were very thorough. I enjoyed preparing the aircraft, planning the flight and briefing the crew almost as much as the flight itself. There was great satisfaction in having the flight proceed almost exactly as planned. After a good job of navigation by Al and only a little sweating on my part while we were in clouds and accumulating ice, we landed in Iceland in reasonably good weather. This being our first trans-oceanic flight, we were feeling pretty smug. We had done it just like the pros.

I can't imagine anyone living in Iceland voluntarily. It is the bleakest, barest, coldest, least hospitable and most uncomfortable place I have ever been. What I remember most is being restricted to the base, being cold and spending a lot of time in the sack trying to keep warm. We did look in vain for a large tree hoping to see the beautiful blonde that is alleged to be behind each one. We soon came to understand the legend. The flight from Iceland to Prestwick, Scotland must have been uneventful, for I remember only sweating being recognized as friendly as we approached the United Kingdom. We had been assigned the code name "forelock-jig" (odd that I remember it, having used it only once) and received a friendly response on our first radio call. We were soon on the ground after one of my better landings.

On a long flight, especially one as challenging as the one we had just completed, there is a lot for the pilot to think about. Most of us navigate in our head, a sort of intuitive dead reckoning that we use to compare with the information we receive from the navigator. We also monitor the aircraft systems along with the flight engineer, and we evaluate weather information as it becomes available. We do a lot of "what if" thinking. If we do our job right, we always have a contingency plan in mind.

Still, there's time for other thoughts, too. As we approached the UK I thought about our future and how little I knew about what lay ahead. We were about to begin the business we had all been trained for. Uncle Sam had a big investment in this crew. I had been in a very expensive training program for 19 months; most of the others for almost as long. Were we ready? I knew that I flew the airplane well and that the co-pilot, navigator, bombardier and gunners were good at their jobs. Outwardly, I was very confident, but there were moments when I wondered about my courage. Would I and the other crew members be able to handle the fear that most normal persons experience when in grave danger? I had no answers to my questions, but felt intuitively that we would do as well or better than most.

The last transmission I had from the Prestwick tower was, "Be sure to remove all of your personal property from the aircraft; you probably will not see it again."

In a few minutes a maintenance office arrived to sign for the aircraft. My beautiful bird was no longer mine. "To have and to hold" lasted about 10 days.

Our stay at Prestwick was very brief. Within 24 hours we were on a train and soon arrived at Stone in the English Midlands. We weren't sure we were still in England. The Midlands dialect is so different from American English that at first we couldn't understand what was being said. Our first evening there we had fun at a pub joshing with the locals who had become accustomed to our speech. They could easily understand us but we had to listen very carefully to their dialect as they laid it on as thickly as possible.

It was here that we saw a P-38 hit a flag pole.

There had been a lot of buzzing. This pass was lower than most. He hit the pole with his right wing, cutting off the pole about eight feet from the top. The cut-off portion cart-wheeled through the air for quite a distance before landing, without injury to persons or damage to property. I would like to have been a mouse listening in the corner when the pilot explained the damaged wing to his CO.

Stone was a "Repple-Depple"—replacement depot—where we spent only a day or two before our gunners were sent to The Wash for gunnery refresher and we officers went to Bovington for a few days of theater orientation. I remember little of Bovington, but I do remember that this was our first exposure to the war. We witnessed an air raid and were fascinated seeing the bombers caught in the floodlights. The flak was heavy and after shrapnel began falling near us we decided that the show could go on without us. We got under cover.

Our trip to Knettishall was in the cargo section of a six-by-six truck that had been sent for us.

Our reception at the 562nd Squadron was not the kind that would give one a swelled head. We did not expect a brass band, but some preparation for our arrival would have been nice. We officers were assigned four spaces in an officers' barracks. These spaces had belonged to a crew that had been shot down that day. Their soiled bedding was still on the cots and some of their personal belongings remained in the lockers. To make my arrival even more memorable, one of the pilots whose cot was opposite mine greeted me as follows:

"What size blouse do you wear? I think I can use it when you get shot down."

I replied that if my blouse would fit him, his would fit me, and asked that he please keep his clean and pressed.

So at long-last we were resident members of the 388th Bomb Group. It was time to step up to the plate, to show our stuff, to pay for all of that expensive training and all the fun we had doing it.

In spite of our unenthusiastic welcome I was glad we were there and I was ready to do the job.

*The Gauthier Crew, from left, Gene Forti, waist gunner; John Dorian, waist gunner; Jack Vann, engineer; John Seeger, radio operator; Jack Gauthier, pilot; Basil Smith, tail gunner; Al Weidenbusch, navigator; Ralph Reese, co-pilot; Harry Montevideo, bombardier.*

# I Didn't Have to Go

From a recorded interview with Joe Capraro
waist gunner, 561st Squadron

I didn't have to go into combat. I was at Lowry Field in December 1941 when war was declared. They had drafted my brother; the draft had already started in 1941. They had drafted all my friends.

I wanted to fly. All my friends had been sent into the infantry; but I wanted to fly, so I enlisted in the Air Corps. I *thought* I was in the Air Corps, until about six weeks later when I found out I was in an ordnance company *attached* to the Air Corps. I didn't even know the word ordnance meant bombs and stuff like that. I thought that they were city laws or government rules.

When war was declared it so happened that I had been a clerk in civilian life and I could type. That was big! Anyhow, we were transferred from Lowry Field, Colorado to Buckley Field, Colorado which was about nine miles away. There was nothing at Buckley Field except a lookout tower and ammunition dumps. We were sent there to guard those ammunition dumps.

Well, since I was in the office as Chief Clerk, I was in charge of the cadre that went to Buckley Field. And then I got promoted; and first thing you know, I was the acting First Sergeant of this ordnance company. And so I spent almost half the war—or more—at Lowry and Buckley Fields. When I started trying to get into flying, my commanding officer would not permit it. He said, "We need you here. You can't go." Well, the adjutant at headquarters said to me behind my CO's back, "I'll sign your papers if you can pass." I took my tests and passed, and then we told our CO and he got very, very upset.

Anyhow, I left. I volunteered to go into battle, in other words. That's what happened.

Then I went into Aviation Cadet training. They washed out about a zillion guys around the time that I got a good start. I happened to be one of them. They gave the staff sergeants and up a choice. They said: "You can go to gunnery school or go into the infantry. Which do you want?" Well, I wanted to fly, so I went into gunnery school. I went to Las Vegas Army airbase, which is now Nelles Air Force Base, and took gunnery there. It was very exciting; very, very good experience.

And then we went into combat training, from Las Vegas to the airbase in Rapid City, South Dakota, and learned how to fly against the enemy. We were shooting at everything we could think of. We were transferred to Lincoln, Nebraska, and at Lincoln they assigned a brand new, shiny B-17 to us. We were all excited that we got this new airplane. And we took very good care of it. We flew it from there to a base up in Manchester, New Hampshire, where we got our orders. We were not permitted to open the orders until we were over the Atlantic. After we left the United States the pilot opened the orders and found out that we had been ordered to Wales. Now remember this beautiful B-17 that we had and were all excited about? When we landed at Wales they marched all of us from the airplane to our barracks, and that was the last time we saw that B-17. Because you see, new crews got the old junky airplanes and the old crews got the brand new ones.

The one we were assigned to when we got to Knettishall was really two parts of two airplanes that had crashed. The tail end of one they had joined onto the front of the other, and that's the one we had. That gives you an idea of what it was all about. However, we did not fly this one on our first mission; we flew *Heavens Above*.

So then we started to fly our missions.

Although we were there in September, I didn't fly my first mission until November 9, 1944. As soon as we arrived, the whole crew—all the new crews—had to go through indoctrination. The second day that we were there at the base we went to an evening class. It was in a building that was next to an ammunition dump. We were in class when we started hearing boom, boom, boom, boom. It was one of the buzz bombs that the Germans were sending over. The instructor said, "That's a buzz bomb." Everybody was squirming in their chair and everything. He then said, "There are shelters right outside the door, right behind the ammunition dump, so if you'd feel better about being safe, go ahead and get into the shelters."

We didn't. Nobody moved. We just sat there. But the sounds just started getting louder and louder, and finally, he said, "Okay, that's close enough. Go to your shelters." And that's what we did.

After that, our indoctrination included a lot of things. It included flying over England and the North Sea. After we were assigned an airplane, the pilot had to get accustomed to it. Although, very frankly, they didn't get much time. After a couple of hours they were supposed to be experienced.

We learned that we were at the Country Club of the 8th Air Force. That's what they called our base because we had dry cleaning and laundry, and we had a Rocker Club and an Officers' Club. We had an Enlisted Men's Club. We had it made! But I'm sure that there were some other bases that were just about as nice. The Rocker Club was where I fit in. If you were a staff sergeant and up, then you were a member of the Rocker Club. And, of course, you paid no dues; you just automatically became a member.

In the beginning, there was no fear. Some of the new guys might have had some fear; but there was no fear in my soul, my mind. Not at that stage. There was no fear in my mind at all—until the third mission. And then I thought maybe I wouldn't make it.

Our first mission was very interesting because we really got hit hard. But since it *was* the first mission, it was all new and it was all very exciting. When I wasn't shooting I was standing at the waist window watching everything that was going on. Flak was going off all around. We'd hear it splatter; we could even smell it—smell the smoke. I thought that was great!

When we got back to the barracks and I lay down on the bunk that evening I got to thinking, you know, that was really an exciting situation. I thought, "Gee that's great!" but pretty soon somebody walked in from the Rocker Club and said, "such and so's crew didn't get back yet." And then somebody else came in and said, "I think we lost three ships today." It was that kind of conversation. I was lying there and I thought, gee, there were only 13 of us up; that means we lost three out of 13. Only 10 of us came back.

And then it began to occur to me that maybe this was not going to be very healthy.

The second mission was pretty much the same. On the third mission I realized that this was very, very serious business. But, you know, I really felt like I wasn't as afraid as many people. I really did feel that I was not as afraid, for example, as our tail gunner who eventually went off his rocker. He had a family and I didn't. He had a wife and two kids. And he got so that it was impossible to do anything with him.

Our pilot blew up, too, and they had to ground him, permanently. He couldn't fly the airplane. Over Hamburg, Germany, we were getting it so bad that he just cowered in his seat and told the co-pilot to take over. The co-pilot actually had been hit in the foot and I had been hit in the face by flak. But the co-pilot took over and flew the plane for the rest of the mission over the North Sea and back to England. When we got back, the co-pilot came to the whole crew. We had a meeting, and he said, "The pilot's not fit to fly these missions anymore." He was jeopardizing our lives. He completely went off his rocker that day, but prior to that, our co-pilot said that he just couldn't stand the flak, the fighters and all that kind of stuff. He had started to get drunk every night. He would go to the Officers' Club and everybody knew him. He was such a wonderful guy, and a nice guy. Very considerate of everybody. He always made sure things were done just so for his crew; and yet, he just folded up. That's all there is to it. I don't blame him for that. Not at all.

So, he had to be grounded and we didn't see him anymore after that. Our co-pilot became our pilot.

Actually, I think I was too stupid to get that afraid. Because anytime anything came up aboard that airplane, they would call on me to take care of it. For example, sometimes when you dropped your bombs, they wouldn't all fall away, and so somebody had to go kick them out. You kicked out bombs in an open bomb bay. You know that narrow catwalk, right through the middle of the bomb bay? You went in there and hung onto whatever you could hang on to, and you tried to kick the bombs out.

Well, it was always me. "Joe, go on up there and get those bombs out of that bomb bay." It was part of what we had to do.

Between missions, we had a good time. We always got as many passes as we could to either the surrounding community or into London. So we always had a good time. We all had bicycles; everybody in my crew had a bicycle. And I think everybody in every crew had a bicycle. I paid four pounds for mine, and four pounds in those days was $16 American. It was a lot of money. We would ride these bikes to wherever we were going, and we even pretended that we were flying. Going around turns and banking, and all that kind of stuff; and sometimes the pilot and co-pilot would be with us as well.

The navigator was a great guy. His nickname was Buck Rodgers. I don't remember off-hand what his first name actually was. He was such a good navigator that he rescued the whole group, because we had been shot up. People lost their direction, and our navigator told the whole group where we were and where to go. We were so good that we became a Deputy Lead crew and also flew as Lead crew.

At first I was right waist, and then, you know what they did? They eliminated one crew member. They eliminated the other waist gunner on all the airplanes. The other waist gunner was sent to the Bloody 100th. He didn't survive.

Do you know about the Bloody 100th? It seems there was an unwritten law of war that if you wanted to give up you dropped your landing gear. And the Germans would escort us to the ground or we would escort them to the ground. So this B-17 in the 100th ran into engine trouble above the clouds, of course, and the Germans were attacking; so the pilot decided to give up. He dropped the landing gear and two German fighters dropped in alongside of him and started to escort him to the ground. They ran into a very thick cloud bank in the meantime, and the pilot got the engines running. He told the crew, "When we break out of the bottom of this cloud, shoot those guys down." And that's what they did. Trouble is, they didn't shoot them both down; they shot only one of them down. Whether this story is true or not, this is the way I got it when I was in England. The fighter pilot got back to his base and reported it, so then the German radio started announcing that from now on the Bloody 100th was going to get it. From then on, whenever the Bloody 100th flew, if you were here and they were over there, the German fighters would likely go after the Bloody 100th.

Not only that, but if there were any B-24 groups around they'd go after the B-24s instead of the B-17s. We could maintain excellent formation, even in combat. The Germans soon learned that they could break up the B-24s. They could break up their formation and then pick them off. We called them very good fighter cover. It was a big joke.

When I came back to the United States after I finished my missions, the war was still going on. When we got to Boston—we came back on a Liberty Liner—when we got back we were welcomed to the United States in a great big theater. We were told that we were not to say anything bad about B-24s because mothers still had boys flying B-24s in Europe.

I don't mean to be putting down the B-24. Fact of the matter is, it was a better airplane. It could fly faster, it could fly higher, it could carry a bigger bomb load. Problem was, it couldn't fly formation and the Germans found out and that was that. It was a better airplane for many reasons, and they did use a lot of B-24s in the South Pacific, because they were over the water most of the time. They didn't have to deal with fighters and flak all the way to the target and back. So the B-24s were very instrumental in the South Pacific.

You know, there were three divisions in the 8th Air Force; the 1st, 2nd and 3rd Divisions. We were in the 3rd Division. The only division that had B-24s was the 2nd Division. And it got so—and this is for sure, we were told—that the B-24s were barely cracking the front lines and they'd drop their bombs and go back because they didn't dare go deep into Germany at that stage of the game. Needless to say, the B-24s were used in some of the biggest raids, particularly in the beginning of the war. Ploesti, for example; the oil fields—the B-24s were there first. They really caught it. Most everybody made it to that target, including our Group.

What was it like getting wounded? First of all, I thought I had lost my face. I don't know if you've ever been hit in the face hard, but I was. Anyhow, we had oxygen masks, and we had goggles. You never wore your goggles, really, until you got into combat, because in case your aircraft started burning, it would help keep your eyes from getting burned. Anyhow, this flak burst that almost got me was also the burst that saved my life. It was so close that it made the airplane lurch—whoom, whoom—and so as it went up and down, the flak came through the Plexiglas window and hit me in the face. There were all kinds of little splinters in my face. One piece of flak that I picked up had lost its momentum; otherwise it would have gone out the other side. It creased my head, taking off a little bit of hair and some skin, and there was a drop of blood. And that was it. And the other piece of flak that hit me was just a splinter; the scar that you see today is due to the infection that set in afterward. But I reported on the intercom to the rest of the crew that I was wounded, and I really did think that I had lost my face because that's the way it felt; yet, it was nothing. Absolutely nothing. My pilot wanted to turn me in for a Purple Heart, but I insisted no; because, after all, I wasn't really wounded. When we got back to the base I went into the latrine, and I could spot little pieces of flak as well as Plexiglas. But it was only skin deep; I mean, you could rub it off. Nothing to it.

*Joe Capraro after his promotion to Second Lieutenant*

You know, we each had a flak suit. I don't know what it weighed, but it was heavy. And we also had a flak helmet. The flak helmet actually fit over your leather helmet and earphones; and it had flaps to fold down over your ears. But most of the time you didn't wear it, because all of a sudden you were under attack, and when you were under attack, you didn't have time to go grabbing your helmet. Although I suppose that would have been the smartest thing you could do. But it was a pretty heavy helmet and, needless to say, I wasn't wearing it that day. Our flak suit was like an apron. It fit down to your waist, both front and rear, as I recall. It would hold off flak or even a bullet, I suppose. It was also very heavy. Once you put that on you couldn't maneuver very well because it just weighed you down. I don't think I wore mine more than once or twice. You didn't have the strength to wear the flak suit and helmet that long.

The backs of the seats for the pilots and co-pilots had a piece of sheet metal about half-an-inch thick. The crew members, including the navigator and the bombardier, would go out and hunt for pieces of scrap sheet metal that we would put on the floor. With flak shooting up toward you, a lot of it came through the floor. In fact, over one of our targets, one piece came through the floor about two inches from my foot. We also spread out our flak suits on the floor and sides.

The gloves we wore were heated. They were leather and they plugged into the rest of your heated suit, just like you'd plug into a wall. Inside the heated gloves there were very thin nylon gloves. The object of these nylon gloves was that if your guns got jammed up and you needed to release the jamb, if you took your gloves off and touched that gun, your hand would freeze to the gun. And if you pulled your hand off the gun, you'd pull all the flesh off, too. That's how cold it was. So your nylon gloves would let you work on the gun so that you could get back to work shooting the enemy down.

I've already mentioned that my brother was in the infantry—he was in the 1st Infantry Division. On the day I flew my last mission, we got out of the airplane, we rolled on the ground and kissed it. The first sergeant handed me a telegram from my parents telling me that my brother had been hit. That's all they said. They didn't know anything else. I knew that since we had flown our last mission, I would be leaving England pretty soon. I decided that I wanted to bail out over the front lines and find out where my brother was.

Well, that was stupid. I know it now, but at that time I was gung-ho and I wanted to know.

So I got permission to go see my Commanding Officer and I told him what I wanted to do. I said, "I know where the 1st Infantry Division is and so does the Group, and so on the Group's next mission, drop me off as close as possible." He was flabbergasted! He put his arms on his knees and said, "Young man, I wouldn't permit you to do that. It would be suicide." He said, "Now, I understand, and I'm with you all the way. It would be wonderful if you could find your brother. But the fact of the matter is, it can't be done."

And the funny thing is that when I met him at one of our reunions I asked him if he remembered anybody who did that, who went to him and asked for permission to bail out, and he said he definitely remembered.

Some of our people were very young. Most of our pilots had about 450 hours of practice before they went into combat. They learned combat by going into combat, and that was it.

We were involved with the 200th mission party, and it was wonderful. I'll never forget it. It was just fantastic. They brought busload after busload of ladies from the neighboring communities: Bury St. Edmunds and Thetford and all around. They always did that. We had such a good time that night, dancing and singing and eating and drinking. You know, not getting drunk, but eating. The group was not involved in a mission the next day and my crew had not been on our first mission yet.

We played different sports during off days. There was also a gunnery range. You could go down and shoot at the range. The first time I ever saw a German jet was when we were playing touch football on the field. We heard this jet noise—never heard it before in my life; and so we looked up but there was no airplane there. He had already passed over by the time we heard the noise. That was quite an experience. We saw him in the distance flying away.

On one of our missions, we were hit by the ME-262s. It was amazing. Our turrets could not keep up with the speed of the German jets as they came through the formation. The turrets—neither the top nor bottom; in fact, nobody on that airplane—could keep up with them. They came right through the formation.

Also, the Germans had a rocket ship. It was called a Kadet and it was a rocket; it was not a jet. It had about enough fuel for three to five minutes worth of combat. What happened was, they'd come up and they'd be out of range of our guns, and they looked like pollywogs up there. And then at some given signal they'd come in. They'd make one pass—that was it.

I'd like to tell you about our beds.

We had a mattress that we called an English biscuit because it was two sections with a space between where you pushed them together to keep from freezing to death. That was our mattress. Nobody had any sheets, even though we were on the Country Club base of the 8th Air Force. But we had blankets, so whenever crews would go down we would "borrow" their blankets. It was cold in England, and cold air would come up between these two biscuits. It was practically impossible to keep warm. The only stove we had was a pot-bellied stove in the middle of the barracks that burned coke. When you ran out of fuel, you couldn't get more. So it got cold. You were allotted a certain amount of coke, and when you ran out, when the old stove went out, that was the end of the heat. Well, we would take these blankets…

Pretty soon, I began to feel numb when I slept. One side of my body was numb. And I couldn't figure out the reason why. Other people were complaining that they were also numb while they were trying to sleep. One day the supply sergeant decided that he needed some blankets, so he came to the barracks and raided all the beds that had more than the allotted number, and guess what? I was no longer numb after that. The weight of the blankets was making me numb during the night! That is a fact. An absolute fact.

As far as sheets were concerned, we went into London; I can't remember where, but I midnight-requisitioned some sheets and took them back to the base with me. I was one of the few guys in the barracks who had any sheets.

Life at the base? It was good and it was bad. Many, many English ladies would bring a lot of pastries and they would serve them every night. You know, they had some kind of refreshment, maybe something very simple, including some of these fruit dyes in sugar, that they put in water. And then you could have the different kind of cookies that they made; very little sugar, if any.

There was no fence around our base. In fact, our barracks was close enough to the village, you know, cottages, so that we could walk from our barracks to these homes. When I first got there, I used to hire my clothes laundered and pressed by an English family. Well, it got so I felt sorry for them. The lady had an iron that was just a solid, heavy piece of iron with a handle that she would put on the fire to heat. Then she'd come back and iron the shirt. It wouldn't last very long and she'd have to go back and heat it again and iron a little bit more. And I thought, man, that is a lot of work, and she wasn't accepting enough pay. Well, I didn't have a lot of pay to give her anyway, but needless to say, I thought, well, I'm not going to let that happen anymore. We did have a little laundry on our base, and I used to then take it to the laundry.

Little kids always used to come around the base. We would usually give them gum and candy.

Also on the base there were two different times to eat. Flying crews got one kind of food, they told us, and ground crews got a different kind of food. Once you were airborne and flying in combat, they didn't want you to get sick. It would be terrible if you got airsick while being attacked by the Germans. Therefore, we got different food than the other people on the base. I don't know what the difference was. I never ate both kinds. But I know that they gave us very, very good food. We did get powdered milk, and we got oranges, for example. That was something the English people hadn't even seen since before the war. Powdered eggs; well, maybe they were terrible, but at that time I could eat, and I did eat. And we must not forget the number of ways that we got Spam.

We weren't supposed to keep a diary, but I thought I could make some notes and leave them at the barracks after every mission and therefore nobody could get them. They'd have to invade England and wipe out the place to get my notes. So, I just left them with my luggage all the time. I didn't know it, but my pilot was doing the same thing; and so was my co-pilot. I don't know who else did it, because we didn't tell each other then.

The Germans had fantastic intelligence. When we were approaching Scotland coming from the United States over the North Sea, the Germans greeted us, believe it or not. We were late, because when we landed at Goose Bay, Labrador, there was a turbo bucket, I think they called it, in one of the engines that was not working right. We had to replace it. But they didn't have the parts, so we sat at Goose Bay for three days while the rest of the group from Rapid City, South Dakota, went ahead. We were coming into Scotland all by ourselves when we were greeted by the Germans. Now, I didn't hear this on our intercom, but our pilot said, "The Germans are greeting us," because he heard it on the intercom. I think what he meant was that they were playing American-style music.

While in combat our orders were that any airplane that points its nose at you, you shoot. In other words, I have shot at our own P-51s. Because, for example, a German ME-109 or a Focke-Wulf would be coming in shooting at us and they'd peel off, but the pilot behind them was a P-51. You didn't stop shooting. The pilot knew that he was not supposed to point his nose at you. Therefore, we just kept shooting.

Some of the B-17s that had been captured by the Germans, perhaps because they had crash landed, would be repaired and used against us. They would get into the air, and then they would try to join our formation, like they were a stray out there. For protection they'd "re-join your formation." Well, that was a no-no, too. If you became a stray, the orders were you were not to re-join a formation. Because they didn't know whether you were a German or a friend, and therefore, they didn't know whether to shoot at you or not. However, needless to say, there was radio, so you could really identify yourself. Each mission had a name, an identification name. And each airplane had a name. Our squadron was Vampire Yellow.

"Vampire Yellow, Vampire Yellow, this is such and so, Vampire Yellow," and so that was the code name of our squadron. If they couldn't properly identify themselves, you shot them down, or they shot *you* down. They'd get into our formation and fly all the way back to England. And, finally, they'd open up on whoever might be closest to them. Then they would peel off, and they'd go back to Germany.

I knew a sergeant whose name was Patrick and he had been in England with the 388th from the day that they were first there. He wanted to go home, and so he would volunteer to fly missions. So this one morning, Patrick was at our table. He was very happy because this was going to be his last mission before he went home. He flew as a radio gunner. Radio gunners did very little shooting, if any. So Patrick had volunteered and flew on his last mission. Well, he didn't make it. A German fighter cut his plane in half. Collided with them and cut them in half. That was the last time we saw Patrick. That was it.

I want to tell you another story about our ball turret gunner. We called him Squirt. He was from Waukegan, Illinois, and his neighbor was also in the 388th and, in fact, in our squadron. To be honest with you, I don't remember the neighbor's name. What happened was that we were on a mission and a German fighter rammed his neighbor's airplane from the back. Evidently, the German pilot got too close and was probably killed by the tail gunner, but the airplane kept going and going and rammed the B-17 in the back, and the B-17 went down. We watched it go down. We would always shout from the tops of our lungs on the intercom to bail out—we were shouting at the people in the other airplane to bail out. Pretty soon we saw somebody on the other airplane bail out. But we didn't see a parachute. So, that was the end of his neighbor, we thought.

When we got back to the barracks, Squirt was worried because he wanted to write a letter to the parents, but he didn't want to say that he saw their son get killed; so he and I composed a letter in which we indicated that there was a chance…chances were that he might have made it. We wrote the letter and that was the end of it. Afterwards, when we were finished in England, we were sent to the Santa Ana Army Air Base in California, because we were heading for the South Pacific. All the 8th Air Force ended up heading for the South Pacific before it was over with. Now, we ended up in Santa Ana on the air base, and I got there first; so I waited for Squirt to get there. When he arrived, I wanted to know how the neighbor's parents had taken the news, and he said, "he beat us home!"

The airplane had, of course, exploded as Squirt's friend was coming down, unconscious. When he came to, he had his chest chute on a strap (we each had a chest chute, usually on the floor, and it was attached to your waist on a strap). So, this guy came to, saw this chest chute flapping up there. He pulled it down, yanked it on, pulled the ripcord and it happened to be close to our own front lines and our troops picked him up. They sent him back to England and from there they put him aboard a ship and sent him back to the United States. We stayed there finishing our missions, and he got back to Waukegan before our ball turret gunner did.

Isn't that interesting?

# HARD LUCK AND BACK

By Paul Arbon, lead navigator
Swift's crew, *Virgin on the Verge*, 561st Squadron

The most exciting and hectic six months of my life began on 14 June 1943 when my squadron left Bangor, Maine. During those six months I lost several friends and comrades, witnessed unspeakable horrors and had more than a few close shaves, but I can honestly say that I loved it.

Foolhardiness? Heroism? It is not for me to judge. What I can honestly say is that I had a cast iron conviction that I would survive. It became a custom among the aircrews for friends to "bequeath" each other personal items in the event of their not returning from a mission. I had an expensive Rolex watch and more than once friends asked if they could inherit it. My reply was always the same: "I'll be back."

In the very early days this attitude had its basis in ignorance; I simply did not know what we were in for. We had the best military aircraft ever invented. We had well-trained crews. We had modern equipment. We had effective aerial armament and bomb loads calculated to knock the stuffing out of the enemy. What we did not have, in the early days, was fighter escort. Our large bombers were inviting targets for Hermann Goering's Messerschmitts and Fokkers.

But all this we did not know as we touched down at our base, Knettishall airfield on the Suffolk-Norfolk border near Thetford. However, I do remember experiencing a sudden twinge as we descended to the runway. The fields all around were luridly red with poppies. Could it be an omen?

In this phase of the war, Allied strategy involved daylight bombing raids on German industrial sites and armament factories. Most of this offensive was carried out by the USAF. All Liberator (B-24) and Flying

67

Fortress (B-17) heavy bomber bases were in East Anglia for practical reasons. It was the closest to the Germans and we had The Wash, a huge body of water, over which we could circle while forming our squadrons into our Group, picking up the late-comers and getting them into their designated slots in preparation to set off on the mission of the day.

Our first mission on 17 July was to attack enemy targets near and in Amsterdam. It was an easy expedition for us to cut our teeth on. These heavy bomber raids were in their infancy and we did not have fighter support except for the brave little Spitfires. We were dismayed to discover that their fuel range was very limited. However, in our enthusiasm and braggadocio we believed we could manage without them.

We could not have been more wrong.

Our first real taste of rugged combat came on the next raid to Hannover on 26 July. We realized that it would be no picnic from now on as we approached the target. We had to wear oxygen masks above 12,000 feet and we were flying at 23,000 feet to avoid the enemy flak.

We were also told that we should always wear our parachutes. This was just one of the rules that was regularly broken. I certainly never wore my parachute, because it got in the way. My job was Lead Navigator and I needed space for the charts and instruments I used to get us to our targets and back again. In addition, I also had to operate two side-mounted machine guns. Another rule which was honored more in the breach than the observance was the order to carry gas masks. We would regularly remove the gas mask from its case and substitute something more comforting, such as a bottle of gin.

Just before nearing Hannover we flew through a very heavy bombardment of flak and almost immediately we were attacked by swarms of enemy fighters. None of us were prepared mentally or physically for this in spite of what we had been told. It was pandemonium. I hardly had a second to register, but saw our left wing plane going down in flames. It was flown by a good friend of mine, Gordon Amos.

We had hardly recovered from this blooding when we were sent off two days later to Oschersleben, 290 miles southwest of Berlin. This time our targets were assembly plants. The German fighters hit us while we were still over the North Sea. I was credited with shooting down my plane's first enemy plane. I saw him spiral down into the water some 60 miles offshore. By this stage of the war Reichmarshall Goering was getting fairly desperate. His Luftwaffe had failed to establish air supremacy and now that American long-range bombers had entered the war, Germany was getting a taste of her own medicine. He was now sending out his best veteran pilots in a frantic bid to stop us disrupting the Nazi war infrastructure. That mission gave us our first sight of the Germans' ace pilots.

They were based at Abbeville and their propellers were painted yellow. Their maneuvers were extraordinary. They usually attacked head on, then turned over and flew down in front of us with only the bottom of their planes exposed. They were magnificent aviators and it was breathtaking to watch their superb aerobatics. That day they came at us and gave us the first demonstration of the tactics we soon came to recognize and dread. Their plan of attack was to fly parallel to us, well out of range, sizing up which group formation seemed to be the loosest and then fly past us in order to attack us head on, in the hope of breaking up the formation and picking off disabled stragglers, one by one. That day we lost 23 heavy bombers and crews (10 men in a crew). Our plane, *Virgin on the Verge,* also had a close shave. Staff Sergeant Robert J. Ponton, our tail gunner, was so intent on his own shooting that he was not aware of having a narrow escape. A shell entered through the floor, passed between his legs and his right thigh and forearm and out through the side of his compartment without exploding.

"I didn't know the shell went through," he told us. "I thought something had hit up in the waist compartment. Then I heard the wind whistling through the holes and I thought it must be a hell of a big hole in the waist. I called up to the waist gunners and asked them if they had been hit." The shell made one hole coming in and hit a brace on its way out.

Pieces of the shattered brace made holes in the side of the plane and filled Ponton's flying suit with metal fragments.

Such skin-of-the-teeth stories occupied much of the conversation in the mess when we got back to base, along with recollections of our friends who had not been so fortunate. Apart from the dramas of aerial combat there was a kind of magnificent poetry about our lives. Each day it would be dark, dreary and cold as we woke up, hurried to get dressed and breakfasted and then filed into the briefing room to hear what our assignment was to be. Only the adrenaline coursing through our veins and the excitement kept us warm—certainly not the pitiful little fires in the stoves. Then we would hurry out to our planes, take up our positions and go through all the pre-flight checks. That done, we would take off and climb up through the dark, murky, overcast conditions. All of a sudden we would break through into blinding sunshine—not a cloud in sight and down below us a white soft cottonwool-like cloud cover as far as the eye could see. Soon, each plane would create a creamy feather plume from the tail fin, known as a vapor trail, an atmospheric condition which would slowly evaporate as we flew on. There was no sound apart from the hum of the engines and all around us just the dazzling blue and white of the upper air. It was a unique experience; no cinematic technique could ever duplicate it or stir the feelings which surged within the airmen who made those day-time raids.

We always knew when a particularly dangerous mission was on the agenda. There would be eggs for breakfast. Eggs were a rare luxury in the middle years of the war and, though we ate them with relish, the significance of their appearance certainly did not escape us, especially when our catering officer cheerfully told us to enjoy them because they might be our last.

The morning of 17 August, 1943 was an egg morning. We were called at about 2 o'clock instead of the usual 5 or 6 a.m., and were given a breakfast of Spam and one egg. In the briefing room we were told that we were to be part of a mammoth operation involving the entire 8th Air Force.

Our target was the Messerschmitt factories at Regensburg, near the Austrian border. From there, instead of returning, we were to fly on to Africa, a 1,400 mile trip. Our flight position in the formation was what had come to be known as Purple Heart Corner.

We formed up into squadrons and groups as usual while circling The Wash. The sky was black with planes—a remarkable sight. This day, of all days, headquarters kept us circling much longer than usual, until we were convinced we would be out of fuel long before we reached Africa. The suicide nature of our mission seemed secured.

At last we were on course and fending off German fighters all the way from Antwerp to the Alps. However, the onslaught was lighter than usual and *Virgin* held her position. We reached our target and our bombing was highly successful. I have a picture on which circles indicate the wrecked factories which once built planes for the Luftwaffe, and yet a hospital is clearly depicted and its grounds are untouched—proof positive of the accuracy of the bombing.

Our fears about the fuel mounted as we left Regensburg and headed south. As we approached Africa, we saw B-17s, one after another, ditching in the Mediterranean for lack of fuel. We all knew that there were hardly any air-sea rescue services available. By now our plane was suffering desperate fuel problems. We threw overboard all guns, ammunition, moveable armor plate—anything that would give us a few more minutes flying time as the fuel gauges went into the red, one by one. All the crew were in constant contact by earphones with Paul Swift, the Lead Pilot. Finally, he said "Well, if we've thrown overboard everything that is unnecessary to keep the plane flying, throw out the Lead Navigator!" That was me. Very funny.

At last we spotted Africa, but where would this huge, disorganized group of planes land? A special field had been built at Constantine to accommodate the 8th Air Force for this mission but we could not possibly make Constantine as we had only minutes worth of fuel left, if that. We spotted a small RAF fighter strip on the coast at Bone and decided to make for it. We had one engine feathered and another just quitting so we were flying on two engines instead of four, with apparently only a whiff of fuel left. We requested permission to land. Because of the wild confusion of planes circling we were denied. The field told us to circle once more. Swift phoned back, as did other pilots, to say "We're coming in." We could see B-17s landing on the small metal mesh mats that covered the sand, adequate for light fighters but not bombers. The few tractors the ground crew had were desperately trying to clear the space, dragging the 17s which had landed off to the side, dumping them anywhere to give the others even a few extra feet.

All eyes were fixed on that postage-stamp landing area as we dropped lower and lower with stuttering engines. Somehow we got down without colliding with other aircraft. No Purple Hearts for us this trip!

A few days later we flew on to Constantine and from there to Marrakesh, the huge international base controlled by the Americans, British and French. The disabled planes flew back to England around Spain, the safest route for machines such as the *Virgin* whose guns lay at the bottom of the Mediterranean. Getting back safely from this outing was a great boost to our morale. We had now flown, and survived, eight missions. So many other crews had been less fortunate. The squadrons' losses were staggering and personnel were constantly changing as replacement airmen came and went.

In another squadron a new replacement arrived and woke after his first night's sleep in a full dormitory. For some reason he did not fly on his first day. That night he was the only person to sleep in the dormitory, as every single plane in the squadron had been shot down. I heard of people suffering mental breakdowns now and then, but these were few and far between. As for me, I still had an astonishing confidence in my own invulnerability.

Of course, the war had its other side. The British were not altogether enamored of their American allies. It was frequently observed that we were "overpaid, over-sexed and over here" and there was a lot of truth in this complaint. We had money, glamour and the devil-may-care attitude which came from knowing that every day might be our last. When we came overseas, we had several built-in advantages. I had deliberately decided not to get engaged to Joanie before leaving the USA. This was partly because of the possibility that I might not come back, but I must confess that it was also because I did not want anything to cramp my style.

We did not get many weekends off—about one a month—but when we did, we sure made the most of them. The place we always headed for was London. The town was really buzzing and absolute heaven for an American flyer. In order to cut a dash, Captain Paul Swift and I had our uniforms especially made by Gieves & Hawkes, with the wings on our jackets embroidered in gold and silver thread. This was much against regulations, of course, but we thought we could do anything and get away with it. I also commissioned Cartier to copy my navigator's wings in platinum and diamonds as a present for Joanie. These were the only wings of this type they ever made. We were always able to reserve the same apartment near Picadilly Circus but we spent very little time there. We would go our separate ways, then meet up at some club or other with the new girls of the moment. I would take Shelagh Macaulay to Claridges, where we always had the same table; then on to The 400—I suppose the chic-est club in town—to dance, and we would end up at yet another club. We belonged to all of them. The fact that the city was in black-out was no problem to us. It just heightened the fun and games.

On one occasion, we could not get our regular apartment. There was a help line for officers who could not find accommodation, so we called it and were given an address: The Cavendish on Jermyn Street. We spent two nights there and when I went to settle the bill the lady who seemed to be in charge refused any payment. She said American flyers did not pay in her place. Rosa Lewis was her name. When my cousin, Dorothy Cooper, heard where I had been staying she was shocked and told me never to go there again. It was nothing but a brothel! Apparently, Edward VII had financed Rosa to buy the Cavendish. He much admired her and also her famous cooking. He would take his favorites there, where he had his own apartment. Her rule was that you paid when you left but if you were on hard times, your bill was put on to someone else's account, who happened to be in the chips. We had no inkling of any of this. It would hardly have made a difference if we had.

Even when we could not get to London we found ways to enjoy ourselves. Swift and I were able to buy two almost-new motorcycles for practically nothing as the English owners could not get fuel because of rationing. We had unlimited petrol and had great fun touring the countryside in our spare time. I must say, this really impressed the local girls and we thought we were the Don Juans of Norfolk. The fun did not last long; our motorcycles were confiscated and locked in a motor pool never to be seen again. High Command told us in no uncertain terms that they had better things for us to do than fall off motor bikes.

Our tenth foray was to Stuttgart. This was a repeat mission, as an earlier bombing run had not destroyed the target completely. It was very dangerous to leave a target half destroyed as the Germans knew by now that we would soon return to finish the job and would be prepared for our arrival. For some unknown reason I wore my parachute on the day in question, maybe because we all knew this was going to be a difficult mission. Over the target, something (I believe it must have been a shell casing) smashed through the window in front of me and hit me on the large metal buckle at the front of my parachute. It hit with such force that I was hurled to the back of the cabin. As we were in the middle of a battle, no one had time to come to my aid or even look at me. Shortly afterwards (I have no idea of the length of time) I came to, felt myself all over and discovered that I had escaped with only a cut to the side of my head from the violent fall; the buckle had obviously saved my life.

That day, when I returned to the base, I had a medical examination and was told that my flying days were over, The rule was a simple one: Any member of an aircrew being rendered unconscious was permanently grounded. My brief blackout apparently counted as unconsciousness.

Naturally, I was upset at this decision, but fortunately the head medic was a friend of mine and I was able to persuade him to forget that the event had ever happened and that someone "up there" was keeping an eye on me. He knew, as we all did, that the squadron could not afford to lose experienced flyers. This was certainly no time to be taken from my crew.

By our 17th mission only five planes of the original squadron were left. There was a severe shortage of flyers at this point, in spite of the replacements. One day I had to fly in another plane and this put me ahead of my own crew on mission count. By this time we were being promised some help that would even up the odds against the Luftwaffe—long range fighters: P-47s and P-51s from America. But for a time that was all we did get—promises.

I have in front of me an entry in my diary, dated 3 November 1943. It reads: "I am looking at a newspaper clipping and photos of us all cheerily returning from the Wilhelmshaven mission, our 19th mission. The clipping says, 'These men have just made history.' We are about to enter the Debriefing Room, get rid of our heavy flying gear and off to the bar for a well-earned drink. There is nothing cheery in my mind. I am furious. It was another day with very little protection from enemy fighters. The P-47s were not there; these fighter escort planes were delayed in shipment from the American factory by strikes for workers' higher pay. We were again exposed like sitting ducks in front of a target range at a country fair."

The *Virgin* was in serious need of repairs, so on about our 19th mission, we were allocated another plane, the *Hard Luck*. Little did we know, when we took off, how aptly named she was. Serious problems arose straight away. Fire broke out in one of the engines and other things also started going wrong, We were not high enough to use the parachutes so we had to make a crash landing. I still cannot imagine how we were all able to help each other free ourselves from the plane and scramble out. We had a quick count and realized that our bombardier, Bowman, was missing. Swift and I returned to the rapidly disintegrating plane and pulled him out. Then we watched from a safe distance as *Hard Luck* blew up.

Later, we were subjected to a roasting for having concentrated on saving lives rather than salvaging an expensive airplane.

That single event, more than any other, made me sick of war.

I have a picture of this escape and one taken at a later date looking at what was left—only part of the tail fin. There was talk of sabotage to the plane, but I think it was just a combination of unfortunate events. Anyhow, yours truly survived again.

*The wreckage of **Hard Luck** is surveyed by Pilot Lt. Paul Swift, left, and Navigator Lt. Paul Arbon.*

Our most important mission was the 21st, although we certainly did not know it at the time. At our briefing we were told that we were going to Norway to destroy a heavy water plant. We had not the remotest idea what heavy water was. We knew nothing of nuclear fission and the desperate race going on in Germany and the USA to develop the atom bomb. So to us it sounded like a total waste of time to fly a 1,200-mile round trip to Scandinavia just to blow up a public utility. It was a long haul and bitterly cold—45 below—as we crossed the Norwegian fjords. We encountered little resistance until we got close to the target at Rjuken. If anything, the German gunfire helped us to find our prey, since locating it in an all-white landscape was far from easy. Unlike earlier missions, which had been directed at specific industrial sites, we were instructed on this occasion to let our bombs go in the center of the town. I recorded in my diary, "This was very disturbing," but, of course, we had to do it. And we did it pretty thoroughly. A couple of days later, newspaper reports went into ecstatic prose about the success of the raid: "Heavy damage was done to an enemy power plant at Rjuken and a war plant in the town making munitions essentials was thoroughly plastered. The Rjuken factory...was one of the world's largest electrolysis works and an important producer of hydrogen, nitrogen, oxygen and essential components of high explosives."

We still did not know what all the fuss was about. Not until after the war did the true significance of Mission 21 come home to me.

On all of our missions, there would be the groups consisting of the B-24s (Liberators). We were always glad to have them join the mission as the German fighters would, without fail, pick on them first. It was a marvelous plane, as I discovered later when I flew it in Florida on my return to the States, but because of its narrow wing construction it could not fly in really tight formation. Thus, the Germans found it easier to break up the B-24 formation and pick off the bombers one by one. However, we did by now have the P-47 fighter escort, which was a great help in distracting the German fighters until the P-51 was brought over. Our P-47 escort would start each mission flying closely parallel to us and always the leader of that group would dip his wing to us meaning "Good Luck" and then go into battle.

By now, only two planes and crews from the original squadron were still in operation, the *Virgin* and a craft captained by a man called Eccleston. On 5 December we flew to Bordeaux to attack German underground submarine pens. A newspaper report of the next day declared, "This raid was more difficult than the costly attack on Schweinfurt." Certainly we had the hottest reception we had so far received. After we had dropped our bombs we were attacked by 50 fighters all the way back to the English coast. Just after the target, Eccleston's ship was hit severely. His position was just to our right. He fell out of formation and kept dropping further and further behind with no protection. He had only two more missions to complete his tour and we desperately hoped that he would not be picked off by the fighters. All of us were desperate, but there was nothing we could do to help. We were kept busy defending ourselves all the way home.

Each of our planes had its own personal ground crew whose job it was to repair, on return from a mission, all damage to the plane and its engines as quickly and efficiently as possible. The ground crews would always be standing at the planes' designated parking spots on our return to help us with our gear, to hear what had happened, etc. That day Eccleston's ground crew waited and waited, refusing to leave the plane's parking spot. We could see them standing in the rain and they stayed there for half the night, willing their plane to make it back safely. They were sure that, by some miracle, their crew would return after going through so much over the months. Eccleston's crew was officially declared missing in action the next day. We were now the only surviving crew of the original squadron.

On 16 December my crew was scheduled to make its last raid—to Bremen. No flyers were allowed to go on more than 25 missions and, for the surviving members of the *Virgin's* original crew—Paul Swift, captain; Bentil Erickson, upper turret gunner and engineer; Robert Ponton, tail gunner; and John Taylor, radio operator—this was it. Because of the extra mission I had flown I was adjudged to have completed my quota and I was not allowed to go. But how could I let my comrades take off without me? It was considered bad luck for a crew not to fly all together. I appealed to the Squadron Commander for permission to fly a unique 26ᵗʰ. He turned me down. So I went over his head to the Group Commander. He reluctantly agreed, but pointed out that I was pushing my luck pretty hard.

I went to Bremen. And I came back.

# THE REPLACEMENTS

By Eugene T. Carson, tail gunner
Ingebritsen's crew, 560th Squadron

*The following stories are excerpted from Eugene Carson's autobiography,*
*"Wing Ding: Memories of a Tail Gunner."*

We were assigned to the 385th Bomb Group as a crew and trucked to our new unit. It was well after sundown when we arrived at our destination. We climbed down from the truck, pleased to be at the end of our journey. But we were told to get back on board. There had been a change to our orders; we were being assigned to the 388th Bomb Group, 560th Squadron.

We were off again on another truck ride to a place called Knettishall. Shortly after entering our new barracks we learned the reason for the change of orders. The 388th had flown its first mission on July 17, 1943. In less than two months, they had suffered a loss of 23 crews; 230 men either killed, missing in action or prisoners of war. A few had managed to evade capture.

We were the new cannon fodder.

In my mind there flashed a picture of the day I took my physical to come into the Army. I saw the second group enter the room as we walked out of it. Just like animals entering the slaughterhouse. I quickly turned off the picture.

It would be nice if I could say we were welcomed replacements. Such was not the case. The older crews treated us with indifference. Someone made a suggestion we not get too comfortable and implied we might not be around very long. Needless to say, we were somewhat confounded by this apparent unfriendly attitude. Later, we were to learn the reason for the defensive attitude. It hurts to lose friends.

Our first combat mission was set for September 26, 1943. During the interim I was promoted from corporal to staff sergeant.

There are two very lonely places on a B-17, the positions of tail and ball turret gunners. Both positions were cramped and both were cold. In the tail, the gunner was on his knees, a great position if there was a need for prayer, which was often. There wasn't much room to move around. Only enough space for a pair of spare gun barrels and a couple of extra boxes of ammunition and a parachute. On the right side of the aircraft, if you are looking forward, between the gun position and the tail wheel, there was a small escape door to be used in the event of an emergency. In the ball turret, Stan Gajewski had even less mobility. He rode in a fetal position, peering out of a circular window between his feet. The guns were mounted alongside of his head. Very few ball turret gunners were small enough to carry a chest pack parachute inside the turret. In the event of an emergency, the guns were rotated to a downward position and the gunner exited via the hatch into the waist area and then out of the waist door. Stan was small in stature. If they could have built someone to ball turret size specifications, Stan would have fit the mold. He was of the right size and he had the ability to ride in a cooped up position for long hours and he could shoot. He never complained. On more than one mission he came out with the cheeks of both buttocks frostbitten. But he never missed a mission.

In the event of a fighter attack, reliable gunners in the tail and the ball turret could mean life or death to a bomber crew. Luftwaffe pilots would take great chances to put the tail gunner out of action. With the tail gunner out, they could press their attack with a great chance of success. Many of the dedicated ball turret gunners claimed the ball turret was one of the safest positions on the B-17. I never thought so. The ball turret gunner flew in an incredible cramped position. Records indicate a rather high casualty rate for both tail gunners and ball turret gunners. In rough air, a strong resistance to air sickness was essential.

Those who flew, no matter what their position, had bail-out procedures etched into their minds to the point where it would have been automatic. It could be no other way. Frequently, there were only seconds between a successful evacuation from the bomber or a howling ride toward certain death while pinned by centrifugal force inside a rapidly disintegrating airplane.

On September 26, 1943, 2nd Lt. Otis "Dingle" Ingebritsen and crew prepared to fly their first combat mission. It was the 388th Bomb Group's 24th combat mission. Immediately after lunch we proceeded to the Briefing Room and watched intently as the curtain was pulled back. Old hands gave a sigh of relief throughout the room when the target selected was Rheims/Champagne, an airfield approximately 50 miles west and slightly north of Paris. The briefing officer noted the rather late take-off time of 14:45 hours and reported the mission would last only five hours from take-off to landing. Anti-aircraft fire was predicted as light and fighters were not expected. Nevertheless, there were butterflies in my stomach.

We were trucked to our parked B-17 where we, as a crew of 10 nervous and scared individuals, followed a ritual destined to become our routine. Pilots Lts. Ingebritsen and Meginnies, along with the ground crew chief, M/Sgt. Paul Irelan and our flight engineer, Sgt. Pepper, carefully checked the airplane. Navigator Lt. Pomeroy nervously went over his maps and charts; Bombardier Lt. Chaklos checked the bomb load, the racks and his bombsight repeatedly. In the radio room, Bill Pross attended to his radio and made sure he had all of the necessary frequencies. Gun barrels were inserted; ammunition was checked. Each member of the crew was busy, doing and redoing, anything to keep the mind occupied. Waist gunners "Windy" Windham and "Pop" Grannis repeatedly checked their guns while Stan Gajewski gave the ball turret a final power check.

They called me "Wing Ding."

*Eugene "Wing Ding" Carson and his tail guns, on the flight line at Knettishall*

I crawled into the tail, knelt in position and shot down a couple of imaginary fighters just to make sure I had the procedure properly established in my mind. With preliminaries out of the way, we turned our attention to our blue, electric heated suits, a type of heated long underwear made of material much like an electric blanket. These blue bunny suits were worn under our sheepskin-lined flying gear and were effective in keeping us warm when in good working order. However, there was one final necessary act to be performed before climbing aboard. We all moved off to the side of the aircraft and in almost comic routine emptied our bladders. The lack of adequate facilities onboard the aircraft and the fact we might be otherwise occupied during a moment of need was reason enough for this somewhat odd preflight procedure.

One by one the engines coughed, smoked and roared. As they were started in unison, each was checked at full power. This was important. The failure of an engine at take-off was always an emergency. Failure of an engine during take-off with a full load of bombs could exceed the emergency category with disastrous results. A green flare arched over the field. Our first combat mission had started.

2nd Lt. Otis Ingebritsen felt a deep sense of responsibility as he moved his B-17F off the hardstand and out onto the taxi perimeter. Countless times before he had followed identical take-off procedures. This time it was no drill. Practice time was over; this was real. On board was a full load of bombs. He was about to fly his first combat mission. He was the pilot, the airplane commander, and the onus of command weighed heavily. On his shoulders fell the responsibility for the aircraft and the fate of his crew.

On September 26, 1943, in the cockpit, there was formed an unbreakable bond. No words other than those of the checklist needed to be uttered. The momentary meeting of eyes of pilot and co-pilot said more than either man could have vocalized. It was a look of understanding. It spoke volumes in its silence. Co-Pilot Ed Meginnies was silently giving his loyalty and faith to Pilot Otis Ingebritsen. Together they would fly and together they would survive. The 388th Bomb Group had already lost 23 crews during its first two months of operation. Ingebritsen and Meginnies were determined not to become crew number 24.

The march of B-17s along the perimeter took on the appearance of clumsy creatures creeping in trail toward the runway. Take-off was in timed intervals with a brief pause at the runway for a final power check, then line up, tail wheel locked, and down the runway. Lift-off came at about 110-115 miles per hour. With wheels up, the once clumsy ground-bound creature became a thing of elegance. The climb continued. The aircraft circled and became part of a formation. Oxygen masks went on at between 8,000 and 10,000 feet. The group tightened up the formation. Far below, the English countryside appeared to be a painting. The coastal area and the English Channel came into view. The B-17s slowly climbed to 23,000 feet. Within the airplane, the tension and fear in the heart and mind of each untried warrior was concealed by an outward and disciplined calm.

A formation of B-17s flying in a clear blue sky is a thing of beauty. But even a thing of beauty can have a flip side. It was a formation of flying machines, each with a cargo of destruction and 10 men—10 men far from home flying in the hostile environment of high altitude and sub-zero temperatures over equally hostile territory, waiting for an opportunity to deliver a cargo of death and destruction.

The order was given to test-fire all guns and keep a sharp lookout for fighters. The ship shuddered as weapons were given a warm-up burst. Ten pair of eyes nervously searched the sky for distant telltale dots of Luftwaffe fighters as the formation of bombers, marked by condensation trails, progressed across the sky unmolested.

At high altitude, personal warmth and oxygen become matters of major concern. The blue electrically-heated suit worn under the sheepskin-lined leather clothing was wonderful when it worked. But it had a nasty habit of burning out and giving the wearer the equivalent of a "hot-foot" at whatever location the short circuit might be located. The hapless victim would immediately disconnect the electrical plug and pull the material of the suit away from the body at the burnout location. The remainder of the ride would then be without heat. Oxygen at high altitude is a basic and essential need if life is to be sustained, therefore care had to be taken to ensure the mask fitted properly and the connection was firmly in place. It was possible for the hose of the mask to become disconnected with fatal results.

When the formation crossed into France slightly below the Belgium border, sporadic flak began to make its appearance. The flak increased in density as we neared the target area, and appeared in black bursts. Each burst spread out to appear to be an octopus. When the red flame was visible in the center, it was too close for comfort and offered its own sound effects. The impact on the airplane came as a dull thump, or sharp crack, depending on its nearness to the plane. The sound was not unlike gravel thrown against a tin building. The proximity of the airplane to each burst determined the aircraft's reaction. The nearer the burst the greater the bounce and reaction of the airplane. There was no place to hide, no place to go to seek protection from the shards of flak spewing from each explosion.

As the formation turned on the bomb run the flak intensified. There was an increased feeling of vulnerability when the bombardier announced, "Bomb bay doors are open." This was followed by a psychological feeling of relief when the bombardier called out, "bombs away," a call which was further accented by a significant surge of the bomber as it was relieved of the extra weight. On this particular mission, old hands reported the flak as meager; however, 16 of the 21 aircraft suffered flak damage. Luftwaffe fighters, as predicted, failed to show. The trip home was uneventful. It was a good day for a new crew. Unfortunately it did not tell us what was in store in the future. We were scheduled to be up early the next morning.

There was no need to awaken me on the morning of September 27th. I was awake, lying in my bunk wondering where we were going. I rolled out and stumbled to the latrine. I wanted to get there early to avoid the crowd. Having a bowel movement while sitting next to another person was extremely alien to me. I quickly finished my morning routine and headed to the mess hall. I was hungry and ate a hearty breakfast of square (powdered) eggs, accompanied with SOS and Spam. I washed it down with several cups of black coffee.

At the briefing, the target was identified as the port area of Emden, Germany. We would approach the target via the North Sea and bomb from about 25,000 feet. Cold is not a good description of temperatures at 25,000 feet; it is colder than cold. Take-off was at 07:30 hours and there was much to be done in a relatively short time. Guns and equipment had to be checked. Time passed quickly and we were soon rolling down the runway. Veterans of one mission about to fly our second.

The tail of a B-17 provides minimal opportunity for conversation, other than to respond to the oxygen and other mandatory checks. Being of a gregarious and loquacious nature, I really needed a little more social interaction, so I devised my own significant greeting. Although ungifted in music, I had learned to whistle the first few notes of Chopin's Funeral March. I think we were at about 22,000 feet leaving the coast of England on our second mission when I first cut loose. The response from the cockpit was immediate. Co-Pilot Ed Meginnies instinctively knew who did it. He yelped, "Wing Ding, this is serious business, knock it off. I don't want to hear the funeral march."

Lt. Meginnies heard it again. He heard it almost every mission and he squawked every time he heard it. I ceased whistling after Mike Chaklos was killed. Somehow it no longer seemed appropriate.

There were 23 aircraft in our formation when we took off to fly our second mission. Seven of those aborted the mission for various mechanical reasons leaving us with only 16 aircraft. The 96th Bomb Group was flying as the Low Group. Our bombardier, Mike Chaklos, reported clouds over the target plus ground haze and an effective smoke screen. Flak was meager and we had P-47 fighter escort to and from the target. However, they would only be able to engage the Luftwaffe for a limited time because of their relatively low fuel capacity. Mike reported the bomb bay doors were open and in about 30 seconds gave the words, "bombs away." The plane gave the usual lurch as it discharged the cargo of bombs. We were at about 25,000 feet. Bill Pross, our radio operator, reported the bomb bay as empty. I breathed a sigh of relief and noticed discomfort in my lower intestines.

My hearty breakfast had turned into a belly full of gas. The pain became intense. The more the pain increased the more I regretted my gluttonous breakfast; however, my problems were soon replaced. Despite our fighter escort, 25 to 30 members of the Luftwaffe made their appearance. Although most of the attacks were directed at the Low Group of the 96th, we had our share.

A single ME-109 came down in a curving attack on our tail. I gave him a short burst. At the time I was wearing a steel infantry helmet, without a liner, over my issue leather helmet. The vibration of my guns caused the steel helmet to jiggle down over my eyes. I could not see! I shoved the steel helmet up, clear of my eyes, and fired another short burst. The steel helmet again jiggled down over my eyes. This time I grabbed it and tossed it to my rear. Then my guns jammed. I had no choice; I lifted the only piece of armor plate in the tail, dove under and cleared my guns. It must have been a healthy move because at the same time all of the accumulated gas in my intestines was released in one long blast. I remember hoping I had not crapped in my pants. Fortunately, it was all gas.

Whether it was the nerves of first battle or a full bladder from the extra cups of coffee, I don't know, but I also had to urinate. I mean I had to urinate *now*, not later. Fighters or no fighters, immediate action was required or I was going to pee in my pants. There was no way I wanted to sit around in wet pants with a shorted-out electrical suit and frozen urine. I could not bring myself to urinate on the floor of the tail gun section. Fortunately, a lull in the action allowed time to recover my discarded helmet. I reached to my rear and found my helmet and then began the arduous procedure of trying to locate my penis under layers of clothing. I finally found it, shriveled though it was from the intense cold. I began the process of extraction. I dug it out from beneath the multiple layers of clothing and cautiously exposed this most important item of personal equipment to the 40-degrees-below-zero temperature. I proceeded to piddle in my steel pot.

"Bandit at 6 o'clock," Bill Pross, our radio operator, calmly stated over the intercom, and added, "Get him, Wing Ding."

It was another 109 making a diving approach on our tail. I could not stop peeing any more than I could have flown without wings. Having grown up a country boy in areas where there were severe winters, I knew well the consequences of having bare skin touch metal. Whatever part touched would immediately become frozen and attached. It sure as hell was not going to be what little bit was left of my foreskin. I held myself with one hand and fired with the other. Tracers streaked into the fighter's left wing. He peeled off and I piddled in peace. Having finished, I tucked everything inside of my flying gear and mumbled some incoherent nonsense. Suddenly I felt faint and dizzy. A glance to my side revealed the problem. My oxygen hose was disconnected. I fumbled with the connection and somehow, while bordering on the edge of passing out, managed the reconnection. I immediately recovered.

I heard the chatter of what I presumed to be the top turret guns and saw a fighter move from our front to our rear, announcing his arrival by decorating the sky with what looked like Christmas tree lights as he used his cannon. He disappeared in seconds. But not before putting three holes in our vertical stabilizer not far from where I was perched. Each hit echoed with a quick thump. It was over almost as quickly as it had taken place. I sat there awed at what had transpired. I responded to the oxygen check and continued to search the sky. Our escort was now all around us.

I noticed my helmet contained a block of yellow ice.

I was outside of our hut, working on my bicycle. It was in my mind to make a trip to the pub. Chuck Allred must have read my mind. He approached me and cautioned, "Wing Ding, don't go anyplace tonight. We are getting up early tomorrow. They are loading extra fuel."

Chuck was right. We were up early. I looked at the crummy weather and thought the mission would be scrubbed. We had the usual breakfast of square eggs, Spam and SOS. The word in the mess was that the mission was going to be a long one. The answer came from the horse's mouth when the briefing room curtain was pulled back.

Schweinfurt.

"Oh, Jesus no, not again," came from the back of the room.

"Holy Mother of God, this is my last mission," came from another corner.

The line stretched on and on, deep into the heartland of Germany. "This is a very important mission," the briefing officer droned. "Germany's ball bearing works must be destroyed." He continued to deliver his message of what we could expect. He assured us we would have fighter escort almost to the border of Germany and they would pick us up again as we returned; however, we would be without fighter escort for over 400 miles. There was minimal talking. Everyone knew it was going to be a rough ride. We were scheduled to put up 22 aircraft and be the Low Group of the Lead Combat Wing of the 2nd Air Task Force. The 96th Bomb Group would furnish the Lead and High Groups.

The day started off poorly. There was a crash on take-off. Lt. Swift, pilot of *Hard Luck*, had almost reached flying speed when his Number 3 engine caught fire. Smoke came from the tires as he hit the brakes. A crash was eminent. Lt. Swift ordered, "wheels up." The co-pilot responded and the take-off of *Hard Luck* became a controlled crash. With its full compliment of crew, bombs and fuel, *Hard Luck* skidded onward with sparks flying. It came to a stop just short of a wooded area. The crew miraculously escaped their burning aircraft without injury. Take-off for the group was delayed until safety procedures could be applied. All aircraft were then diverted to another runway and the area cleared in anticipation of the explosion. When it came, it was spectacular.

The formation climbed up through the cloud cover. We were in clear skies and out over the English Channel; however, with one take-off crash and five aborts for mechanical failure we were quickly reduced to a formation of 16 aircraft. I think we had been in the air about 45 minutes. I was busy checking my gear and test-firing my guns. Something did not seem right. It was not. My parachute was missing. In my mind I visualized my parachute bag sitting on the ground at the hardstand! We were now 23,000 feet up and more than 100 hundred miles from our base.

I sat at my gun position trying to decide what to do. I knew if I reported my parachute as missing, Dingle would turn back, probably abort the mission. It is not possible to describe my thoughts. Terror would be a grossly inadequate description. I could not bring myself to tell the crew. All I could do was hope for the best. I am sure I sneaked a few quick prayers in for good measure. I felt weak and afraid. Then I heard a female voice clearly state, "Trust me." I quickly checked my oxygen to be sure I was not suffering from anoxia. My connection was in place. A sense of calm came over me.

What would I do if we were hit and the crew had to bail? My plan was probably ridiculous, but it was the only plan I could think of. I would try to make it to the cockpit and fly the crippled bird back to England, or crash land. Good plan or not, there were no options. My basic thought was a simple, "Oh, Jesus."

We crossed Belgium, and near the German border our fighter escort gave us a final apologetic waggle of wings and turned back. The Luftwaffe arrived on the scene moments later. Obviously they had been waiting in the wings for our escort to depart.

Their attack came with unbelievable ferocity. They outnumbered us at five-to-one or more. I watched in amazement as they lined up and barrel rolled through the other formations with guns blazing. I could only assume they were doing the same to our Group as fighter after fighter went streaking past the tail. They offered no opportunity for even a quick shot. Others sat behind the formation, out of range, and lobbed rockets into the formation. Again and again I watched the Luftwaffe line up on other groups and fly head-on, wing tip to wing tip. Their courage was unquestionable. They came in six at a time; diving and turning in attempts to draw fire while another fighter tried to make the kill. From the beginning of the first fighter attacks the Luftwaffe stayed with us. Long before we arrived over the target the sky was filled with a host of bombers and fighters going down in flames. Some were falling out of control with crews pinned in by centrifugal force and still others were exploding with bodies and debris falling through the formations.

Parachutes were everywhere. B-17s and Luftwaffe aircraft were going down and exploding. The ground below was marked with blazing debris and the black smoke from the rubble of aircraft wreckage. Through some miracle, all 16 of our aircraft made it to the target. The scene was one of carnage beyond imagination. It was frightening.

We dropped our bombs and turned for home. The intercom was a constant chatter as the crew called out Luftwaffe fighter locations. I knelt in silence. I had nothing to say. My tail guns were doing my talking in short nasty bursts. No one had to tell me there were bandits at 6 o'clock and there was no need for me to report their presence. The Luftwaffe was everywhere. I was up to my ass in empty shell casings. We were being mauled. I watched the decimation of the formations below and around us. I could not see how we were going to make it home. There was, however, a calmness in my heart; I felt as if someone was watching over me.

When we reached the Belgium border I searched the sky for signs of our fighter escort. They were not to be seen. Our escort was weathered in, still on the ground in England. The Luftwaffe continued to have a field day. Shell casings piled deeper at every gun position. All gun positions were complaining about being short of ammunition. Although I had quietly carried extra boxes on board before take-off, each of my guns had fewer than 100 rounds remaining. Almost every round had been needed.

As we left the coast of Europe, the Luftwaffe disappeared. I bent forward, rested my head on the window and began to shake and cry uncontrollably. I stopped long enough to take a deep breath and say, "Thank you God."

I could not tell to this day from where came the voice with the words, "Trust me." But in my heart I knew I had not been alone in the tail.

As I was about to enter my barracks I heard the unmistakable sound of a honking goose.

I looked and saw someone coming toward me with a large white goose under his arm. I recognized Jimmy Jones, another tail gunner.

"Jimmy, what in the hell are you doing with a goose?" I asked.

"Gonna eat him, Wing Ding," he said. "I'm sick of eating mess hall junk, canned meat and powdered eggs."

At first I did not believe him. But when he got his knife out, his intentions became clear. Fortunately, those of us who were country boys knew enough to take the goose outside for the decapitation ceremony. The goose, honking in protest, died hard. Blood squirted everywhere. The now-headless goose twitched and kicked his last.

Once the goose was dead and dry plucked, the question of cooking came up. Being the only one with any real cooking experience I was tempted to volunteer for the job. I decided against volunteering. One of the gunners was dispatched to the mess hall with instructions to come back with the largest frying pan he could find.

The goose was cut up and prepared for cooking. Chopped goose would be a good description. Smokey, the waist gunner who had been sent to the mess hall, returned with a large pan and one of the cooks. The cook brought half-a-dozen nice-size real potatoes plus salt and pepper. We agreed to let him share in our feast in exchange for his expertise. The stove was stoked to full blast. Our chopped goose soon became frying goose. The aroma had us all drooling.

However, we were soon to learn the drool-producing aroma of the cooking goose was an illusion. When it came time to eat the goose, we found the old gander was as tough and chewy as a piece of shoe leather. Only those with strong molars were qualified to chew the old bird. Our age brackets so qualified us and before sunset there was nothing left except bones.

A crewman quipped, "The goose was cooked."

Rather early on the morning of October 16th we had visitors. A British constable accompanied by a farmer came to our barracks. The officer apologized for bothering us and explained the purpose of his visit. He was looking for a family pet, a large white goose. Jimmy Jones was the first to speak.

"No goose around here," he said.

I could not help but notice how his quick denial brought forth more than a little interest from our Sherlock Holmes-type visitor.

"You gents don't mind if I just look around a bit?" he asked.

Of course no one objected.

Sherlock was not on the case for long before he spied a few feathers in a corner of the barracks. He picked them up and with meticulous care put them into an envelope. He soon found other evidence when he strode outside to the decapitation site. "I say gents, the goose must have been visiting here," he said wryly and fixed us with a stern gaze. We could see he was not buying our story. But we were staying with it. How could we tell them we had killed and eaten a family pet? Then, as they were about to leave, the constable glanced above the door. There, on the outside, above the door, spread out like a huge fan, were the wings of the goose.

The farmer's eyes followed those of the constable. He stared at the wings. For a moment he was silent, then he spoke.

"Oh, I say lads, you know, the goose, he was a family pet."

I think we were truly ashamed of our act. A helmet quickly made its appearance and was passed around. Eager eaters became eager donors. The farmer left with enough money to buy a dozen geese. He was smiling at our generosity and telling the constable he had no hard feelings. The case was closed.

It was too late for breakfast, so I went directly to the armament shack and worked on my guns. I discarded my old gun barrels and spent the next two hours checking the ammunition we would be using the next time we flew.

The notice on the bulletin board indicated a group of ladies, members of the WAAC from 8th Air Force headquarters, would be touring the base and visiting the service club. Stan Gajewski, our ball turret gunner, decided to go and see what real American-speaking girls looked like. Having enjoyed a good service club experience while at Denver, I was in favor of having a look-see. Chuck Allred told us not to waste our time. "Bunch of bats. You can't do any good with anyone from the WAAC," he said. Chuck's admonitions were ignored. Stan and I showered, put on our best Class A uniforms and peddled our bikes to the service club. The band was playing and there were about 20 members of the WAAC there. I quickly noted they were under what appeared to be control or supervision of the more mature members of the outfit.

One young lady in particular interested me; a beautiful dark haired girl, younger than most of the others. She stood out like a bright star. Her name was Genevieve Marie. She came from a dairy farm in Minnesota. I spent the evening talking with her. I was captivated. She was clean, wholesome and as fresh as the early morning dew. I fell in love. I had to see her again. But how could it be arranged?

Since we were still standing down on October 17<sup>th</sup>, I decided to find out how to travel from Knettishall to Pine Tree, the Air Division Headquarters, and make it back in time to fly. I made contact with the sergeant who drove the Message Center Jeep to and from Pine Tree. He agreed I could ride with him as a passenger. The courier Jeep would leave our base at about 17:30 hours and start back at about 22:30 hours. The schedule was like clockwork. I could rest on the return trip by sleeping. The safety belt would keep me from falling out.

Needless to say, my first unannounced visit was a genuine surprise to Genevieve. However, I was well received and it soon became obvious that Genevieve felt the same way. Our instant love seemed to be glowing and growing. I tenderly gave her a goodnight kiss on the cheek and caught the courier Jeep back to Knettishall in time to get ready for a mission.

The 388th was to provide 22 aircraft for the mission of October 18th to Duren, Germany. This would be my ninth mission. Take-off time was scheduled for 10:43 hours. The group would form and leave the English coast at approximately 14:00 hours. We were to bomb from 29,000 feet. It was cold. Eleven aircraft aborted our formation for various malfunctions before we even crossed the English coast. Three more aircraft aborted soon after. We were now down to a formation of eight operational aircraft.

Dingle's voice came over the intercom. "I need help in the cockpit. Chuck and Mac have both passed out."

Dingle was making reference to our engineer and our co-pilot. We were at 29,000 feet. The temperature was between 48 to 52 degrees below zero. The intense cold had caused the bomb bay doors to malfunction. They had to be closed if we were to keep up with the formation. Chuck Allred, our engineer, had used a portable oxygen bottle and had proceeded to the bomb bay. He cranked the doors to the closed position and attempted to return to the cockpit. His oxygen supply exhausted, he collapsed as he crawled into the cockpit. Without a thought for his personal safety, Co-Pilot Ed

Meginnies climbed out of his seat and gave his own oxygen supply to the stricken engineer. Chuck had not even had time to recover before Ed, too, collapsed on the flight deck. Dingle had no choice. We were flying in formation and he could not leave the controls even for an instant. He could only watch in anguish as his flight engineer and co-pilot remained inert on the flight deck. Chuck, now with fresh oxygen, a gift of life from Ed Meginnies who had surrendered his own oxygen, responded. He quickly reconnected the stricken co-pilot's oxygen and helped him back to his seat. The act was a typical demonstration of the personality of Ed Meginnies. He never gave thought to his own safety when he surrendered his life-giving source of oxygen to save the engineer.

Fortunately, we were recalled while over Belgium. This was truly a milk run. There were no Luftwaffe fighters and no flak. We landed at Knettishall at about 16:30 hours. Returning to base with us were many complaints about frostbite. The cold had been intense and had taken a heavy toll.

I caught my ride to Pine Tree and went to the WAAC dayroom where I was to meet Genevieve. Instead of Genevieve I was met by a bevy of older WAAC women. They asked me, "What are your intentions? Will you be nice to her? Genevieve is innocent and a good girl. She does not know about aircrew members."

I weathered the interrogation by the self-appointed guardians of Genevieve as they assured themselves her virtue was to remain intact. I convinced the ladies of the WAAC detachment of the absence of ulterior motives on my part. They were satisfied. I was in love. After stern warnings they allowed me to visit with Genevieve. We shared a wonderful evening by the huge fireplace. Later in the night when I departed it was Genevieve who led the way. She wrapped her arms around my neck and passionately kissed me goodnight.

She whispered, "Please be careful when you fly."

# MIDNIGHT REQUISITION

From an oral history by Elliott Hewes, engineer
Tom Dennis' crew, 561st Squadron

My third mission, I guess the most outstanding mission as far as the Group was concerned, was the Regensberg shuttle raid, the first shuttle that was flown by any Air Force for any country.

We left England, bombed Germany and landed in Africa.

We took off one morning about 5 o'clock and proceeded across the Channel and the whole thing was going great. We started getting a little flak now and then along the route and a few fighters would come in and hit us.

Just before we got to the IP, all hell broke loose! Fighters got on us real, real, good; shot the hell out of us. And then the flak started hitting about that time as the fighters started pulling out after they had made about six, seven passes in all.

We lost a lot of aircraft. A lot of aircraft went down on that raid. Our squadron was fortunate up until that point; we hadn't lost anyone. We got back into formation pretty well, and about that time the flak hit us and knocked the top half of Number 2 engine completely off. Well, that left us with three engines and we started trailing. We fell out of formation and we didn't think we were going to be able to make it, but we managed to go to maximum power and, with the three engines we had, got back into formation and got our bombs away on the target.

Our bomb statistic on that raid is that we hit our target 100 percent. We wiped it out. We went on through past the target and, oh, I guess it must have been about six minutes after bombs away and we were starting to break out of the flak area—we had numerous holes all over the airplane from flak—and it started feathering down a little bit, and the fighters hit us again.

97

They were making passes from high and low, front and rear and all the way around, in fact. One of them kind of slid underneath us and fired and knocked out Number 3 engine. So we were left with just two engines, and no one thought we'd ever make it.

We started to put max power on everything else we had. We only had two engines so we put max power on those and finally got up to the pass to go through the Alps. And we got over it. We just cleared the pass by maybe 50 or 60 feet. And while all this was happening the waist gunners and tail gunner were taking all the armor plating out of the back of the airplane and throwing it overboard to lighten the aircraft. And we still continued to lose ground.

After we got past the Alps and it looked like we were pretty clean, as far as fighting was concerned, we all started stripping our guns out. We took all of the guts out of our machine guns and threw them overboard. Then we threw the ammunition out, and anything else that was loose in the airplane; we threw it out. Even including the little walk-around oxygen bottles. Extra clothing that you might have. We threw everything overboard.

We'd come down from about 23,000 feet as the last things went out and we'd got over the end of Italy, over the Mediterranean. I guess we were down to about 600 feet. We maintained that plane between 500 and 600 feet until we got almost to the coast of Africa and the old engines—the two that we had—started crying because they were hurting. We had to cut back a little on the power, and we began to lose more altitude, and when we got to Africa to land, we called and made a straight-in approach. If we'd have had to make a go-around, it would have been impossible. Not only were the engines running out of power, we were running out of gas. When they serviced the airplane—it held 1,532 gallons of gas—they put in 1,507 gallons. We only had 25 gallons of fuel remaining, totally, onboard the airplane!

When the main gear hit the ground it was all right, but when the tail gear hit the ground the engines cut themselves. There was no more fuel. The fuel slipped into the back of the tanks and there was no way for it to get to the engines. So we landed and started servicing that airplane, which was foolish because we couldn't take off. But we serviced it anyway.

We put about, I think it was 900 gallons of gas onboard, and I'm glad we did because late that evening Lord Haw Haw came on the radio and said if we didn't leave now they were going to blow us off the face of the earth the next day. So we took off on two engines and got the hell out of there.

We went to Marrakech, where we landed on two engines again, and we knew we could not go any further. We had Number 1 and Number 4. They were balanced. They say you can't take a plane off the ground with two engines on one side, but I say we would have tried like hell. It was either that or we'd have no chance at all anyway.

In Marrakech we had to put in requisitions for engines. In the meantime, the Group had gone back and bombed Bordeaux, France on the way to England and left us, and no one knew where we were so we were listed as Missing In Action. They thought we'd gone down in the Mediterranean.

While we were in Marrakech I requisitioned the engines, and they told me they would get them there when they could ship them. So we didn't know how long we were going to be there. But while we were there I found out that Teddy Roosevelt (President Roosevelt's son, who was a Brigadier General in the Army) had a B-17 that they had rigged up for him as his personal airplane to fly around checking these different outfits. I also found that they were going to change the engines on his airplane and those engines were in a hangar right there in Marrakech.

So myself and the rest of the men on the crew and one officer (I'm not giving any names other than my own) did a little what we called "midnight requisitioning." That's when you open a door whether it's got a lock on it or not and get what you want out of it and that's it. So we stole the engines and put them on our plane and took our old engines and put them back in the boxes so that he had some goodies when he got ready to have his engines changed.

We got the engines on and got everything running good. It was about four or five days to get things going. I had to do some scrounging and "midnighting" for tools. I still had a few tools on board that I could not throw overboard, because they were in a place where I couldn't get to them; they were in a wheel well. I always carried something like that in the airplane I flew in so that if I did go down somewhere and had to do some maintenance I would have some things that I could work with.

We decided that we would load up the bombs again. The group had gone home ahead of us and they'd gotten a mission going back. So we loaded up 500-pound GP bombs, coasted out with a full load of gas, took off, went across the Mediterranean, and went in on the border line of Spain and France and flew right straight across instead of going out and then coming back in. We went across that way and then turned north/northwest and went in over Bordeaux from the opposite direction—one they would never expect anybody to come from—and we solo-bombed Bordeaux on our way back.

We went on out to sea and over the Atlantic, and then turned north and went into England. We were flying at a lower altitude because we didn't have any oxygen. I think that we had seven guns, and we had put them in strategic spots so that we would have some protection. We did away with the guns in the ball turret, because we were so low that nobody could make a pass under us, so we put guns in the waist, guns in the tail, guns in the upper turret and one gun in the front. And that's the way we came back.

We were flying at low altitude—it takes a whole lot more gas at low altitude to cruise like we were because the air is so much heavier—and we started running low on fuel. We went in to Land's End. As you look at the map of England and the British Isles, there's a little tip that sticks out on the southwest corner of it, runs out there just like a little finger. Well, there was an airbase right on the edge of that thing. At the bluffs there's a landing strip. And that's where we landed and serviced, and then we went on back to base the next day.

When we got back they wanted to know where the hell we'd been, what had happened and everything; and we told them, but we didn't tell them about where we'd got the engines. And things got a little bit sticky when they began to ask questions. You know, they don't appreciate when people steal stuff from the general.

We finally told the Group Commander about it. Bill David was the commander at that time. He was flying with us one day and he just came right out and asked me, "Where in the hell did you get them?" and I told him.

He said, "Well, that's one damn time a general gets his pants took off." And so that's the way it worked out.

# And Then There Was the Time

A ground officer who came to England in late 1942 told about when the 388th was on the East Coast just prior to being shipped overseas. Security was very tight, and no one was to ever mention the Group's name or where it was headed. All letters came under the scrutiny of the officer in charge of censorship. After the Group was on the ship headed for England, the colonel commanding the 388th congratulated all personnel for the fine job in maintaining security.

The first evening that the Group arrived at Knettishall, a small German plane circled overhead and from its loudspeaker came this greeting: "Welcome 388th Bomb Group to Knettishall."

Still circling, it named the Group's Commanding Officer and other staff officers. It then picked out one crew and named all 10 crew members. In addition, backgrounds of each crew member—home towns, education etc.—were provided. The final message was that if crews survived being shot down, there would be space in the stalags for them. The personnel of the 388th were surprised that the Germans knew so much and their effort to maintain tight security had seemed a useless exercise. This points out what a gigantic spy organization that the Nazis must have had in the United States.

John W. Dixon, bombardier, 560th Squadron

This happened to a 560th navigator who slept in a nearby bunk. In October, 1944 a piece of flak, or shrapnel, hit him in his upper back. After his plane landed, he was taken to the base hospital where the doctor cleaned his wound and sewed it up. After missing two missions, he resumed flying again.

In December, he complained about having a funny sensation in his index finger. A few days later it became very sore, and it appeared as if a boil was forming. A couple of days later, he pulled from his finger what he thought was a splinter. It turned out to be three-and-a-half inches of wire from the electric suit which he had been wearing when wounded.

We wondered whether this wire would have caused a serious medical problem if it had traveled instead from his upper back to a critical part of his anatomy.

John Dixon

After our arrival at Knettishall, our crew spent quite a bit of time in training. The days were flying by, but we were getting tired of being mere spectators as the 388th took off and returned from missions. Having a gap in our training schedule, we decided to bicycle to Bury St. Edmunds, about 10 miles from our base. Because of the sorry shape of the bicycles that had been issued to us, it was to prove a strenuous ride. The route to Bury St. Edmunds was on a paved but narrow country road. We were bicycling around slowly and peacefully enjoying the countryside when we heard a loud roar behind us. Turning our heads, we saw a convoy of British lorries bearing down on us. Our only escape was to an uneven verge which slanted into a ditch. We barely got off road before the convoy roared by. Before reaching Bury St. Edmunds, we had to abandon the road several times to get out of the way of convoys.

It was about lunch time when we pedaled into the town. We headed for the nearest pub to enjoy our first English pub lunch. Afterwards, we decided that it would be best to explore the town on foot. We really enjoyed this old and historic town; but Meyer, our pilot, decided to do some roaming on his own. The three of us agreed to meet him back at the pub where our bicycles were parked a little before 5 o'clock. When we got back, Meyer was at a table surrounded by several English girls. He was reluctant to leave, but we dragged him away.

We knew our ride back to the base would take longer than it took us to get to Bury St. Edmunds. We were all very tired and had to make many rest stops on the way. When we finally reached our barracks, we collapsed on our bunks and were comatose until it was time for our mile-long bicycle ride to the mess hall for supper.

We awoke the next morning with bones aching. I suppose that our expedition could be called a success, but never again did we get the urge to ride our bicycles off the base.

John Dixon

*Sgt. James Jones, right, with Crew Chief "Doc" Mitchell*

"S/Sgt. James F. Jones, 21-year-old Fort tail gunner from Baltimore, fell out of his ship without a parachute and lived to tell about it.

"It happened at night and Jones doesn't know how far he fell. It was far enough for him to pull his parachute out of his pack, but not far enough to give the 'chute time to open. Nobody in the crew was able to say definitely what the altitude was at the time. Crew members' estimates range from 25 to 100 feet. The distance was probably under 50 feet, Jones believed.

"The Fort was returning in darkness from a late afternoon raid on the U-boat locks and pens at La Pallice, France. The ship was over England, but was temporarily lost in clouds and darkness. The pilot was unaware of his dangerously low altitude because of a 1,000-foot error in the altimeter reading, said to have been introduced by a storm center. Suddenly, the Fort struck and ricocheted off the top of a hill and immediately zoomed upward. The impact threw Sgt. Jones against the escape door in the tail section of the ship and, as the Fortress careened upward, the door opened and out Jones went.

"Fortunately, Jones fell on soft ground. He was knocked unconscious, but his only injury was a slightly sprained leg and minor cuts and bruises."

From *Stars and Stripes*

On 14 April, 1945, on my 46th mission, I flew Wing Lead to Royan, France. Several of us had stayed up all night to find out what the target was. By the time we found out that were going to France, it was too late to go to bed in that our take-off time was 04:37.

During briefing for the mission, I was alerted to the fact that the Command Pilot assigned to us was well-known for sleeping during missions. With that in mind, after bombs were dropped, I set the autopilot on a course and declining altitude toward Knettishall, calculated to arrive back in England at the proper altitude. I then confided to our flight engineer that I would feign sleeping so that the CP would be forced to stay awake!

However, having had no sleep the previously night, I actually *did* fall asleep. I awoke over the English Channel, only to find that the CP, too, had fallen asleep, was still asleep and wouldn't wake up until we were over the Thames River.

I am certain that none of the 36 aircraft flying on our Lead ever realized that they were following an aircraft with only the flight engineer awake in its cockpit!

Hal Bigelow, pilot, 562nd Squadron

*Virgil Hodge*

I was a cook in the enlisted men's mess hall for maybe a month, then I was transferred to the officers' mess hall for the rest of the time—like two years and two months. Sgt. Gearheart was in charge of us. We had two shifts. You'd be on the night shift for awhile, then change to the day shift. I often think about making lemon pies all night long for the next day...

Virgil F. Hodge, cook

The Gremlin Band was not a military band. It was a swing band.

When it went overseas, the band was just a small group—just some guys who liked to entertain. The small group went to a 14-piece band. I became a member while I was serving in the armament department. I played lead alto. Playing in the band was on my own time. Rehearsals were at the Red Cross.

The following is a list of where the band played: Rainbow Corner USO Club in London; London Palladium; BBC broadcast from Rainbow Corner to the States; Officers' Clubs; Rehab Station, Cambridge; EM Clubs, and, of course, for the GIs at Knettishall.

I'll always remember my relationships with the band members. I still keep in touch with Isador Rozosky and Leon Robins. One member, Morty Wyman, I haven't seen since 1945. We were together a lot; played gin rummy on most of our time off. I still owe him a few shillings.

I want to thank the Red Cross for being there at all times and allowing us to rehearse there. It was a home away from home.

Alfred Arellano, Gremlin Band

The following is a humorous event that occurred during interrogation. This followed a Berlin raid April 29, 1944. We were shot down and imprisoned before being released one year later by General Patton. On April 29, and for several days later, we were transported under heavy guard to St. Giles Prison at Brussels, Belgium. I was confined in a cage or cell about 6 ft. by 6 ft. and had one bowl of soup per day and one call to "be excused," with the guard. Then, after about three days, I was interrogated by a German captain with flowers on the table who offered me a cigarette. The conversation went something like this:

*Question:* "What was your IP where you started your bomb run?"

*Answer:* "I don't know. I can only give you my name, rank and serial number."

*Question:* "What was your target?"

*Answer:* "I don't know. I was a replacement and was not told."

*Question:* "What was your bomb load?"

*Answer:* "I don't know. We were not given that information."

*Question:* "When are you going to run out of manpower? How can you keep sending crews over when you are losing so many?"

*Answer:* "We will never run out. There are always others to replace us."

*Question:* "What was your position on this mission? We know there were 10 of you and all the other nine have been here and told us their positions so you might as will tell us your position."

*Answer:* "Well, by the process of elimination you know the other nine positions, so I am the only one left. You can certainly guess my position."

*Question:* "Ah yes, my dear Watson, I'm familiar with Sherlock Holmes mysteries, but I know that you know the answer but do not wish to tell me. If you will tell me the answer to the five questions I have asked you, I can send you over the other side of the fence to be with your crew buddies and you can eat Red Cross parcels."

I never gave any information other than name, rank and serial number. I later learned that my interrogator had lived in the United States in California and had attended one of the leading universities in that state. While he interrogated me, he opened a dossier on me and read where I lived before entering the Flying Cadets program, where I went to high school, when and where I was trained for the Army Air Corps, when and where I graduated. It was amazing the amount of information he had on me.

Donald B. Wiley, bombadier, Joe Cogner's crew

*Lt. Donald Marble, gunnery officer*

I returned to visit the 561st the day of the 200th Mission Party only to find I didn't belong anymore.

The fellows were almost all replacement crews. The crew that I had flown my 25th mission with went down in a mid-air collision on their next mission. On top of that, I was a Tech Sergeant when I was there last time, and now I was a 1st Lieutenant—no longer an engineer/gunner but now a gunnery officer. I know it was an odd situation for these enlisted replacement crews, and they didn't relax with me as I desired.

I roamed around the base, watched a ball game for awhile, went to the mess hall for lunch and took off for my new home with the 486th.

Sometime during my visit that day I was standing in the far end of the barracks when I head a loud shot, which I recognized as from a .45. We rushed down to the other end of the barracks where three guys had been sitting together on one's cot. I think they had been looking over a .45 Colt when it went off. It struck one man near the knee, the next in the calf area and then hit the last man in the foot. Surprisingly, the least injured man went into shock. I don't know where the medical personnel came from, but they were there promptly. No one seemed to be seriously hurt, but that, on top of my strange reception, just turned a party mood into something else.

I left Knettishall shortly after and never went back.

Donald E. Marble, gunnery officer

I have a twin brother, Harry C. Stiles, Jr. He enlisted first, and got in the Air Force in Fort Worth, Texas in B-17s. I went in January, '43 and went to Ft. Hood, Texas, in Tank Destroyers. We then found out that there was a War Department order out to put twins together.

So, I tried to get transferred with Harry and he tried to get transferred with me. His company commander said, "let your brother do it." My company commander said, "let your brother do it." I then got in ASTP and assigned to North Texas Teachers College. Harry wanted to get with me. The same thing happened with the company commanders. Then Harry, who was a tail gunner, was shipped to England.

When France was invaded they closed all the colleges and wanted all the warm bodies they could get for the Infantry. I was put in Company F, 103rd Infantry Division as a machine gunner, given basic training and landed in Marseilles, France, Oct. 20, 1944. We moved up to the front. Around Thanksgiving time, I was hit by a sniper and sent back to England to a hospital.

Meanwhile, Harry's crew was picked to be Lead plane; the pilot was made co-pilot and the co-pilot went to the tail gunner position and Harry was out of a job! He finally trained as a radar operator (called spot jammers) and by April 1945 had been on 27 missions. When I got well (I was hit in the arm near the wrist) I wrote a letter asking to be put with Harry. Harry's company commander okayed it, so I arrived at the 562nd Squadron on about April 9. My brother Harry showed me how to use the jamming device and three weeks later I flew my first mission. I was able to get another mission in before the war was ended in Europe in May, '45. Harry had 29 missions. We went back to the U.S. on the *Queen Mary* and celebrated the end of the war with Japan on our leave at home in Chicago.

Walter R. Stiles

The time of the mission had to be in late 1944 or in early January, 1945. We were in a three 12-plane (36 planes) formation, followed by many other such formations.

As we approached the target, the 12 planes on the right of Lead Group peeled off to go over the target. Then, the Lead Group followed suit. Our formation, the Left Wing Group, was supposed to follow over the target; however, the group behind us, which was not from the 388th Bomb Group, had overtaken us and went in ahead of us over the target. Our Group was forced to make a 360-degree turn in order to go over the target. The Group that cut us off was hit by German fighters. The fighters came in all at once instead of by single-plane attacks. If this 80 year-old mind remembers correctly, eight of the 12 B-17s were taken out.

Our turn came again to go over the target. Our Number 2 engine began to smoke. As the engineer, Sanford Pike, and I discussed the proper procedure to follow, I allowed the plane to lag somewhat behind the formation. The fighters came back to hit any stragglers, of which we were one.

One plane, however, was farther back than we were. That plane was taken down by the fighters. This could have been us.

The Number 2 propeller was feathered and the smoke ceased. A one-inch oil line had a flak hole in it and was losing oil. Fortunately, no fire occurred. We pulled back into formation, which was on the left wing of the Lead plane. Our plane had flown only three missions and therefore had plenty of power with three engines. We had dropped our bombs just before the engine began to smoke.

I feel that the Power Above was with us three times that day: Once when we were cut off from the target and when there was a plane farther back than we were which the fighters took down and finally, when the engine stopped smoking as the Number 2 propeller was feathered. Praise the Lord.

James M. L. Comer, pilot

Because our crew was on stand-down status one day, we were preparing to use the opportunity to go on pass. Jack Gauthier and I had just finished an early-morning bath and shave routine. As we emerged from the bathhouse hut, we looked aloft in time to see our B-17s beginning to assemble overhead for that day's mission. Procedure at that time was to have the Lead plane's tail gunner deploy a flare which gave a brilliant white light to guide other planes into formation. This flare was supposed to slide down a long steel cable to a stop which would trigger the ignition. Instead, right after it ignited, the flare broke loose from its tether, and came crashing down right at the spot where Jack and I had stood only seconds before! Pieces of white-hot magnesium splattered all over the area. It was a mighty close call, but fortunately neither of us was injured. That was just one of many scary incidents during our exciting life at Station 136 in England.

Ralph M. Reese, co-pilot, Gauthier's crew

*Medic Vince Howie, center, and friends*

I took my trumpet overseas with me and we formed a kind of band—the drummer's name was Ted Holden; I don't remember the piano player's name. I sang all the vocals. There was a pub about four miles away and I used to bicycle down there with my trumpet on the handlebars. We'd play there sometimes. I remember one night in particular at Christmas time. I was singing and the place was packed with women. When I went to the bar to get a drink I had to pass under some mistletoe in the hallway and I got kissed there by so many women that I never did get to the bar. I was mobbed. I almost didn't get back to the band.

Vince Howie, medic

A funny thing happened to me on my way to the air war in Europe. They took away my bomber.

I spent six weeks at Smyrna, Tennessee in B-24 First Pilot Transition School, picked up my crew and trained with bombing missions at Chatham Field, Savannah, Georgia. Flew a brand new B-24 aircraft from Mitchell Field, New York, across the northern Atlantic route to England, where they took my B-24 and gave me train tickets to Thetford and the 388th base.

Image our shock, a B-24 crew on a B-17 base. Where do you start?

The 563rd assured me that I was at the right base. There was a war on and they needed crews. So the crew and I quickly learned how to fly the B-17. I think it was the short course. We flew our first combat mission to Darmstadt, Germany, Dec. 24, 1944.

I have concluded that being sent to a B-17 Group in a B-24 was probably the best thing that ever happened to me and my crew in the military. Switching to B-17s at the last moment could have very well saved our lives. I completed 25 missions without getting scratched.

John W. Hoff, pilot, 563rd Squadron

You will say, "I never heard of it," and I say, "you're right;" and that's why I am writing this story.

The 563rd Pound Club was evidently unique to the 563rd Headquarters Hut. In the large end-room, the troops would gather after the evening meal and someone would say, "Who's on for a Pound Club?" Pound notes would be placed on the table and the junior officer—me—would gather the money, take the squadron Jeep to the Officers' Club and procure beverages equal to the funds. Back at the hut, as the evening passed, conversations ranged from war stories to politics, back-home tales to jokes. But the highlight of the evening came when Roger Swihart would be persuaded to recite, in his own inimitable way, *Casey at the Bat*." His "flighter" on backwards, he would step up to the plate and his words would flow. The word "impressive" doesn't do justice to his rendition.

Roger brightened our social time and made the war a little bit shorter. I shall never forget it.

John Hoff

Lt. Paul Schwartz    my wife Madelene    "Me" Herman Teifeld

*Herman and Madelene Teifeld and their Best Man, Lt. Paul Schwartz*

The 6th of June, 1944, was to have been my wedding day.

I was a 24-year-old 1st Lieutenant, U.S. Army Air Corps, assigned to the 388th Bomb Group, Knettishall, England. I was one of the two Group Radio Officers (S). The "S" stood for "secret" because it denoted radar, which in itself was secret. Early in the morning on June 6 my men and I were assigning and installing radar jamming devices and metallic chaff aboard our B-17s.

I met my future wife, Madelene, in England in September, 1943, after attending an electronics school near London.

We were told to advance our wedding plans from June 6 to May 1, which we did, because all leaves in June were to be canceled. As it turned out, all leaves were also canceled in May! But Col. David was a very under-standing person and put me on special orders:

*1st Lt. Herman H. Teifeld WP London on TD for a period not to exceed four (4) days o/a 27 April 1944 to carry out instructions of the Commanding Officer.*

Madelene and I celebrated our 50th anniversary on May 1, 1994.

Herman H. Teifeld, group radio officer (S)

The 388th was going to bomb German columns in support of ground troops trapped in Belgium during the Battle of the Bulge. I knew my brother was in that approximate area. He was with the infantry and had also been at Omaha Beach on D-Day. But the weather in England was ferocious. It was just terrible. We couldn't see the ends of our own wings. You couldn't see anything at all, so you couldn't take off. That was on the 16th of December. We went down to the revetments to go bomb, to help out the troops who were involved in the Bulge, and we couldn't take off. I knew my brother was there. Maybe not right at the Bulge, but in that general area. Each morning we went out and got ready to fly, but the weather stayed bad and they called off the missions.

Finally on the 24th of December we got the signal to go.

On Christmas Eve, we successfully dropped our bombs to help, then we came back and went to church. The choir was singing *Adeste Fidelas*— Come All Ye Faithful.

You know, I sat there in church and wondered—we went out and killed all those people and here we are singing about goodwill and peace toward men.

But, that's the way it was.

I was never really able to sing that song again.

Joe Capraro, waist gunner

*Fireman Floyd Palmer at work during a demonstration on base*

As a fireman, I was stationed at the end of the runway one day where planes were landing from a mission. One aircraft landed with brakes shot away and many other problems. It continued off the end of the runway, turned and came right at our fire truck. A prop cut the back side off the foam tank as we were trying to get away. What a scary day *that* was! Life on the base was pretty good, but we would get calls day and night for fires in the surrounding area—lots of them in straw rolls close to the base.

Floyd Palmer, firefighter, 434th Service Squadron

April 17, 1945—Mission to Dresden:

We are somewhat surprised today to learn that we fly as B Wing Lead, which means that we will lead the 388th Bomb Group. We taxi at 10:05 and, since we are the first ship to take off, clear the ground at 10:15. We make a visual climb to the left to 2,000 feet, form our squadron on the racetrack pattern and leave the field at 10:55. At 10:58 we make Wing assembly on time and fall into our position in the Division column. Col. Mallory of the 45th Combat Wing flies the right seat as Command. The colonel is quite new and this is my first Group Lead.

As we reach our IP the weather is very hazy and contrails become dense and persistent. We have a rough time approaching the target as a squadron from another group—with bomb bay doors closing—appears in our faces!

In a split second, it is over as two Forts collide and explode.

We are thoroughly shaken at this confrontation and, just as bombs fall away, I make a sharp left turn from the bomb run, fearful and that another squadron may be on its way.

Our course from the IP was 350 degrees; the other squadron had missed its IP and turned to re-enter the bomb run in the opposite direction.

Back at 18:20. Total time, 8:05 hours. Celebrate tonight with Charlie Gault, who finished his 30 missions today, and then to bed at 24:00.

From the mission diary of Franklin D. Little, pilot

Quite a bit has been written about the Aphrodite missions, so I will eliminate the technical details and get on with my experience.

Our plane and her crew arrived in England in June 1944 after D-Day. Our first mission was on July 28, 1944. After six or seven missions, around the middle of August, my pilot, Casey Sulkowski; myself (co-pilot); navigator, Fred Ulbrich and engineer, Bob Crowell were ordered to take our B-17 up to a field near Fersfield, which was just a hop from home base.

We knew that we would be staying for a few days, and we brought a change of clothing and our ditty bags. We were put up in a hut, and spent the next three or four days relaxing and enjoying some rare English sunshine. There were all sorts of rumors that our mission was highly secretive, and that we should not relate anything regarding it, even when we returned to base.

Finally one morning, we were called into operations and introduced to a couple of Navy pilots, Kennedy and Wiley. Coming from Massachusetts, I should have recognized the name Kennedy. It was not until later that I realized he was the eldest son of Ambassador Joseph P. Kennedy.

An old B-24 had been stripped of all excess weight and loaded with thousands of pounds of very high explosive. The two Navy pilots were to fly the loaded aircraft outfitted with sophisticated equipment that would allow the plane to be controlled by a mother ship after the two pilots had bailed out.

Our job was to escort the B-24 to the English coast and report their position. We went to our B-17 and prepared for take-off. We became airborne and circled the field at around 1,200 feet. Finally, the B-24 lumbered down the runway and became airborne. At that time, we were at the opposite end of the runway and had to make a 180-degree turn to catch up with the B-24.

We were closing the gap on the B-24. It was hard to recall just how close we were to it, when there was a blinding flash and explosion, and the B-24 was gone.

Had we been much closer, I am sure I would not be here to relate the story. The blast tipped our plane practically up on one wing tip, and those who were not secure in their seats were thrown to the floor of the plane. When we circled the area, the only thing visible was a seared spot on the ground.

In the late 40s, after returning to the states, I was going with a girl whose aunt had a place adjacent to the Kennedy Compound in Hyannisport, MA. Word got out to the Kennedys that I was on the mission when Joe Kennedy was killed. One day, when I was on the beach, John and Ted Kennedy came along, introduced themselves and wanted to hear my story.

William W. Worthen, co-pilot, 562nd Squadron

One day our squadron Executive Officer came to our barracks mad as all get out. A local farmer had come to him complaining that someone had stolen a couple of his chickens. Of course, no one in our outfit knew anything about said chickens. However, the Executive nosed around a bit and returned a couple of hours later saying that he had found a bunch of chicken feathers outside in back of our barracks. Still, no one knew anything about the situation. However, the Executive figured that in order to keep on good terms with our neighbors, it would be a good idea if we were to pay the farmer for his loss. Without admitting any knowledge about this chicken deal, we paid up.

William B. Forrest, navigator on William Kelly's Crew

At the end of the war, I was on two of the Chow Hound flights to drop food to the Dutch. On one of the missions, a box of food somehow broke open a bit during loading into our aircraft. Said box contained large cans of bacon. Now, we had not even *seen* bacon for at least a year. No one knows how it happened, but a can of said bacon showed up in our barracks after we returned from the mission. Boy, did that bacon taste good cooked over the coal-burning stove in our barracks.

William B. Forrest

Right after the war in Europe was over, our group had a mission to fly a number of our own ground crew members on a sightseeing trip over sections of Holland. The plane that I was on as navigator flew over Rotterdam,

Amsterdam and the low countries to show our ground personnel what some of the war damage was. When we started back to base, the pilot decided to give the boys a real close view of the countryside. We dropped down to about 30 feet above ground level. This was very, very level and flat country. As we approached a dike and canal, we had to pull up just a bit to clear the dike. As we did so, a farmer leading a cow was right in our line of flight. As navigator, I had a great view of the action. The farmer fell to the ground, but the cow was so frightened that it jumped into the canal. This was a great story to tell later around the bar in the Officers' Club. We were really just kids and we thought that it was all great fun. But later on we wondered if the farmer thought the same as we. I think not.

William B. Forrest

On May 8, the war in Europe ended. There was little celebration; all personnel had been restricted to the base, so many of us just sat around and talked about where we might go from here.

Those of us who had not completed our tour of missions speculated that we would be sent for B-29 training and then fly missions over Japan. This was not a happy thought.

On the night of May 11, our crew, along with others, was scheduled to take what they called "training flights" around England—or, as we called it, "an end of the war celebration flight." So we took off, circled real low over London (which I found out later, in no uncertain terms, I shouldn't have done) then on down the coast to Land's End, just leisurely flying around, somewhat relaxed, while listening to the BBC and enjoying the lights of England.

Around 11 o'clock, I switched back to our military frequency and heard our plane's identification being called:

"Fog is rolling in. The British Isles are in danger of completely closing in. Come in immediately."

Wow, what a revolting development. Why didn't I at least have some crew member monitoring the weather reports? Hadn't I been in England long enough to know that fog can form in a hurry and often does? We flew back to Knettishall and made two passes, but couldn't land. Visibility in fog can be deceiving. It seemed to be sufficient while looking down from above, but as I started the letdown on final approach, all visibility disappeared. Landing was hopeless. It was a terrible feeling. What do I do now if there is no place to land? My thoughts were that I was in real trouble. How could I have been so careless?

While I was still mulling over the alternatives, air traffic control came back with some welcome instructions. I was to go to a certain Royal Air Force Base where FIDO was available. I don't recall having heard of this before that night. FIDO stands for Fog Intensive Dispersal Operation, developed as an emergency measure by the British Petroleum Department in 1943. This is the burning of fuel, probably kerosene, along both sides of the runway in sufficient quantity to clear a spot in the fog so pilots can find a place to land. We circled around and started a descent through the fog toward the blazing fires and on into the "inferno," then with great relief the wheels touched and we were on the runway and on into the fog again to finish the roll.

I had lucked out. No injuries, no damage except that probably our government had to compensate the British. Five other 8th Air Force planes had a similar experience and joined us. All I can say is we were lucky, but not too smart, and thankful to whoever thought up this procedure.

In addition, I learned a valuable lesson that night.

Noah C. Thompson, pilot, 560th Squadron

# *DAILY BULLETINS*: FEBRUARY, 1944

## No. 32, 1 February 1944

SPECIAL SERVICES:
Today—*"Bombers Moon"*
Feb. 6—*"This is the Army"*
Feb. 7—*"Mexican Spitfire's Blessed Event"*
Feb. 8—*"The Man from Headquarters"*
Feb. 12—*"Stormy Weather"*

———

There will be a rehearsal of the military band today at 15:00 hrs in the Aero Club Snack Bar. All instruments are available. Openings on trombone, French horn, etc.

———

Glee Club rehearsal tomorrow at 19:00 hrs in Aero Club Snack Bar. All others interested are invited.

———

All organizations will turn in Council books and supporting papers to the Air Insp. Office before 5 February for inspection.

———

Mobile Sales Units handling officers, nurses and WAC officers clothing for sale will be installed and opened for business at locations and times as stated:
Great Ashfield—19:00 hrs. 5-2-44 to 17:00 hrs. 12-2-44
Eye—09:00 hrs. 26-2-44 to 17:00 hrs. 27-2-44
Mendlesham—05:00 hrs. 1-3-44 to 17:00 hrs. 2-3-44

———

452nd Sub-Depot salvage yard, located across road from the sheet metal shop, is off limits to all personnel unless authorized by Sub-Depot Engineering Officer. Anyone caught taking any equipment from the area will be subject to disciplinary action.

———

The following named officers of this Station have books overdue to the Station Library, and will return them without delay: Capt. Fulkerson, Capt. Samuel.

———

LOST: Bracelet with embossing consisting of wings and St. Christopher Medal. Finder please return to Base Sgt. Major's office. Reward.

FOUND: Bracelet belonging to William R. Fitch. Please claim at Base Sgt. Major's office.

———.

Cashing of Vollar Instruments: 1) Money orders will be cashed at local APO. 2) Express money orders and travelers checks will be cashed at local Finance Office. 3) All currency will be converted at local Finance Office.

———

AERO CLUB:
    Monday—Board of Governors' Meeting at 20:30, also Bingo
    Tuesday—Battle of the Paddles Ping Pong Tournament
    Wednesday—Dancing Lessons
    Friday—Lower Grades Dance
    Saturday—Photo Quiz—Projection of Kodachrome films

———

Officers Bed Allotment, Reindeer ARC Club, London, 7 beds for this Station. EM bed allotment, Hans Crescent Club, 21 beds. Bomb Squadrons allotted 3 beds. All other organizations this Station are allotted one bed.

## No. 35, 4 February 1944

All officers scheduled for duty as inspectors will assemble in the Ground Executive's office at 09:00 hrs Saturday morning for instructions.

———

All flying officers upon completing their tour of operations from this Station will turn in the following items of flying equipment to the Sub-Depot Supply before being cleared:

1 pr gloves flying, type A-10
    or
1 pr gauntlets, flying winter, type A-9
1 pr goggles assembly type B-7
    or
1 pr goggles, flying VII or VIII (British)
1 ea helmet, flying winter, type B-6
1 ea jacket, flying type A-2
    or
1 ea jacket field, lined (battle jacket)
1 ea jacket, flying, winter, heavy, type B-3
    or
1 ea jacket, flying, winter, medium, type B-6
1 ea mask, oxygen type A-10 or A-14
1 pr shoes, flying, winter type A6 or A9
1 ea suit, flying summer, type A-4
1 pr trousers, flying, winter, heavy type A-3
    or
1 pr trousers, flying, medium type A-5
1 ea vest, flying, winter type C-2

———

Protestant Services—Coney Weston Church of England

06:45 hrs—Rev. Morgan, Preacher
09:46 hrs—Chap. Fulkerson
14:00 hrs.—Chap. Fulkerson
Catholic Services—Sunday Mass
09:00 hrs and 17:15 hrs.
Confessions before Mass

## No. 38, 7 February 1944

Effective this date, all Jeeps assigned to individuals or sections are limited to two gallons of gas per day. Instructions have been given to gasoline disbursing attendant not to put more than two gallons per day in these vehicles. In the event some vehicle requires more than this amount on any particular day, the responsible officer will have to contact Transportation Officer and explain why it is necessary to secure more gasoline.

## No. 41, 10 February 1944

The Station S-4 has brought to the attention of this Headquarters that there are a number of abandoned bicycles in the various Sites with warped wheels, missing sprocket chains, etc. Apparently these are not being claimed by any officers and have been allowed to stay out in the weather. Officers in charge of Living Sites and Unit Commanders are requested to make a survey of their Sites to ascertain if any such bicycles can be found. Those that are found without ownership will be turned in to the Station Ordnance immediately.

———

There has been a tendency to pull rank on and disregard the MP station at the Control Tower during mission take-offs and landings, with the result that the tower is congested and AAF Regulations are violated. Henceforth, only the following personnel will be admitted: Col. David, Col. Henggeler, Lt. Col. Cox, Lt. Col. Satterwhite, Maj. Ball, Maj. Forrest, Maj. Relyer, Maj. Chamberlain, Maj. Goodman, Capt. Jones, W/O Gillespie.

## No. 42, 11 February 1944

The Weekly Progress Reports heretofore prepared and submitted each week will, effective this date, be submitted monthly and be known as the Monthly Progress and Problem Report. The monthly report will be dated the last day of the month for which the report is written and prepared so as to reach the Adjutant's section, in duplicate, not later than the 5th day of the succeeding month. The report will follow along the same general lines as the weekly report heretofore submitted and, in addition, will present any particular or difficult problems confronting the section or department.

———

"Bitching Sessions:" Officers and enlisted men are again reminded that any complaints (bitching) that they might have to make regarding anything in their organization or on the station generally may be made to Major Boardman C. Reed, Air Inspector, this office in the Technical Site on any Saturday. On those Saturdays in which Major Reed is not available, CWO Charles E. Oakes will be there. Officers and enlisted men are assured that any complaints that they may have will be treated as secret and confidential and, if desired, the complainant's name will not be disclosed and that all matters worthy of consideration will be taken up immediately with the proper authorities.

———

The Station Utilities Office has approximately 250 pounds of grass seed for issue to the squadrons on the base. The following procedure should be followed per instructions of the Clerk of the Works in sowing this seed;
A. The area should be mulched where seed is to be planted.

B. Seed should be mixed with sand or covered over lightly with earth to keep the birds from eating the seed and to ensure retention of moisture and proper germination.

C. Seeded areas should not be trespassed upon.

Seed may be obtained at the Station Utilities office at any time between the hours of 08:30 and 05:30 each day. Containers for seed should be brought by the squadron desiring issue. All areas will be seeded between 25 February and 10 March. The Section Officer in each Living Site will be responsible for the seeding in that Site.

## No. 43, 12 February 1944

Gifts may be ordered at the PX for special occasions. Come in and place your orders on Thursdays, Fridays and Saturdays. War Bonds may be purchased on the same days.

———

Glee Club rehearsal tonight at 19:00 hours in the Aero Club.

## No. 44, 13 February 1944

SPECIAL SERVICES:
    Today—*"Panther's Claw"*
    Feb. 14—*"Mr. Smith Goes to Washington"*
    Feb. 15—*"Holy Matrimony"*
    Feb. 17—*"Casablanca"*

———

Through the good offices of the Chaplain, arrangements have been made to pick up 36 London daily newspapers. These papers will be divided at this Headquarters into three packages; one for the Aero Club, one for the Rocker Club and one for the Officers' Club. There will be a charge for each club of one pence for each paper per day, which will be payable at the end of the month. Papers delivered to the clubs will be made available for all members.

————

The practice of cannibalizing parts of GI bicycles will cease immediately. Members of this command are referred to AW 96 which directs the punishment of such offenders.

————

The Medical Liaison Office of the American Red Cross, APO 887, has informed this Headquarters that prophylactic stations for the prevention of venereal disease have been established in the following American Red Cross Clubs:
Edinburgh—53 Princess Street
Henley—Stoke-on-Trent
Plymouth—4 Elliott Terrace

————

Effective this date the public house located on the station known as the "White Swan" is declared off limits as is also the public house known as the "Royal George" near Site No. 5. These restrictions affect all military personnel. Organization Commanders are directed to bring this directive to the attention of all in their command. The action taken in those premises is in no wise a reflection on the management of those public houses.

## No. 51, 20 February 1944

There have been one or two instances of late where soldiers, in an attempt to ridicule prisoners, have counted cadence for the prisoners. This will serve as notice that anyone who hereafter counts cadence, ridicules and degrades prisoners while at work or on their way to the mess hall will be arrested on the spot and dealt with severely.

―――

The coal and coke supply on this station is facing an acute shortage. Unless steps are immediately taken to drastically reduce consumption, only mess halls and the dispensary will receive allotments of fuel. Organizational commanders will see that wood is burned whenever possible.

―――

FOUND: One wool knit scarf (OD). Owner call at S-4.

LOST: One wool knit scarf (OD). Finder please return to Cpt. Rabinowitz of the Sergeant Major's office.

# THE INCREDIBLE JOURNEY BACK

From the *Hartford, Conn. Courant*, November, 1989

MANCHESTER—"You can imagine what a profound and lasting impression you have made on me!" the letter read. "To get the privilege of lodging an American during the German occupation of our country was something quite uncommon and, I dare say, even exciting for a little boy."

That boy, Paul Windels, is now 58, and the letter's recipient, John Maiorca of School Street in Manchester, is 70. The letter from Belgium ended 43 years of silence between the two men; Maiorca, an Air Force lieutenant whose plane was shot down over Belgium in 1943, and Windels, at the time an impressionable 13-year-old.

They were never supposed to meet.

"I was coming back from boarding school on a Saturday; I went upstairs and found a man," Windels said in a telephone interview from Belgium, speaking in French. "My parents were very embarrassed that I found out, but I didn't tell anyone," he continued. "If the secret wasn't kept, the immediate result would be the firing squad."

The letter, the successful result of persistent efforts by Windels to get in touch with Maiorca, also contained an invitation. "It would be wonderful if you could fly over to Belgium again. You certainly would do it in much better circumstances than formerly."

Maiorca accepted, and returned from a two-week trip to Belgium earlier this month, completing what he has named "The Incredible Journey." Incredible, because he found the exact spot where he parachuted into Nazi-occupied Belgium; because he was reunited with a half-dozen Belgians who had helped him escape, some of whom, made aware of Maiorca's visit by newspaper and radio notices, did not meet each other until the reunion; and because he discovered—contradicting his own

129

assumptions—that younger generations are interested in World War II and the lessons that can be learned from it.

"I thanked Paul for his father's saving my life," Maiorca said, surrounded on his sofa by albums containing hundreds of photographs of the trip and of his erstwhile protectors, and even a blurry black-and-white shot of his plane's wreckage which was taken furtively by a member of the Belgian resistance.

In helping to save American lives, Paul Windels' father lost his own.

Marcel Windels and Joseph Duthoy, another member of the Belgian underground who helped Maiorca begin a two-month odyssey to freedom, were killed by the Germans in 1944 shortly before their village was liberated. They were shot as they tried to help two other Americans escape, Maiorca said.

After 45 years, the details of Maiorca's first, unplanned trip to Belgium as a 25-year-old Air Force bombardier are indelible in his mind.

In the early afternoon of a sunny day,, Nov. 5, 1943, Maiorca's plane, a B-17 Flying Fortress, was hit by anti-aircraft fire over Germany. Attempting to return to Britain, it was hit by fire from a German fighter over Belgium, killing two of the plane's 10 crew members.

"The plane took a dive, and the pilot ordered us to bail out," recalls Maiorca, a member of the 8th Air Force 388th Bomb Group. "I decided to free fall, tumbling in the air, just to see what it was like." After falling about 4,000 feet, he reached for his ripcord. "It wasn't there, and I had never parachuted before." He finally found the cord over his left shoulder.

Maiorca landed softly on flat farm land, his comrades nowhere in sight. He rolled up his life jacket and parachute, hid them and ran. Forty-five years later, at the end of his recent trip, a man approached Maiorca with a package.

"By the way, what's your serial number?" Maiorca said the man asked. "He said, 'You don't know, but I was following you. I watched you'." Maiorca unwrapped the package to find a faded yellow life preserver, still bearing his name and serial number.

After his jump, Maiorca decided to head toward France, hoping to get help from the underground. One man put him up for the night and offered to accompany him on a train to the French border. Maiorca declined after the man told him he would be shot if he was found to be helping an American. So, dressed in civilian clothes the man gave him, Maiorca began a 27-mile walk during which he encountered, uneventfully, German soldiers.

After passing through the city of Gent, rain soaked through his shoes and he started to shiver. "I must have looked like a drowned rat," Maiorca said. "I decided then that I had to throw myself on the mercy of the Belgian people."

He knocked on the doors of a half-dozen homes whose residents turned down his pleas for help—but neither did they turn him in. A man named Modest Vandenbrouck, nicknamed Al Capone because of black-market business affairs, then accompanied him by train to the town of Waregern and members of the resistance there. They asked him a lot of questions, but Maiorca would, at first, only give them his name, rank and serial number.

"Young man, if we are to help you we need information!" Maiorca remembers one of them saying. "I think I'll trust 'em," Maiorca said he decided—a decision that sits well today.

For two weeks, Maiorca alternated between the homes of Marcel Windels and Modest Vandenbrouck, the shades of his bedrooms always drawn. It was during that time that Paul Windels, then 13, stumbled into Maiorca's bedroom. "I said, 'Hi kid, how're you doing'?" Maiorca recalls. Soon after, he forgot about the youngster.

Marcel Windels and others helped Maiorca begin a slow ride on the resistance's underground railroad. Carrying false papers identifying him as a deaf mute, he traveled to and even did some sightseeing in Nazi-occupied Paris; went by train to Bordeaux; traveled by bike and by foot south; walked across a neck-high stream into Spain under the cover of night and finally found freedom in the British crown colony of Gibraltar.

During the two-month escape, members of the underground told Maiorca and other Americans that their families knew they were safe.

"Ha!" said his wife, Betty Maiorca, who was in Manchester those months with their newborn child. Her husband was listed as Missing In Action and she had received no other information. Making matters worse, a local newspaper printed Maiorca's obituary.

"But," she recalls, "nobody could convince me he was dead. He wouldn't dare go off and leave me alone."

On Jan. 4, 1944, she received an "all's-well" telegram from her husband.

"I said, 'Oh, God,' and with that I passed out."

# Col. David's Story

From an 8th Air Force news release

With his pilot wounded and the cockpit in flames, Col. William B. David, 31, of Calhoun, Georgia, nursed his Flying Fortress out of an 11,000-foot dive to fly it 500 miles to a safe landing in England. Nine of the crew, including the Colonel, were treated for injuries. The enemy is missing four fighter planes.

Col. David, Commander of an 8th Army Air Force Heavy Bombardment Group, was in the co-pilot's place as Command Pilot of the formation. The bombers had finished blasting a German airfield near Bordeaux, France and were headed home over the Bay of Biscay.

The Colonel's ship, the Fortress *Big Red,* which had started out as Group Leader, was now in Tail-End Charlie position—last plane in the last squadron. Enemy fighters made a furious attack. Col. David remembers seeing a German fighter peel off to the right, and he saw gasoline pouring from a right wing tank; the Fortress had been hit by 20mm cannon shells. At almost the same instant bullets slashed into the cockpit from a head-on attack, one of them wounding the pilot in the leg, others drilling the hydraulic system and an oxygen tank.

Col. David found himself in a sea of flames that burned his hair, his face and hands, and shriveled his flying jacket.

For some seconds the ship flew wild. Then the Colonel put the plane in a dive. "My first thought was to get down close to the water so we could ditch the aircraft; we were too far off shore to have any chance if we bailed out at altitude," he recalled.

While the ship plunged from 21,000 down to 10,000 feet, the fire burned itself out. His eyes peeled for enemy fighters, carefully Col. David pulled the big bomber out of its dive. The wings stayed on, the ship flew level and the leaking gasoline tank did not explode.

"My plan was to head straight out to sea and make a run for it," the Colonel explained. Enemy fighters returned to the attack, aiming their tracers at the flood of gasoline streaming from the bomber's wing. Col. David, alone in the cockpit, flew evasive action. In a 20-minute battle, his gunners knocked down four of the German planes and drove off the rest.

The Fortress' wounded engineer, T/Sgt. John J. Thomas, 29, of Gloversville, New York, succeeded in transferring gasoline out of the damaged tank and the torrent of escaping fuel stopped. *Big Red* headed home.

In the end, it was Col. David in the pilot's seat and the bombardier, Capt. George Bartuska, 23, of 1212 E. Donald Street, South Bend, Indiana, in the co-pilot's place, who brought the ship to a safe landing at the home field. They had flown far out to sea to avoid the Brest Peninsula.

This was the 16th time that Col. David has led his Group in attacks on German factories and installations.

*Col. William B. David, Commanding Officer*

# THE MILK RUN

From the Baltimore, Md. *Sun,* January, 1944
By Price Day, Sunpapers' War Correspondent

A United States Bomber Station Somewhere in England, Jan. 14 (By Cable-Delayed)—The ambulances at this base had nothing to do today.

No returning Fortresses dropped red flares asking landing priority because of wounded aboard. The only lights were from the ground—pairs of flares to assist the big ships home through the dusk.

Today every ship that went out from here came back. Unlike last Tuesday's, the day's mission was a milk run, with prompt delivery on the targets just inside the "rocket" or "invasion," or, as the Germans call it, "reprisal" coast of France.

"It wasn't anything," the 21-year-old pilot of the Fortress *The Princess Pat,* Lt. Arthur B. Pack, of the 4300 block Groveland Ave., Baltimore, reported. Standing before his locker in a hut, with a cup of hot, rich cocoa, Pack pointed out the importance of the word "The" in the name of his ship—"I think it adds distinction to it"—and expressed hope that there wouldn't be powdered eggs for dinner.

Lt. Pack's navigator, 2nd Lt. Robert S. Izat, of Lonaconing, Md., his map case under his arm, agreed that the day had been uneventful; a little flak, no enemy fighters, excellent protection by the escorting Mustangs, Thunderbolts and Lightnings.

The two young officers moved off toward the briefing room for interrogation. Other men drifted in and grouped themselves by crews and stood quietly talking. All looked solid and chunky in their heavy clothes. Some still wore once-white parachute harnesses and bright yellow "Mae West" life jackets.

In a few minutes they followed Lt. Pack's crew to sit around tables and tell their composite stories to Intelligence officers.

All day the men left behind on the ground had anticipated that the mission would be an easy one. But "easy," in bombing terminology, is a relative term.

Indeed, well before the Forts were due to return, small knots of men gathered on the edge of the field watching the skies, now and then saying a few words through the roar and rattle of the giant bulldozer trying to worry a few drops of water out of a small sea of thin black mud across the road from the headquarters hut.

The men who never take part in combat, but who are indispensable to any mission's success, waited as eagerly as any.

Among them were two Baltimore staff sergeants, William H. Helfrich, of the 3000 block Brendan Ave., who once worked at the Maryland Drydock Co., and Bernard Thanner, of the 2600 block Chesterfield Ave., a meat cutter before he entered the Army. Sergeant Thanner is an Operations Draftsman. Sergeant Helfrich is assigned to Group Operations.

Major Walter V. A. Harrison, Intelligence Officer, who before the war had his law office at 100 St. Paul St. in Baltimore, interrupted his discussion of the beauties of the base's new rustic bar to watch a plane coming in over the far end of the field.

"Bring her down, boy," he said to himself, but the plane was too high at that moment. The pilot took it around the field once again and then came in to make a beautiful, three-point landing.

By now it was almost dark. In the briefing room the Flight Surgeon, Maj. James R. Bell, who studied medicine at the University of Maryland, stood smoking his pipe, his back to the stove which heated a small area of the large hut.

"The more days like today, the better," he said, inhaling deeply and nodding his head.

Today's mission, however—though important—will create no big splash in the communiques or newspapers, and no one cared. Everyone knew they had done their job well and were grateful for the bloodless outcome.

Every man also knew that most missions would neither be as easy as today's, nor as "rugged" as some others. Either way, the bomber crews are ready and eager to take them as they come.

*From left, Thaddeus Hense, bombardier, Arthur B. Pack, pilot, and Robert Izat, navigator*

# THE MISSION DIARY OF AUBREY R. STANTON

Ball turret gunner, Campbell's crew, 561st Squadron

Thursday, Dec. 30, 1943: We took *Berlin Ambassador* on what should have been our first mission. We had to come back because we lost the oxygen from the right waist. We were up from 9 'til 12. We got as far as the Channel. What a time we had this morning; no heated equipment and we didn't know where our plane was. By the time we found our plane we had about 30 minutes to clean guns and get them in the plane. This afternoon we got a lecture and cleaned our guns.

Friday, Dec. 31, 1943: Today we took *Jimmy Lee* on what should have been our second mission. We had to abort again because the oxygen went out. The bombardier and co-pilot had no oxygen. We made a perfect landing both yesterday and today with a big load of gas and bombs. We had twelve 500-pound bombs today. Think I'll start the New Year off right by going to bed.

Tuesday, Jan. 4, 1944. First mission, Munster, *Miss Fury*, #853: The night before the first mission I slept like a log from about 9 'till 2 when they woke us up for 3 o'clock briefing. I was so scared and shaky I could hardly get my clothes on. As usual, we walked to the mess hall for breakfast of tomato juice, hot cakes and bacon. Then a truck took us to the briefing room. First, we had to get heated clothing from other crews who weren't flying. That was really a headache because of the shortage of heated clothing. Then we went to the briefing. It was a very tense moment just before the curtain went up uncovering the target for today, Munster. We also learned the route we would take, that we would have plenty of P-47 escorts and that the flak would be heavy only over the target. Take-off time was to be 6:55 a.m. Next, we got all of our equipment together and got on a truck to go to the plane. Some of the crew who had looked at the dispersal area chart thought they knew where our plane was located, but apparently not, for we looked first here and then there, always on the wrong side of the perimeter. Finally, we got off the truck—a bad mistake—thinking our plane was in the next revetment. It wasn't, so now we were on foot carrying about 100 pounds of equipment. At last we found it, #853 *Miss Fury*.

Next, we cleaned our guns in the nearby armament shack. I got my guns in the ball turret and had time to start dressing before take-off. We had some trouble getting into formation due to darkness. It didn't get light until after we were over the Channel. We test fired our guns. Everyone's guns fired and we began scanning the sky for fighters. After reaching the enemy coast, P-47s met us and stayed with us from there to the target and back. We dropped all our bombs through solid cloud cover with the aid of the Pathfinder ship. I didn't see a lot of flak, but the gunners above did, exploding close enough at times to hear and to make a lot of holes in the plane, which we didn't know about until we landed.

Shortly after leaving the target, our pilot, Ray Campbell, noticed that the gas tanks were getting very low. He sent the engineer, Anthony Kawalec, back to see if the Tokyo tanks were open. They were open, but were apparently empty or wouldn't drain. The pilot immediately figured we wouldn't have enough gas to make it back and was in doubt as to whether we would even make the Channel. We had a 120-mile-per-hour headwind to buck and one engine gone. It couldn't be feathered so it windmilled all the way back. The pilot gave the order to throw everything overboard that wouldn't be needed—guns, ammunition, flak suits and radio equipment. Next, we got the order to prepare to bail out over France, since it looked like we could not reach the Channel. I got out of the ball turret, put my chute chest pack on and sat shaking with fear that we were going to have to bail out. The next order was, "Man your guns. Enemy fighters approaching." I was practically back in the ball when it was reported that the fighters were our own. I put my chute on again and

waited for the order to bail out. I should have fired all the ammunition in
the ball turret, but didn't, thinking we might need it. The P-47s escorted
us all the way back and no enemy fighters were seen. Just before reaching
the Channel, the pilot gave us the order to prepare for ditching. We had
left our formation long ago due to losing so much altitude. We had been
flying slowly on a very low RPM at about 130 miles per hour to conserve
as much gas as possible, since the tanks were registering very low.

To prepare for ditching, all of us in the rear of the ship were on the floor
of the radio room. I crowded into the right front corner with my head pro-
tected by putting my heavy jacket behind my head. Brooks, the assistant
engineer and waist gunner, was leaning against me. McIntyre, the radio
operator, was under his radio table. Miles "Tex" Johns, the tail gunner, was
against the bomb bay door and Marr, the other waist gunner, was in front
of Tex. From our positions in the radio room, we could see nothing and
were expecting to land in the Channel. We were surprised, to say the least,
when the plane came scooting in on hard ground. After coming to a stop,
we got out as fast as we could, expecting a fire and possible explosion.
Neither happened. The pilots had made a perfect crash landing. With
wheels up, the ball turret had crumbled under the plane and the fuselage of
the plane had broken. The pilot then told us we had run out of fuel as we
were circling a large green pasture on a small island just off the coast, southeast of London. Because there was so much water all around the field and
drainage ditches across the field, the pilot wisely decided to make a belly
landing to prevent nosing over in one of the ditches. Just as we were making
the final approach, the third engine cut out and the tank on the turret threw
grass and dirt up through the camera hatch into the radio room.

To our surprise, we had landed near an RAF air base. Their ambulance
and fire truck came to pick us up. The name of the RAF base was
Eastchurch. After looking the plane over we found it had a lot of flak
holes, several in the wings, nose, waist, and a large one in the tail section.
The plane had to be salvaged because the center section was so badly broken. We were treated royally at the Royal Air Force base. The next day we

returned to our base by truck and air. Our operations officer took us back from a nearby Spitfire base.

Tuesday, Jan. 11, 1944. Second mission, Braunschweig. Flew *Blind Date*, #195. Had to spend about and hour cleaning guns this morning. They were very dirty. We flew *Blind Date* on the plane's 31st mission. I got my guns in but didn't have time to check them. The solenoid wouldn't fire the right gun. The only way I could fire it was with a screwdriver. I test-fired the guns but didn't have any other use for them, thank God. We ran into quite a bit of flak. We were fortunate to get no holes in our plane. A few enemy fighters were seen, but no attacks were made on our formation.

I got sick and threw up all over the turret.

Just before dropping our bombs my oxygen had gone down to 100 pounds. After getting back, I found that I had been on pure oxygen, the reason for using so much. There wasn't enough pressure in the waist to fill the bottles up to more than 120 pounds. So, as soon as they dropped below 100 again, I came up and got on oxygen in the radio room. Shortly after this, Mac passed out from anoxia. I found a twist in his oxygen hose. We had a hard time reviving him. Marr, Crabb and I worked on him. He kept stiffening up and then he would breath very hard and fast. He seemed to be all right when we reached the base, but went to the hospital just to make sure. He had a slight frost bite on his fingers and one foot. We were called back before we got to the target because the weather was closing in at the base, so we dropped our bombs on what looked like open country except for a few small buildings. We were lucky not to have run into fighters. Other groups lost very heavily today; 59 bombers were reported lost. Two from our group were lost.

Friday, Jan. 21, 1944. Third mission, Calais area, France, coastal installations: I got up about 9 a.m. for 10 a.m. briefing. Had hot cocoa before the briefing. We flew on #176, *Flak Suit*, today. We took off at 12:30 p.m. We made three runs on the target before the clouds had moved far enough away to see the target. I followed the bombs all the way down. Looked like we got a perfect hit with our 12 500-pounders. What an explosion! Smoke came up a mile high. We encountered no flak or fighters today. Got back about 4:30 p.m.

Monday, Jan. 24, 1944. Fourth mission, Frankfurt. Flew *Return Engagement*, #1214: Up at 2:30 a.m. for 4 a.m. briefing. We got as far as the Dutch Coast. Test-fired our guns and saw a little flak; no enemy aircraft. The weather was bad and difficulty was experienced in making formations. After crossing the enemy coast, the formation was recalled due to a weather front moving in over England.

Saturday, Jan. 29, 1944. Fifth mission, Frankfurt. Flew *Miss Lace*, #842: Up at 3 a.m. for 3:45 briefing. Drank some pineapple juice for breakfast this morning. We climbed singly through the clouds and got in formation above the clouds. I was in the ball turret for about five hours and still had 200 pounds of oxygen left. Bombing was done through the clouds from 24,000 feet. Enemy aircraft were in the target area but attacked other formations with no attacks on our Group. They threw up a very heavy barrage of flak but it fell behind us. It was quite rough flying today. One plane was shot down by flak over the target.

Sunday, Jan. 30, 1944. Sixth mission, Brunswick. Flew # 849: Up at 4 a.m. for 5:30 a.m. briefing. Ate a few prunes and a little grapefruit juice for breakfast. We had solid cloud cover from the coast to the target. Just before we got to the target the formation split up because of vapor trails so thick you couldn't see. We got back in formation an hour later. I was in the ball turret about four hours; had to get out on the way back and change shoes. My heated shoes went out. We dropped our bombs on target from 26,800 feet. Enemy aircraft were seen in the distance but none attacked. There was lots of flak over the target. We lost one plane from our group.

Thursday, Feb. 3, 1944. Seventh mission, Wilhelmshaven. Flew #849: Up at 4 a.m. for 5 a.m. briefing. Mac, our radio operator, was sick, so the pilot sent him to the hospital and called for another radio operator. If he couldn't get another operator, I was going to take over. I was all prepared to be the radio operator when a fellow on his last mission showed up. I was sure glad to see him. We had to go up to 28,000 to keep above the clouds going in. Coming out we couldn't keep above the clouds. We flew through soup so thick I couldn't see the loop antenna at times. We practically dived down through the clouds. We had a stiff headwind coming back: 120 miles per hour ground speed. Going in it was 360 miles per hour. Not much flak and no enemy aircraft today. A navigator on another plane was hit by flak and died after being admitted to the hospital. It was 50 degrees below zero today. I was quite comfortable in my heated suit, except for one foot which was very hot. We carried 100-pound incendiaries. I cleaned my guns up good tonight.

Friday, Feb. 4, 1944. Eighth mission, Frankfurt. Flew #849: We were up at 4:30 a.m. for 5:30 a.m. briefing. I ate no breakfast. We carried 500-pound demolition bombs. Bombs were dropped from 23,999 feet. Flak was very heavy and accurate. We got several close bursts; one hole just in front of the ball and one hole through the waist and down through the floor just behind the ball. It was 46 degrees below today. We were up for six hours. We think we missed the target. We ran into flak both coming and going. We did not encounter any enemy aircraft today. We were very fortunate not to have been hit by enemy fighters because we had no fighter support on the way back. Germany was covered with snow today. This was our roughest mission since Frankfurt. I felt and heard four bursts right beneath the ball turret. One plane in our B Group right behind us got a direct hit on the right wing. It went down in a spin. The wing fell off, the engine was burning and the plane blew up as it went through the clouds. All crew members were killed except the bombardier and radio operator who managed to bail out. Very tired tonight. Seven days out of eight we have had to get up early. I was in bed by 8 tonight.

Tuesday, Feb. 8, 1944. Ninth mission, Frankfurt, plane #240: Up at 3 a.m. for 4:30 a.m. briefing. We started out in #393, a new plane with closed waist windows. We got halfway down the runway going 110 miles per hour. Tail was up, Number 2 engine was pulling over 70 inches, so the pilot stopped the plane and came back. Then we took a standby ship, #240. We got 68 miles into France and the Number 1 engine was running away. The pilot feathered the engine and told us all to get our chutes on. The engine was beginning to windmill.

I came up out of the ball and sat in the open door of the ball shaking like a leaf for fear of having to bail out.

Then the tail and waist gunners began calling out fighters, so I got back in the ball, only to find out it was P-47s. I had just gotten out of the ball again when Tex, the tail gunner, said that six fighters were coming in on us out of the sun. As I was getting back in the ball he decided they were probably P-47s. I had only one gun that would fire, so I was very thankful that enemy fighters were not attacking us. We dropped behind the formation and came back alone. We dropped our bombs in the Channel.

Thursday, Feb. 10, 1944. Tenth mission, Brunswick, #849: Up at 3 a.m. for 4:30 briefing. The 388th furnished one Group of 18 aircraft, which led the 45th Combat Wing, which was the last Combat Wing in the 3rd Air Division. We were supposed to have lots of fighter escort. We crossed the North Sea and the Zeider Zee. We were 10 or 15 minutes late. Enemy fighters attacked us shortly after leaving the Zeider Zee and stayed with us all the way in and all the way out to the coast. We saw B-17s being knocked down all around us, a horrible, terrifying sight. There were more enemy fighters than friendly fighters. Enemy fighter opposition was the most intense that this Group had seen since receiving long-range fighter support. Three of our crews were shot down. Losses from the Group on our right were much heavier. Our escort did a wonderful job, but they didn't have enough gas to stay with us long enough. One large group of FW-190s would come up and attack our escort and scatter them all over the sky, then another group would attack a formation and stop for nothing. We saw at least a dozen Forts shot down. The sky was full of chutes and planes going down. Out of 192 Forts, 29 were lost. Intense flak was encountered at the target where 13 of our aircraft received major flak damage. As we neared the target, JU-88s fired rockets into the formation. The most surprising thing I saw was a B-17 with one engine flaming coming head-on towards us. At first we thought it was an enemy fighter and the bombardier and I were already to shoot when the bombardier said, "Hold it, I think it's a 17." Sure enough, it was, with what we thought was an enemy aircraft on its tail. For some reason, I couldn't believe it was a JU-88. I thought I saw four engines and was afraid it might be another B-17. Apparently everyone alive had bailed out of the 17. The other plane was right on its tail.

At the time, I was either afraid to shoot or afraid I would hit the 17. Anyway, I let them go by right under me, so close I could see the pilots in the JU-88. I got a long burst in on one enemy fighter and a short burst on another. It was very cold today, 45 degrees below zero. The guns were still frosted up even after landing, though none of our guns froze. We had no escort whatsoever all the way back. We had to fall out of our group on the way in because of a Fort falling in front of us. The group we got in was very poor on flying formation. Everyone bunched up in a tight group and did no evasive action whatsoever, making a perfect target for the rocket ships. Very few stragglers got back. As soon as a plane fell out of formation, dozens of fighters would shoot him down.

I was in the ball over seven hours. I used all my oxygen and most of my ammunition. The ball was very jerky in elevation and quit working for awhile. I had trouble with my knees.

March 4, 1944: Eleventh mission, Berlin. Flew #291: Briefing at 4 a.m. I flew with Malmberg's crew as radio operator. I was separated from my original crew because they were assigned a Pathfinder ship and the radar equipment took the place of the ball turret. We got deep into France and had to abort because of the lack of oxygen. About 30 minutes later our entire group had to turn around and come back because the cloud cover was higher than the planes could climb. I had a little trouble with the radio; couldn't pick up Wing (L.T.L.) and had to interpolate to get the MFDF station to identify coming back.

April 26, 1944. Twelfth mission, Brunswick: Flew as radio operator with Littlejohn's crew. We carried five 1,000-pound bombs today. Sammy and I went to the dance in Hopton. We got to bed just in time to get up again at 1 a.m. for the 2 a.m. briefing. I didn't even get to sleep. Sure had a hard time staying awake while flying today. We took off at 5 a.m. and got back about noon. I got sick just before landing. My ears gave me a little trouble also, as usual. Bombing was done on a flare from the leading PFF aircraft through 10/10 cloud coverage. Target was the Hildeshein-Hannover area. Meager flak was encountered and no enemy aircraft were encountered.

May 9, l944. Thirteenth mission, Juvincourt. Flew #017: Flew as tail gunner with Gabler's crew. We carried 38 100-pound bombs. Briefing was at 3 a.m. and we were back by noon. The target was clear and the bombing was done visually. I had trouble clearing my ears and got sick just before we got back. There were no fighters and very little flak today.

June 2, 1944. Fourteenth mission, Pas de Calais, Boulogne area. Flew #096: I flew as radio operator on Newell's crew. We had a brand new ship, which made its first mission today. We carried 12 500-pound bombs, which were dropped on signal from the leading PFF aircraft at an altitude of 25,300 feet. No enemy fighters were seen and very little flak. We came back with one engine out.

June 3, 1944. Fifteenth mission, Pas de Calais, Boulogne. Flew #851: We were up at 3:30 for 5 a.m. briefing. I flew as radio operator on Newell's crew. The mission on this day was against coastal defenses. The 388th flew as Low Group in the 45th Combat Wing; 10/10 clouds prevailed over the target and bombs were dropped by PFF methods. Bombs were away at 11:24 hours from 22,900 feet. No enemy fighters were seen and only meager flak was encountered. All of our aircraft returned to base by 13:15 hours.

June 4, 1944. Sixteenth mission, Pas de Calais, Cape Gris Nez. Flew #849: We were up at 5 a.m. for 6.30 a.m. briefing. I flew radio operator position on Newell's crew. We bombed visually from 23,900 feet. The A Group missed the target and the B Group had a loose pattern on the target area. Flak was moderate with two of our aircraft suffering major battle damage. No fighters. All returned to base.

June 6, 1944. Seventeenth mission, D-Day, French coast, 10/10 cloud cover: We were briefed at 11 p.m. on June 5th and took off at 2 a.m. on June 6th. On D-Day, the 388th flew three separate missions sending 72 aircraft with only one abort. Our group led the 8th Air Force on the first bombing in direct support of the invasion. Orders were as follows:

"Guns will be manned but not test-fired at any time. Gunners will not fire at any airplane at any time unless being attacked. Bombing on primary targets will be carried out within time limits prescribed. Otherwise, secondary or last resort targets will be bombed. No second runs will be made on the primary target. Take-offs will be accomplished according to schedule—regardless."

All available heavy bombers of the 8th Air Force were dispatched in waves to attack coastal defenses between Le Havre and Cherbourg in France. The attacks were in direct support of the Allied Invasion Forces, which landed immediately after the bombing of the beach area was completed. Our A Group led the 8th Air Force D-Day attacks. Some difficulty was encountered in securing formation due to darkness and because the buncher went out. Bombs were dropped by PFF methods because of complete cloud cover. Bombing was done by groups with squadrons lined up abreast. Bombs were dropped from 15,050 feet at 06:56 hours by the A Group and from 13,850 feet at 07:03 hours by the B Group. No enemy aircraft or flak were seen. All our aircraft returned to base by 10:43 hours. Immediately after returning, we took off again to attack tactical targets just inside the French coast. This operation was in support of the Allied Invasion Forces, which had an hour earlier landed on the coast. We returned to base about 12:30. No enemy aircraft or flak were encountered. About 5:30 we were off for the third mission of the day. Our group did not attack its primary target because clouds obscured it. Instead, a railroad choke point in the southern part of Flers was attacked as a target of opportunity. It was another milk run. We got back about 10 p.m. I was dead tired. We got credit for one mission today, even though we made three bombing runs. It was a 23-hour day from first briefing to last touchdown.

June 7, 1944. Eighteenth mission, Nantes. Target was a railroad bridge: I flew the radio operator position on Newell's crew. We encountered no enemy fighters and only moderate flak. Bombed visually, got back about dark. After eating and cleaning guns I just got in bed and had to get up to fly again.

June 8, 1944. Nineteenth mission, Tours. Flew on Bonnicelli's crew: Our target was a railroad yard at Tours. We took off about 4 a.m. Bad weather over England made formation assembly very difficult. Over the Continent, weather improved and the target area was clear with bombs away at 08:31 hours from 21,000 feet. No enemy aircraft were seen and flak was moderate but accurate at the target.

I was completely worn out and had to throw up just as we landed. My ears plugged up again. I ate an orange and drank some hot cocoa, then had to throw it all up before I got back to the barracks. I didn't feel like eating any dinner. Slept a couple of hours and woke up with a sick feeling in my stomach. I went to see the doctor. He gave me some pills to take and I went to bed without any supper.

June 12, 1944. Twentieth mission. Target was a German-occupied airfield in Northern France. Flew on *Blind Date*: The largest force of heavy bombers ever to be dispatched by the 8th Air Force was sent out to attack German-occupied airfields in Northern France. The 388th furnished the three Groups for the 45th Combat Wing, a total of 42 aircraft. I flew the right waist gunner position on Little's crew. We took off about 5 a.m. and got back about 11 a.m. We went on a sight-seeing tour of France and got plenty of flak, all for nothing. Didn't even drop our bombs. We got several flak holes in our plane, one directly above my head. We saw no enemy fighters.

July 13,1944. Twenty-first mission, Munich: Up at 1 a.m. for 2:30 briefing. I flew radio operator position on Cooke's crew. Cooke led the B Group and Campbell led the A Group. It was a nine-hour trip to Munich. The flak was moderate to intense. We saw no fighters. It is known that, following our bombing, the cities of Stuttgart, Nuremberg and Salzburg were told to send all available fire fighting apparatus to Munich.

July 14, 1944. Twenty-second mission, secret mission to Southern France: Didn't get to sleep last night. We were up at 11:30 for 1 a.m. briefing. I flew the radio operator position on Deskin's crew. It was Deskin's 30th and last mission. We flew #096. We took off at 3:30 and got back at 1:30. The mission was flown in support of the Maquis. We were loaded with C3-type bombs. The bombs were large boxes of supplies, which were dropped by parachute. Strike photos showed excellent results for all groups. No flak or enemy fighters were seen on this mission.

August 1, 1944. Twenty-third mission, special mission deep into France: I flew the radio operator position with Campbell, PFF 542B, on his 29th mission. We carried "C" 300-pound projectiles with supplies to the Maquis. We took off at 10:30 am. We were back at 8 p.m., a nine-and-a-half-hour mission. We saw some very beautiful country. The Brenner Alps—they were amazingly high, with little farms on the steep, smooth slopes. Snow covered the tops of the higher peaks. We flew off the right wing of the lead ship as an extra navigational aid. We missed all the flak and saw no fighters. We had a communications officer. I wore my heated suit and nearly roasted. I got sick on the way back; so sick I didn't feel like living, let alone copying weather messages, etc. So I heard about it from the colonel when we got back. We had flown around the Alps at treetop level at times, up over the peaks and down through the valleys. We saw pine trees and deep gorges with beautiful little streams. We dropped our bomb load from 500 feet, visually.

August 2, 1944. Twenty-fourth mission, Mery-Sur-Oise, an ammunition dump north of Paris: I flew radio operator position with Campbell on his 30th and last mission. We flew PFF-666. Flak over the target was very accurate and intense. Our ship was riddled from tail to nose; at least a hundred holes. The navigator was hit in the hip quite seriously. Another piece of flak nicked the waist gunner. Another piece just missed our Mickey Man. Several pieces came through the radio room missing the three of us by inches and less. One piece nicked my heavy flying boot and stopped inside Tex's boot just before going through his heated shoe. We lost about half of our oxygen over the target. Five of us were on bottles. One gas tank was hit, the control cable to the tail wheel was out, the Number 3 oil line was hit and that engine had to be feathered. The supercharger on Number 2 engine was out until I changed amplifiers. We took off at 1 p.m. and got back at 7 p.m. We saw no fighters and too much flak. Six crew members were wounded by flak and one aircraft was shot down. It was a very strenuous mission. Hard on the nerves. I went to bed early tonight.

October 9, 1944. Twenty-fifth mission, Mainz: Up at 7 a.m. for 8 a.m. briefing. We took off at 10:30 a.m. I flew on Bigalow's crew in #296 as radio operator. No fighters. Plenty of flak, but inaccurate. We received no holes in our ship. It was quite cold: 36 degrees below. We bombed from 23,900 feet using PFF methods. All of our aircraft returned to base safely. We were back by 5 p.m. I had trouble with my ears.

October 14, 1944: I celebrated my 21st birthday with Myrtle Ward at their farmhouse near Market Weston.

November 5, 1944. I boarded a cruise liner for my return trip to the USA. We arrived in New York City on November 17th. It was a very pleasant trip, with no seasickness coming back.

# A Soft Landing

By Robert E. Scalley, tail gunner, *Satan's Sister*, 563rd Squadron

On 30 Dec. 1943, the 388th BG A Group took off between 08:31 and 08:43 hours with the IG Farbenindustrie Chemical Works at Ludwigshaven as its target. The 45th Combat Wing was to be led by Major Hank Henggeler, the 388th Group Leader. Henggeler had to abort some 15 minutes after the formation crossed into Germany, at 11:20 hours. The Deputy Leader, without PFF equipment, took the Lead, but then advised the 388th B Group, whose complement included a PFF aircraft, to take the Lead instead. This was essential in view of the 10/10 cloud cover.

I was the 6-foot-tall, skinny, 18-year-old tail gunner in *Satan's Sister*, aircraft #42-31131-D, a B-I7G, and our crew was on its seventh mission. For the first time we were in the High Group flying at 25,000 feet.

At the IP another group cut in front of the 388th A Group and we experienced severe prop wash; this occurred at 12:35 hours.

*Satan's Sister* initially tipped up on her right wing, came back down, then went up and rolled over on her left wing (in other words, a slow roll with a full bomb bay!). The last report on the intercom was the pilot saying, "We're going over." Needless to say, we went over and into a tail spin. (Later, back at Knettishall, returning crews erroneously reported that our ship had exploded on entering the clouds some 5,000 feet below the formation.)

At this point, I assume Lt. Art Carlson, pilot, and Lt. Ben Scroggin Jr., co-pilot, were wrestling with the controls in a desperate attempt to recover from our dive and spin. Unfortunately, *Satan's Sister* could not take the strain and she broke in two at the radio room.

Lt. Edgar F. Slentz, our bombardier, took off like a football fullback and plunged headlong through the plexiglass nose without a parachute. Lt. John R. Bassler Jr., the navigator and the sole married man in the crew, who always put on his chest chute at the first sight of flak or fighters, went through the nose after Slentz, coming within inches of the inboard propellers, which were still revolving at full power.

Jim A. Neal, the right waist gunner, put his chute on and went forward to check the radio room. He opened the door, took one step, and found he had involuntarily bailed out!

G. H. Parizo, the other waist gunner, went to the ball turret to extract Sgt. F. S. Brincat, then put on his chute, opened the waist door and promptly froze. Brincat tried in vain to budge Parizo, but the latter's vice-like grip and his extra weight (180 pounds to Brincat's 110) held him in position. Brincat gave up and bailed out of the right waist gun-gate.

For me in the tail, it was a case of up, down, up and over. From my kneeling position in the tail, my back and head (the latter saved by my steel helmet) hit the top of my confined compartment. After the complete roll, I ended up on my stomach where I was pinned down at times due to centrifugal force. It seemed a very long time, possibly three minutes, before the cables all snapped around me and I was able to get up off the floor.

The tail section was whipped around like an autumn leaf from a tall oak tree in a high wind. This time, although I was scared as hell, I did not know what had happened, but there was no noise of any kind.

I released my flak jacket and, finding my chest chute, snapped it onto my harness. I pulled the release on my escape hatch. Nothing happened. Struggling to escape, I banged the door with my shoulder and it finally blew out with Yours Truly following.

Seeing the ground very close and spinning around, I reached for my parachute D ring. There was nothing! If I had been as scared as hell two minutes ago, I was now absolutely terrified. I looked down at the clouds and then saw the D ring by my left leg. It came to me that I was upside down, and that in my haste I had only hooked the left ring in my chute pack to my harness. I reached up and pulled the ring and was struck full in the face by the canvas cover. Everything went black.

The following was related to me by Frank Brincat, the ball turret gunner. He had come down in a farm yard and had sustained broken ribs and an injured back. I landed in the same farm yard on a pile of horse s—t, which evidently saved my life. I now love horse manure! My right leg was broken and I had shrapnel in my back, head and hand, as well as a bullet in my left thigh. I don't remember being hit and it is possible this occurred on my way down in the chute by fire from the ground.

Evidently, I was trying to get off the manure pile when a couple of civilians, probably farmers, approached me, whereupon I pointed my .45 at them. The weapon was wavering and one man walked up and took it from me—anyway, there was no shell left in the chamber.

Obviously, I was semi-conscious at this time and was thrashing around on my pile of soft horse manure. I remember nothing of this.

The tail section of the B-17 had crashed onto the farmhouse. Frank was recovering and wanted to retrieve a first aid kit from the aircraft. The farmer said, "Nicht! Boom, boom!," thinking the yellow oxygen bottles were bombs. Frank eventually got the kit and gave me a shot of morphine. I only became fully conscious some six days later in a hospital in Heppenheim, about 20 kilometers from Ludwigshaven. Frank and I had really lucked out, because the tail section from *Satan's Sister* had killed a woman and child in the farmhouse.

I have often wondered why those Germans did not execute Frank and me.

# FORECAST CAVU—CEILING AND VISIBILITY UNLIMITED

By Edison D. Jeffus, Station 136 Weather Officer

Weather is extremely important to all aircraft, but especially to manned aircraft. As a matter of fact, bad weather can create a hostile environment for such aircraft which can be as destructive, or more so, than enemy action during war.

Almost 60 years after the fact, I continue to be both pleased and proud with having had the opportunity to serve the 388th Bomb Group (H) in the European Theater of Operations during World War II as the Army Air Force (AAF) Station No. 136 Weather Officer at Knettishall, from 14 Dec 1943 until the Group left England to return to the United States in June and July, 1945. I was among the handful of American soldiers who remained at Knettishall to close up business after all other flight and ground personnel returned stateside.

Before describing my specific duties as a Station Weather Officer, let me describe an incident which introduced me to the reality of air warfare over Europe. On or about 15 Nov. 1943, I was sent for one week of temporary duty at AAF Station No. 155 at Great Ashfield where the 385th Bomb Group (H) was stationed. During that week, I attended my first few early morning briefings for bombing missions to European targets. One of those briefings was for the very first scheduled daylight mission for the 8th Air Force to Berlin. When Operations mentioned that the primary target was Berlin, intense trepidation and quietness smothered the flight crews who were being briefed. Poor local weather delayed the scheduled take-off time not once but twice. Subsequently, the mission was scrubbed and shortly thereafter, at mid-morning, the Commanding Officer declared over the loud speaker system that the base's bars were "open for

155

business." After having felt the gravity of that situation until the mission was finally scrubbed, and having seen the resulting jubilation of the flight crews, I joined the party.

Attending bombing mission briefings to present weather summaries became rather commonplace for me, but I can't remember another briefing which caused that same level of apprehension. In all probability, the reaction of flight crews to bombing mission briefings remained about the same, but a young Weather Officer can feel only once for the first time that "war is hell."

Generally speaking, there were two types of Weather Officers associated with a bomb group in the ETO during WWII; Group and Station. Both had the same Military Occupational Specialty—8219. Lt. Elmer T. Poppendieck was the Group Weather Officer. He was assigned to the 388th Bomb Group (H), served on the Commanding Officer's staff, and was subject to relocation with the Group. He was the liaison between the Group and the Station weather detachment, with some oversight responsibility in ascertaining that his Group was being provided satisfactory weather information and forecasts for their operational use. The Station Weather Officer and his detachment of officers and/or enlisted men were assigned to 18th Weather Squadron while serving the Group on an attached basis. The Station Weather Officer had the responsibility for the actual operation of the weather station at a particular base regardless of which bomb group might be assigned to that location.

In theory, if the 388th had been transferred to another location, Lt. Poppendieck would have moved with his Group, but I would have remained at Knettishall to serve any replacement Group.

The Weather Room was located on the lower floor of the Control Tower. A small, well-ventilated weather station containing instruments to measure various atmospheric conditions was mounted on a four-foot-high stand near the control tower, but away from the influence of other buildings. Enlisted men who qualified as weather observers made hourly measurements of atmospheric conditions, including wind direction and speed;

air temperature and dew point; barometric pressure and changes over the past several hours; amount and types of clouds and ceiling height; weather type, including visibility restrictions; and the amount and type of precipitation. These data were converted to a plotting code and then transmitted by teletype to Eighth Bomber Command, including 18th Weather Squadron Headquarters. Similar data from all reporting stations were summarized and re-transmitted to each AAF station for preparation of synoptic meteorological charts—weather maps—every six hours. Enlisted personnel decoded the weather data and plotted them on maps of the ETO, including the North Atlantic Ocean.

Other than hourly weather observations by our personnel at all AAF stations in England, three factors should be mentioned to indicate just how comprehensive our data collection system really was:

• U.S. weather observation stations in southern Greenland and Iceland provided valuable information because major weather systems passing those locations usually arrived on schedule in the British Isles about 24-48 hours later.

• We transmitted coded weather data from one location to another by teletype (a closed system), but the Germans transmitted similar data by radio (an open system). Their radio transmissions were intercepted by U.S. and British personnel and decoded for our use. Moreover, the Germans, their allies and other countries who collaborated with them had weather observation stations throughout Europe. This intercepted data was most important in making more accurate weather forecasts for European targets.

• U.S. and RAF flight crews returning from missions over Europe and the Atlantic Ocean and Allied naval vessels all provided valuable weather information for our use.

Weather Officers or higher ranking non-commissioned officers who were qualified as weather forecasters completed the maps for the hours 00:00, 06:00, 12:00 and 18:00 Greenwich Mean Time (GMT). The finished weather maps showed high- and low-pressure systems, frontal systems and areas and types of precipitation within air masses and made it possible to prognosticate future movement of these systems and the effect that these changes might have on future weather conditions within the area with good accuracy, especially over the short term. Official weather forecasts for bombing missions were made at Bomber Command and transmitted by teletype to the various bases for presentation during the bombing mission briefing by Weather Officers or enlisted weather forecasters.

The local weather staff, which was available to flight crews around the clock, was responsible for providing forecast information for individual flights and for Group practice missions.

I do not remember how I selected, or was assigned, living quarters upon arrival at Knettishall, but other details about that life may be of interest. I think that most of the officers on the base were housed in Nissen-style quarters in their respective squadron, headquarters or unit areas. However, I lived in a relatively small non-Nissen-type building which contained one large room and two smaller rooms. The large room had a large coal-burning, pot-bellied stove near the center. An officers' latrine and shower room was across the street and butted up to a fenced-in coal compound. These quarters were conveniently located just in back of the base movie theater and very near the Officers' Mess Hall and the Officers' Club. However, this living area was not near the Weather Room in the Control Tower, nor the primary Briefing Room. Riding on a bicycle to the Weather Room between 02:30 and 04:00 hours on a cold foggy morning to prepare for a mission briefing was no simple chore. Once, we had ice fog which lasted almost three weeks.

When I first moved into the larger room, which could accommodate up to six officers, I remember that Lt. Vance W. Dortch, 560th Bombardment Squadron Armament Officer, and a civilian instrument specialist from Pratt & Whitney Corporation were among the residents. Lt. John H. Meyer, Quartermaster Corp, and Lt. Walter J. Heatherington were living in the middle, smaller room, and Lts. Alfred A. Windsor and

Herman H. Teifeld, both Group Radio Officers, occupied the other smaller room. At various times during my residency in the larger room, other roommates were Lt. Michael G. Zdeb, 587th Postal Unit Officer, and Capt. Wilfred F. Tooman, who was associated with the Aphrodite Project at Fersfield, and who made routine visits to Bomber Command to discuss this highly confidential operation. Capt. Tooman was one of the most interesting, knowledgeable and well-traveled flying officers I had the pleasure of knowing during WWII.

The 388th officers had great parties nearly every weekend on Sunday night. English girls from nearby towns, and as far away as London, routinely attended these dancing/drinking parties. Although single and available at the time, I remember that ground personnel such as I seemed to be non-competitive with the more glamorous flying personnel in gaining the attention of the British girls at those parties. (The "sour grapes" long ago turned to vintage wine...) I used to wonder how a young ground officer might be assigned to report to Major Cox at the Motor Pool "to serve as escorts in convoys to pick up lady guests." Such an assignment might surely give a ground officer a head start, but I was never so lucky.

Between songs at one of those dances, I managed to get the name, address and telephone number of one of the prettier, more provocative British gals. I wonder what might have happened to "Chic" Hardcastle of Manor Lane, Horringer, Bury St. Edmunds, phone: Chevington 235?

During leaves of absence from the base, I usually visited London or Edinburgh. Both were very nice places to visit; however, London was being bombed frequently by German aircraft and later by V-1 buzz bombs, especially at night for maximum psychological disturbance. Having been in several bombing attacks while visiting in London, I can assure everyone that I always wished vigorously and prayed that I could be elsewhere.

We frequently heard bomb alert sirens at Knettishall at night and stood outside and watched V-1 buzz bombs pass overhead at altitudes of about 2,000 feet on their way to London.

Visiting Scotland was a real pleasure, because, most importantly, it was away from the war, but Scotland also had beautiful scenery, pretty lassies and friendly people. The Scottish people told me that Hitler never bombed Scotland because he planned to make his summer home there after the war. One Scottish lassie, Dorothy Dewar, during a weak moment on my part, persuaded me to have my picture made while wearing a kilt since I have very diluted Scot blood in my veins.

Several months after I was assigned as Station Weather Officer at Station No. 136, 2nd Lt. Norman J. Putnam, originally from Tulsa, Oklahoma, was designated as Assistant Station Weather Officer. As such, he worked into the rotational shift schedule with Lt. Poppendieck, M/Sgt Louis A. Pennow and me. One day, he was on duty serving as senior weather forecaster in charge of the weather station when he was asked to make a forecast for a special flight to Prestwick, Scotland.

This particular flight was to serve as the infrequent but routine "whisky run" to obtain supplies for the various bars on the base.

The 388th had great parties at the Officers' Club and, no matter how much we and our guests drank, we never ran out of Scotch, Irish whisky or gin—but American-made bourbon was always in short supply. (One may not fully realize just how much alcohol is required to maintain high morale among a bombardment group's wartime flight crews and their supporting ground personnel, but it is not inconsequential.)

Desk-bound flying personnel and others, such as the medics, qualified for flight pay provided they acquired a specified minimum number of flying hours per month. Therefore, officers in these categories were assigned and readily accepted duties such as making whisky runs to beautiful Scotland.

On the particular day under discussion, Lt. Putnam, using the best available meteorological information and tools, forecast that there would be satisfactory visibility and a minimum ceiling above 800 feet at the time of arrival at their destination. Unfortunately, the weather conditions at time of arrival were much worse than forecast, which played a part in the

B-17 crashing into a cloud-shrouded mountain near the intended destination. As a result, all of the flight crew and several medics were killed in the accident. The plane was *Skipper an' the Kids*.

I truly believe that Lt. Putnam never forgave himself for missing that forecast and shouldered more of the blame for his tangential involvement in the crash than was proper.

Immediately after V-E Day, several senior officers at 3rd Air Division Headquarters arranged a special tour over war-torn Europe in a B-17. My friend and fellow weatherman, Major Jay Jacobs, was among that group of officers.

Major Jacobs was not so much a personal friend as he was an excellent role model for young, inexperienced weather forecasters such as I.

The primary purpose of the air tour was to let officers who had not served in significant combat roles observe first-hand the extent of damage inflicted in Europe, primarily by the air war. Since the war was over in Europe, the touring aircraft was flying at a leisurely pace at a fairly low altitude when it crossed the continental coast near Dunkirk, France. All of a sudden, and quite unexpectedly, bursts of flak disabled the aircraft sufficiently to make the flight crew realize that the plane would crash.

Apparently, the anti-aircraft firing from the ground was coming from an unsuspected and isolated pocket of German resistance which had not been notified that the war was over. At the moment that it was decided that this disabled aircraft would crash, it was determined also that there were not enough parachutes for everyone aboard. Major Jacobs, after much pleading, finally convinced a full colonel to let him jump from the plane locked arm-in-arm with the colonel. (I did know but have forgotten the name of the colonel.) Unfortunately, when the colonel's parachute opened, Major Jacobs plummeted to earth and his death.

This tragic incident so infuriated other officers at Third Air Division Headquarters that they considered bombing the "isolated and un-informed pocket of German resistance" to kingdom come, but that idea was "nixed" by cooler heads and/or higher authority and it never happened.

*Edison Jeffus, front, Station 136 Weather Officer, with Lt. Col. Robert Satterwhite and Lt. Elmer Poppendieck*

# ANY GUM, CHUM?

By Percy Prentice, David Calcutt and George Stebbings

*Station 136 was located in fields near, in and around villages in East Anglia—Coney Weston, Barningham, Market Weston and Hopton, among others. The villages and farms were home to numerous children, many of whom saw the American servicemen as friends and the machines and activities of war as intriguing adventures. The children were no strangers to the base. Following are the reminiscences of three of those young boys who, today, remain good friends of the men of the 388th.*

**You Are My Heroes**—Percy Prentice

It was spring 1943 when I walked from my home in Market Weston toward our school. Two men on a tandem cycle stopped me near the school. I was frightened until I saw they were in uniform. The tall guy in front said, "Hey kid, do you know where we can we get some eggs?" I took them to Mr. Ward's farm where they purchased a dozen.

The men asked if I would like to go to the base with them to get some candies. I had no cycle, so I ran alongside them. There they filled a large sack with chocolates, gum, shelled nuts, Baby Ruths and Hershey bars—as much as I could carry. I said, "Thanks a lot!" When I got home to Mum and opened the sack, she cried when she saw all the goodies. We were down to just mini-rations which was hardly a mouthful, so this was a real feast for the children in my neighborhood.

It was a busy area. For two years a small village became a city. The roads were full of traffic and skies were thundering with aircraft engines. When I saw aircraft in the sky, I used to think the boys were safe up there. In later years I realized they were riding in a death trap if hit by flak or fighters.

There were also terrible accidents on the flight line with planes loaded with gasoline and bombs.

I started going to the base and I'm afraid I missed quite a bit of school, but I loved the military life—especially the Other Ranks Mess Hall and Red Cross, places that were great for eats. They called me Chow Hound, but the white goat with "Lend" on one side and "Lease" on the other in red paint was usually the first in line. It would eat nearly everything edible.

In about two months, Pop White, the cycle man down past the fire station, made me a super bicycle. It was really appreciated. I wore shorts then and it was cold on base, especially at the bomb dump and ammunition huts near the old Knettishall church. I used to fill 100-pound practice bombs with sand, which were dropped at Redgrave Fen.

Martin Kozelka, an armory sergeant, sent back to the U.S. for a uniform for me. It was great! Long pants and warm legs. Really appreciated. In 1944 I made Private First Class and Capt. Leo H. Rector presented me with a bolt action 22mm Mossberg rifle. It was a lovely gun, but one of the local farmers reported me to the police and there were problems. My sister Norma later told me that Dad took the gun and threw it into a big pond near our home. It must still be there.

Roy Torgeson and Ray Sherman used to cycle 10 miles to and from the Bury Dance Hall. They were two of the best jitterbuggers in town. Roy and Ray also made bracelets and necklaces with Plexiglas, English silver threepenny pieces and a reel of silver wire. They'd sandwich a threepenny between two sheets of Plexiglas in a wire frame about two to three inches off a heated stove top. They would then cut the heat-sealed Plexiglas into a heart shape and polish it with Duraglit wool polish. Finally they would drill small holes, two at each side of the coin, and thread in the silver wiring. The trade in these necklaces and bracelets was very good.

I remember the great movie theatre on the domestic site. The seats came from bombed out theatres in London. We had free movies for all the children.

There was plenty of gambling on base. I once saw Mac, the barber who cut my hair on Site 11 opposite the base hospital, throwing dice. Mac pocketed about £100 that day. The boys really enjoyed their leisure time, which was not too long. They worked very hard around the clock, some of them. We had several boys visit our home; they were very careful with their money and bought War Bonds with it.

One night over the Tannoy system there was a gas warning alert. I was pretty scared. Boys were running around hunting up a spare gas mask for me as mine was at home with Mum and Dad. After about 5-10 minutes we got the all clear, thank God. Another night, two doodlebugs came over the base flying east to west about three minutes apart. The noise was nearly beyond bearing.

We used to watch ships leave for missions and meet the assembly ship. There was plenty of activity on each mission. When we lost planes it was very bad. The day we lost 11 ships was really below the belt; a terrible loss of good men.

Mum was a lovely laundry lady and the day *Skipper an' the Kids* crashed in Scotland killing Capt. Littlejohn and all the crew, their laundry had all been washed and pressed, but no one to wear it. All the family cried. We were heartbroken.

The 200 Mission Party Day was great! Plenty of drinks and eats. I had the honor of meeting Gen. James Doolittle, a wonderful man. In the evening we went to the Number One hangar for the big dance. The crystals used to absorb moisture in cargo packaging were scattered on the floor to help the dancers. It was a great night—truckloads of women. They chased me around the inside of the hangar until I climbed up a steel frame where I stayed until the end of the dance.

In winter time the cold was so severe, I still wonder how the engineers and ground crew worked on that cold metal. The stoves in the huts were a bonus to come home to—glowing red hot—you could then thaw out. The flyers had problems with their heated suits; there were plenty of malfunctions and bad frost bite. Cold was the number one enemy.

I think we had some 250 dogs on base. After the boys went home the dogs were either destroyed or taken by English families. There was also a massive "grave" not far from Number One Hangar where motorcycles and bicycles had been flattened by a bulldozer and then buried.

When D-Day came all the base went crazy—guns and flare pistols were fired and every truck and Jeep blew their horns in harmony. Peace was here at last.

When the trucks lined up on the road in front of Coney Weston Hall near the 562nd Squadron area to go to Thetford Station, it was time to say goodbye. It broke my heart after two years of friendship. I realized later that the boys had wives and families to go home to; then the hurt was not so bad.

I think the 388th was tops in the ETO. They fought and died for the peace we have enjoyed and to all the boys that returned home, thanks fellows, you are my heroes.

It's been a great honor to have such wonderful friends. God bless you all.

*Percy Prentice and General James Doolittle during the General's visit to the base.*

**The 388th and Me**—David Calcutt

I commenced school in Coney Weston in 1941. The building still stands, but was closed as a school in the 1960s and converted into a house. Around this time, 1942, an aircraft crash-landed in a field on the outskirts of the village, and, as they do, the local boys went to look. It didn't seem too badly damaged, but what intrigued us was the pile of bombs stacked nearby. With hindsight I think they were probably incendiaries. A day or two later the aircraft was dismantled and taken away on two or three large trucks. As it went through Coney Weston Street it touched the trees on both sides of the road. Shortly after this my father started working for a company building an airfield locally. At holiday times I would go with him to collect materials or arrange for delivery, such things as sections of buildings from Thetford Rail Station, or truck loads of wood chippings which were rolled into the surface of runways to create grip for the aircraft that would use them very shortly.

When the Yanks and their aircraft and vehicles arrived, it changed the area beyond recognition.

All the country lanes had been widened to make room for the numerous Jeeps, command cars, large trucks and ambulances that proliferated, it seemed, overnight. By this time we had moved two miles down the road to Hopton, to a small cottage right on the road, which meant the road was slightly wider at that point, an opportune place for two six-wheeled Studebakers or GMCs to pass. I remember on one occasion two of these trucks tried to pass a few yards down the lane and became locked together. I can see now one of the drivers standing on the load in one truck with a crow-bar, levering the sides apart, while the other drove slowly along. And the load in the truck? Bombs! They were from the main storage depot near Thetford, heading for the bomb store at Station 136, Knettishall.

From where we lived it was only a few hundred yards to the airfield and, I learned much later, the dispersal area of the 562nd Squadron of the 388th Bombardment Group. I and many other local boys would visit the airfield often, at weekends and holidays, to get close to the Flying Fortresses parked there. The favourite cry was, "Got any gum, Chum?" whenever we met a GI.

As well as gum, we were well looked after. When it came time for the ground crew to go to chow they would hoist us kids up on the truck and off to the mess hall, there to feast on a large plate of meat and vegetables consumed with a borrowed spoon, probably with tinned peaches on the same plate for dessert.

If I was on the airfield when the planes returned from a mission I would get a job clearing up empty shell casings from the floor of the plane. I have regretted many times not making note of aircraft names or serial numbers that I could refer to in years to come; but, when you are only eight or nine years old, you cannot see 40 years ahead when these memories might be important. Maybe I have met crew members of these aircraft in England or the USA since, but have no means of knowing.

I remember on one occasion some pals and I were making our way home past an aircraft with one of the tail-planes removed. The ground crew wanted someone to crawl inside it for some reason, and a nine-year-old boy was about the right size. We were asked to help but, to a nine-year-old, nothing gets in the way of mealtime, so we carried on. The next day I returned and asked if they had found someone to do the job. They had.

The nearest I got to actually flying in a B-17 was being on board while the engines were being run-up. That, in itself, was quite a thrill. Also a bit frightening.

On another day, while in school at Hopton—which has long-since closed and been converted into a private house (I seem to have this effect on schools)—we had a message that a B-17 had crashed on take-off and was likely to explode at any time. We all had to get on the floor under our desks. Before long, there were loud explosions and, when we eventually emerged, the desk tops were covered in paint and plaster from the ceiling. I learned many years later that the name of the aircraft was *Hard Luck*. The navigator was Lt. Paul Arbon. Paul has a home in London now, and we have corresponded. Paul visited the base area on October 15, 1995, and was taken to the crash site, where, among the fields of potatoes, small fragments of *Hard Luck* were still to be picked up.

Back to the 1940s. The base cinema was visited by us local kids, where we got in for free. We sat in the front row, or, if the cinema was full, on the floor. If our clothes got dusty we told our parents it was a cowboy film and it was dust kicked up by the horses. I don't think they believed us.

Other highlights were the Christmas parties given by the base for all the local schools. We were picked up from school in American trucks and taken to the base where we had film shows, a meal with more food than we had ever seen and a present off the tree from Santa Claus. I still have a book received at one of these parties, *"Meetoo and the Little Creatures."*

As I mentioned earlier, my Dad worked on the building of Knettishall base, and then worked on the base for the rest of the war. As part of his wages he received 200 cigarettes a week, and a small cupboard in our kitchen was full of packs of Lucky Strike, Pall Mall, Chesterfield, etc. As boys do, an occasional pack was spirited away and my pals and I would enjoy a smoke among the bushes in the fens that were nearby, probably making ourselves sick in the process.

I would watch the planes take off in the early morning, then when we heard them returning in the late afternoon or evening I would call Mum and we would rush across the fields to the end of the runway and watch them land. Occasionally, there would be a red flare from one of the planes signaling wounded on board. We didn't like to see that. If they landed in daylight they came so low over our house we could read the names on the nose. A friend who lived along the road mentioned one day that she hadn't seen *Old 66* flying over lately. A while after this I saw the fuselage of the aircraft laying near one of the hangars. It wasn't until many years later, in 1993, that I learned from a book written by Richard Bing that *Old 66* blew a tyre on take-off on August 13, 1944, and ground looped off the runway, virtually destroying herself.

Although living so close to the airfield we—the kids anyway—didn't feel in any danger. One evening, at about the time the planes returned from a mission, we heard this noise and my father said, "That plane is making a funny noise," and went outside to look. He then rushed back inside and shouted,

"Get under the table, it's a doodlebug!" This was the nickname of the V-1 flying bombs that the Germans were sending over. We crouched under the table and listened until the sound died away; we knew that as long as we could hear the engine we were okay. When the engine stopped, the Doodlebug crashed.

One of Mum's sisters, Auntie Elsie, met a GI from the Medical Center, Reg Brown, who, among other things, drove an ambulance. Whenever an ambulance was seen the cry would go up, "Ambulance, Elsie!" in case it was Reg driving. At the end of the war Elsie went to the States and married Reg. They lived in New York State, at a place called, if my memory serves me right, Napanoch. Reg worked in the Prison Service after the war. They had no children and both passed away some years ago.

Came the end of the war and all of a sudden peace descended on our corner of Suffolk, as it did around all the airbases in East Anglia. At the height of the war, it was said you couldn't go more than five miles without coming across an airfield. We settled into peacetime, although we still had rationing—food and clothes mainly.

*Christmas was a special time at the base for the local children*

**Seeds of Friendship**—George Stebbings

Our village school owned, a small distance away, a small plot of land where youngsters could be taught the rudiments of gardening, aptly named, of course, the school garden.

I was quite surprised to find, early in the war, that our headmaster brought a substantial box containing various seeds, explaining that these seeds had been shipped over to us from unknown American citizens. These seeds were to be used to help toward our own efforts to provide produce for the use of the British people. At that time we were severely rationed and food stuffs of any sort were in short supply.

I tried to conjure up some sort of image of who these caring people were, and understand their kindness, as America at that time was not involved in the conflict. In my eyes the USA was a million miles away.

Later, I realized that those seeds had been sent over by the very parents of the servicemen and women who would later arrive in our midst. Even so, I was still wondering why America could not come to our aid in those dark days, as it had in the Great War of 1914-18.

How could I ever begin to dream or later to comprehend that as we fulfilled yet another dream to build our own home—which was to be sited on that self-same very spot, the old school garden—that shortly after its completion we would have as our guests, post-war, numerous sons and daughters of the self-same parents who had made the initial donations of those seeds, seated on the very spot within our home where they had been sown. Those seeds of friendship had well and truly been planted way back in 1940.

It's true to state that my involvement with the 388th at Knettishall has had a lasting effect on my life, a situation I would not want to change, ever.

Here I will report on my first official visit to Knettishall with the Air Training Corps Cadet Squadrons, of which I was a member—illegally and underage. We had received an invitation to visit Knettishall, a first for all of us. Our involvement with the 388th was due to a directive issued by the base commander, Col. William David, that British Air Cadets could gain air experience where possible with aircraft of the 388th Bomb Group. The arrangements for our visit where made possible by our Squadron Commanding Officer and full-time school teacher Maj. D.C. Reed, the original 562nd Bomb Squadron Commander.

The invitation began with a luncheon in the Officers' Mess on a Sunday afternoon. With our party of 20 or more, it was quite obvious that very few, if any, had ever experienced such an occasion, bearing in mind that it was wartime and that we had been accustomed to quite stringent rationing. It revealed a whole new world to all of us. I must add that our manners on that day were actually impeccable.

From the Officers' Mess, we were next introduced to the station gymnasium. We were shown various methods of self defense, unarmed combat, along with techniques to attack a potential enemy. Following this we went to the parachute school and learned the art of folding and packing a parachute. I, for one, took great heed of these instructions as I'm sure, in the back of my mind was, "well, just supposing." The thought of putting your trust in a parachute and the particular person who packed it is sobering, indeed. But at 14 years old, I suppose I didn't question anything, especially those whom we'd now have to trust with our lives. After all, these guys were so confident and highly skilled at their jobs.

Next, we made our way to the Military Police Station where we were introduced to a variety of small arms, then to the 1751st Armory Section where we were instructed to take apart a .50-caliber Browning machine gun, after having previously watched a demonstration on how this was to be carried out, step by step, by the real experts. And it amazed us that every gunner had to carry this out blindfolded. I understood, but again thought, "Supposing someone were blinded. He'd have no need of a machine gun."

That visit to the armory paid great dividends as our newfound friends informed us that we could visit their living quarters at any time and, if cycling, could leave our bikes there in complete safety. On our next visit we made use of our invitation. But further than this, these men of that particular section became great friends. Time after time we left our cycles there and we were always made welcome. This is probably where I discovered how the average GI thought and behaved, insofar as their presence over here was concerned—their thoughts of home, their own part in the conflict, the top brass, their thoughts on the survival of the air crew, their comparisons with the American infantrymen—this after D-Day; "There were no fox holes at 25,000 feet," my favorite saying.

We also became involved in a friendly banter as to the role of the Royal Air Force, being told that only the Americans dared to fly in combat during the day and that the British only operated under the cover of darkness. We retaliated by saying that the B-17s and B-24s couldn't even fly at night— that they could get lost over Britain even in daylight. Also that our Lancasters carried 15,000 pounds of bombs in comparison to the 5,000 pounds of the B-17 and B-24. These friendly arguments were usually replaced with references to pub crawls, drinking, gambling and English girls, but not necessarily in that order. If, as a very young teenager, I was not aware of the facts of life, I became very much aware by mixing with guys who gave the impression they were all Romeos and Clark Gables, or so at least they thought. This is all part of how we saw the average American GI.

But, after all, they loaned us, without question, their eating knives, drinking utensils, etc. They gave us the latest copies of Yank Magazine. We in return brought them fresh eggs, a priceless commodity to anyone within the confines of the 388th. So, actually, we thought, "all's square."

Here I must return to that very first visit. From the confines of the armory, we made our way to a radio signals building, just short of the Group Headquarters building, but immediately opposite. We were given a demonstration lecture on the various methods used to contact and, if desired, control aircraft in the vicinity of the airfield.

Next, we went to the all-important Group Headquarters building itself, probably for us the most interesting of all. Here, we were informed that within these walls the whole of the Group operations were controlled, each and every day, in relation to tasks carried out by the Group's B-17s on Hitler's Europe. I noted a large wall map of Europe with targets near and far, but mainly the long-haul targets deep into Germany. I also noted the board referring to the Group's B-17s and pilots, with reference to the four squadrons comprising the 388th. Much of this was of a highly secret nature, which we were warned of, so I was most surprised to be shown the various methods used to identify the various targets—the system of maps leading up to whatever target had been chosen. In fact, it appeared that almost every major town or city was a potential target and that the 388th, along with the rest of the 8th Air Force, could launch an attack on almost anywhere.

We were given a great insight into how the 388th would and could operate.

I, for one, was rather over-awed being a guest of the top brass, but more than a little intrigued as to their apparent friendliness and tendency to drop everything in their efforts to make us welcome. And here we were in the middle of a war, fighting for our very survival. They must have wanted us to think we were, after all, partners and to be treated as equals, as well as guests, by these strangers in our own country—a kind of situation I still recall with great pleasure to this day.

Our final Port-of-Call was to the nearby Number One Hangar. Here was the real reason for our being there, because here stood the first of the Group's B-17s I would ever go into. And, after we were shown around the now-familiar Boeing Flying Fortress from the outside, we were then invited inside where a mechanic pointed out or described the various crew positions, the .50-caliber arms, the bomb bay, the radio operator's compartment, plus the various escape hatches if need be. Since I had already experienced my first B-17 with the 385th Bomb Group, which carried the Square D symbol, I found myself immediately at home in a strange kind of way. And, with the eagerness and sharp mind of a typical teenager of that time, everything I had noticed in my previous flight in reference to the B-17 had been stored and memorized, and I retain much of this, even to this day.

So to my next visit, which meant cycling four-and-a-half miles or so.

We had been invited by Major Reed back to Knettishall for a fast flight in one of the Group's B-17s. I can't recall how many of my ATC friends were on board, but I was astonished to discover we were to land at a nearby RAF station, which, at that time, was using a four-engine, short Sterling bomber. This airport was less than two-and-a-half miles due south of Knettishall. In fact, their circuit was dangerously close and by some kind of miracle there were never any collisions.

To resume my story, after a very brief meeting between the Royal Air Force and a United States Army Air Force Major, we then proceeded. This was to be the first of many such flights from Knettishall, as we had been informed that if we presented ourselves at the Group Headquarters building there was the possibility of taking further flights and we had been also advised that our squadron had been officially adopted by the 388th.

The technique used to hopefully obtain a flight was to approach a pilot or pilots just short of entering the Headquarters building. It follows that even if the answer was a negative one, we only required the one affirmative. So we were on our way. But there was still one other stumbling block. That was to present to whosoever was in charge a warrant, signed by our parents, which consented to any such flight.

I always felt about six inches too short in the presence of the others, simply because I knew I was the youngest there and had joined these cadets somewhat illegally. I was just 14 years old at that time, the legal age being 16. Luckily, the signed warrant didn't state my age, so that aspect was never queried.

I have referred to our official adoption by the 388th, which in fact gave us permission to eat at the Airmen's Mess, among many other things. I soon discovered the difference between dining at the officers' mess and the lower ranks', mainly the enlisted men's. Many stories abound, even to this day, of the fabulous food to be had at any American mess hall, so I will add at times the food offered was not of the best, but hasten also to add that after four years of wartime rationing, just anything was more than welcome.

I also recall those were the days of various "leg-pullings," asking us who would be paying for the meal, then someone saying Uncle Sam had to foot the bill for us "Limeys"—which again reminds me that prior to our presence at Knettishall, we had never heard the term Limey; but I was extremely careful in not referring to our hosts as Yanks.

Taking this one step further, I felt intrigued and fascinated by the unfamiliar, foreign-sounding names, discovering that although many had well-known English names, a great number had German, Italian, Polish, Czech or Scandinavian surnames. And so it dawned on me that these American crews could well be dropping high explosives on various relatives down below. We of course, although perhaps of Saxon origin, had no such worries, our connections long since severed with our European forebearers.

Sundays were taken up by these visits and flights. We were instructed to sit down, usually in the waist; or, if on my own, maybe this was in the radio room area. It occurred to me that whichever crew we went with there was always a kind and clear consideration shown for our safety and well-being on board.

Each time we went up we presented ourselves at the parachute room. Normal issue was a chest-type pack with the ever familiar words ringing in our ears, "Remember, if it doesn't work, just bring it back. And don't take that home for your big sister to make a silk dress." Familiar words to us for sure. And if we went in a Royal Air Force aircraft about that time, those same comments were always part of the parachute ritual.

Once airborne, we would listen in on the chat over the intercom, as there were normally spare sets of headphones and throat mikes which had been handed to us. Depending on the length of the flight, we were able to move around much as we desired, although we were normally told not to go back in the tail gunner position which was rather remote, because if we removed our headphones to go back there and an emergency arose, we would be none the wiser. My two favorite positions were either lying down in the nose compartment, which offered a fantastic view, or standing behind the two pilots observing every movement made, as well as keeping a keen eye on the instrument panel. I cannot remember anything instructive as to where to be on landing, although usually we'd be asked out of the nose position, again for obvious reasons. Just supposing the landing went badly wrong, which happily never occurred.

We were issued flying logs by our Air Cadet squadron. So it became part of the ritual to obtain the pilot's signature. The duration of the flight was also recorded, type of aircraft and number, if Royal Air Force, or serial number if U.S. Army Air Corps. A column for remarks gave the reason for the flight. This log, which I retain to this day, has become one of my most treasured possessions.

I was fortunate enough to go on practice mission flights, practice formation flying, practice bombing, etc. Probably—or better still, most definitely—the best experience for me, ever, was on one particular flight to be called on the intercom to go forward to the cockpit, where, to my astonishment, I was then informed that, as I was there, I might as well get some stick time in. The co-pilot retired his seat and motioned me to occupy his position. The pilot then advised me as to the basic acts necessary for straight and level flight, rudder movement, how to rely on the artificial horizon indicator and to follow any instructions from the navigator as to our position. The next 20 minutes or so, yours truly was in control, even making a necessary turn successfully.

The pilot was Lt. Eugene Yarger who had helped me, possibly, become the youngest ever person to take control of a B-17 at the age of 14 years.

Maybe a world record; maybe not.

But it was the kind of experience that no person of my age could ever forget.

# THEY WILL NOT CATCH ME

By Lt. Norman P. Kempton, pilot, 560th Squadron

Many U.S. Airmen were shot down over Europe during World War II. Most were taken prisoners by the Germans. A few evaded capture. This is the experience of one who did escape.

The story began at 4:30 a.m. on 5 January 1944 at Knettishall. Our crew was briefed for a mission to bomb a German fighter training field near Bordeaux, France. Take-off was scheduled for about 7 a.m. We were to fly High Element Number Three position in the squadron, the best position in the formation.

The mission was a bit screwed up from the beginning. While taxiing, the left tire on the aircraft seemed very low. It had to be checked. We lost our position for take-off. Another aircraft took our position. We had to take the most vulnerable position during formation, Low Number Two, Second Element—Coffin Corner.

We reached Bordeaux, a trip of about 500 miles, at 11 a.m. flying, at 21,000 feet. As we approached the target, we were attacked by German fighters, ME-109s and FW-190s. Heavy flak pounded around us and under us as we approached the target. Our Number 4 engine went out and I was unable to feather. A fighter pass set off flares behind the pilot's seat. Co-pilot Paul Davis and Engineer Sgt. E. E. Taddeo smothered the fire. Another fighter pass hit a waist gunner. Bullets passed over my head and smashed into the co-pilot's instrument panel. Number 2 engine lost manifold pressure to 25 inches and was losing oil pressure. We dropped our bombs over target on the Lead aircraft's drop with Number 4 engine windmilling; we could not feather, and the vibration was severe. Number 2 engine was going out. Our tail was hit by flak. In order to stay level and hold the nose down, I had to use my knees on the control wheel to get enough forward pressure to keep from stalling out.

The squadron moved away fast after dropping its bomb load. We were under heavy fighter attack and, with two engines out, we couldn't keep up with the Group. I tried to take a position high on the following Group for protection, but could not keep up with them. I followed the formation out over the Atlantic Ocean in a northwest direction, still under fighter attack.

The ball turret gunner was wounded. Vibrations were so severe I thought a wing or engine would tear loose. It was 500 miles back to England, most of the way over enemy territory with probably more fighters and flak. We were losing fuel and oil. The possibility of making it back to England was extremely remote and landing would be nearly impossible. I decided to give the crew a better chance of survival by turning over land and allowing them to jump.

We were gradually losing altitude. We lowered the landing gear to signal to the German fighters that we were returning to land. An FW-190 was following us but did not attack. By the time we were over land on an easterly-to-southeasterly heading, we were down to 8,000 feet. I gave the order over the intercom to bail out and rang the alarm bell. The crew bailed out over a distance of approximately 10-15 miles over forest and swampy countryside. I sent the co-pilot back to see that all the crew were out. He returned and indicated that all were out; then he took a pack of Lucky Strike cigarettes from his pocket, ripped them in half, put half in my jacket pocket, said "so long" or something to that effect, and went to the bomb bay and jumped. A very cool character.

*Back row, from left, Lt. Norman Kempton, pilot; Lt. Paul Davis, co-pilot; Lt. Stanley Plytynski, navigator; Lt. Harry McKenna, bombardier. Front row, from left, S/Sgt. Emil Taddeo, engineer; Sgt. Raymond Evtuch, waist gunner; S/Sgt. Hamp Nicholson, tail gunner; Sgt. Norton, gunner; S/Sgt. Louis Mostardi, radio operator and Sgt. Melvin Larson, gunner.*

I held the nose down and tried to put the aircraft on auto-pilot, but couldn't. The attitude was 4,000 feet and going down. I backed out of the pilot's seat, holding the wheel forward with one hand, then made a dash for the bomb bay and fell into it. At the same instant, the aircraft stalled and the nose fell. I was floating in the bomb bay, not touching anything, but could not fall out. The aircraft was falling at the same speed I was. It seemed like a long time before the aircraft started to pull up and I finally went out. The roar of the aircraft was suddenly gone. I seemed to be floating, spinning on my back in absolute quiet. I had no sensation of falling. I was wearing a chest parachute. I looked down at it and thought, "shall I check the pins to see if it will open?" then thought, "it's now or never" and pulled the D ring.

Because I was spinning horizontally on my back, the chute trailed out straight in front of me. The shroud lines wound up, leaving only a very small canopy at first. The shock of the opening was hardly noticeable. Then, the shroud lines began to unwind, the canopy became gradually larger to full size, 22 feet. I looked around to see the aircraft above and going away from me in a stalled attitude. It stalled, fell off on the left wing, and spiraled down toward me. For an instant I thought it would come back and hit me. I thought to myself, "it's going to run me down." However, it turned away from me. It stalled again, then spiraled into the ground about a quarter of a mile away from me with a tremendous explosion.

By then I was only a few hundred feet from the ground. I put my feet together with my hands on the risers and landed easily in a semi-sitting position. It was about 11:15 a.m., 5 January 1944. The weather was clear and cool.

While I was coming down, a German FW-190 fighter was circling; however, he did not attack. He was probably radioing my landing location to ground troops. I had landed in the middle of a large, treeless open swamp in about a foot of water and grass about five miles from the coast. There was no cover or trees for at least a half-mile in any direction. It was like a very shallow grassy lake, maybe a mile or more in diameter. I could easily be seen from the surrounding woods. I rolled up my chute, removed my harness and pushed my chute under the water in a small drainage ditch. I also removed my sheepskin boots and hid them under the water and grass because they impaired my movement. The purpose for hiding my chute was to prevent the Germans from having a starting point in their search for me which I was sure would follow soon.

I had come down within a zone occupied and intensely controlled by the Germans. I had to get out of sight as soon as possible. The nearest cover was about a half-mile away; a small island, about 100 yards in diameter, of woods and brush in this large swamp or grassy lake. I ran toward the island in order to get out of sight as soon as possible. Going was slow because of the water, mud, and swamp grass that was about three feet high. I finally reached the island and went through the woods and brush to the opposite side. There was nothing but wide open swamp for a mile surrounding me. If I tried to cross in broad daylight I could be easily seen and I knew the Germans would soon be searching for me. I picked a small patch of high grass and dense dry reeds about 30 yards off the edge of the island, dug in, and covered myself with reeds to await night and darkness. About a half-hour or 45 minutes later, I heard voices and footsteps. They were searching the island.

They came within 20 feet of me. I caught a slight glimpse of two German soldiers with an American between them. He was a big guy, and I thought it may have been Paul Davis, my co-pilot, but I couldn't see enough to be sure. I finally had time to think about what had happened and then began to feel scared but very, very lucky.

I kept telling myself, "They will not catch me."

I stayed hidden until it was completely dark, about 9 p.m. It was a very clear but moonless night. I picked out the North Star for directional reference and started walking out of the swamp in a south-easterly direction. We had been instructed, if downed, to try to go south to Spain and east to the interior of France, called Vichy France, which was supposed to be less occupied by the Germans. It was a clear, cold night; temperature about freezing. I must have walked a mile to get out of the swamp area. I came into a pasture, or meadow, fenced in, and I realized I was approaching a farm house. I had been walking in foot-deep water and I was soaked up to above my knees. After leaving the water and swamp, the legs of my flying coveralls began to freeze and, brushing together, made what I thought was a terrible noise.

Fortunately, I had plenty of clothes. I was wearing two pair of long underwear, one cotton and one wool, my wool O.D. uniform pants and shirt. Over that, I had my O.D. flying coveralls and leather flying jacket. I had two pairs of socks, one heavy wool, and a pair of British high-top lace shoes, my evasion kit and, of course, my .45 automatic in an underarm holster. Although I didn't know it then, all were to become very beneficial to my evasion experience later.

As I approached the farmhouse, the noise made by my frozen coverall legs seemed deafening. The night was pitch black—only starlight. I came to the barn first. I could hear animals; cows I believed. I opened the door and went inside; but I could not see anything because of the darkness. I had hoped to find a dry place to rest; however, about that time a dog began to bark and I could see somebody stirring in the adjoining house, so I decided I had better take off. I went back the way I had come, then took off into the woods. I walked though dense brush and woods for what seemed liked many hours. The moon had come up and I could see fairly well, even though I was in a dense forest. At one point I skirted a small lake-like depression of dense brush so thick I didn't think I would ever get through. About 2 o'clock in the morning I came into a clearing in the woods. In the center of the clearing was a small hut which turned out to be a woodcutter's hut. It was about six feet square and had a fireplace and a stack of fire wood. I was very tired, hungry and cold. I decided the hut was isolated enough that I could start a fire. I started a fire in the fireplace, dried my clothes, lay down on the bench and got two or three hours of sleep.

About daybreak I woke up and, assuming someone would probably be coming to use the hut, took off into the woods again. I walked for about a half hour in easterly and south-easterly directions. I came out on a narrow farm road through the dense woods and brush. As I was crossing this path, I looked down the road to the east and, around a turn about 50 yards away, came a Frenchman pushing a bicycle. He stopped and looked at me. I thought, "This is it. Is he friendly or pro-German?" I needed help. At worst I could only be taken prisoner.

He was a French farmer, I would guess in his early 30s. After he saw my flying suit and recognized me as an American airman, he came up with a big smile, patted me on the back, jabbering in French. I could not understand a word, but with his "boom booms" and pointing at the sky, I knew he understood I was a downed airman. I didn't realize it at the time, but I found out later that a number of aircraft had gone down in the area during the previous day's raid. I knew I had found a friendly Frenchman.

By his pointing at my wrist watch and using sign language, I understood that I was to wait for him in the brush until he returned. An hour or so later he returned with a bottle of hot milk and coffee, a piece of hard baloney and a chunk of hard, dark bread. Nothing ever tasted so good! He hid me in the brush and I understood he would return that evening after dark. He pointed at the time on my watch.

All day I lay hiding in the brush. Several times during the day, German ME-109s, flew by, once at a very low altitude. I remember that once I took out my .45 and thought if he came any closer I could shoot him down. Foolishness.

About 9 o'clock that night the farmer came back and took me to his house. He fed me potato soup and dark bread. I drank a couple of glasses of wine on a near-empty stomach. I slept in a feather bed that night, 6 January 1944, and didn't care much what was going to happen to me.

Early the next morning, the farmer brought me clothing. I had indicated with sign language the night before that I needed civilian clothing. I could not speak a word of French nor he a word of English. Because I had had two years of Latin in high school, once in awhile I would understand the meaning of a French word. I gave him my O.D. uniform pants and shirt, my .45 and shoulder holster, and my O.D. flying coveralls and leather jacket. He gave me a well-worn black beret and dark suit with a striped blue shirt, tie and a black topcoat. All were a couple of sizes too small for me; evidently they were his and he was about three inches shorter and weighed about 20 pounds less. I kept my two pairs of long underwear and my two pairs of wool socks. Later on, they turned out to be lifesavers. I, of course, kept my uniform insignia and the dog tags around my neck. When I dressed, the pants were pretty high and did not cover the brown British hightop lace shoes I was wearing. This worried me somewhat. I had lost my O.D. wool gloves and leather helmet when I jumped. My evasion kit, a small box about 6x6x1 inches, which I had carried in a buttoned pocket of my flying suit, consisted of a fabric handkerchief-like map of Germany and France, dextrose tablets and chocolate candy, Benzedrine tablets for keeping awake, halogen tablets for purifying water, a quart-size rubber bag with draw strings, a small (about ½-inch diameter) compass and some matches. I stored in it the lining of my coat. The kit also contained French money—a 500 and a 100 franc note; new crisp bills. I don't recall what they were worth in U.S. dollars or British money. I had not carried a wallet on the mission. We were only allowed to carry dog tags and uniform insignia.

After eating breakfast, which consisted of a chunk of dark, heavy bread and hot milk and coffee (the coffee was actually made from roasted barley; they had no real coffee), the Frenchman indicated I should follow him. It was still very early morning and still dark. The only other person I saw at this farmhouse was his wife. I didn't hear or see any others. He gave me a bicycle and indicated that we were going to take a bus. I followed him on the bicycle over a narrow winding farm road for maybe a couple of miles. We came out on a main road or highway with a bench alongside and a highway sign which I realized was a bus stop. He again indicated I should take the bus and then took both bicycles and disappeared down the road on which we had come.

I was again on my own. The farmer had indicated by pointing at my watch about when the bus would come. I waited quite some time. The sun came up and maybe about 8 or 9 o'clock I heard the bus coming down the main road. There was a road sign nearby which had Bordeaux and the number of kilometers on it. The bus stopped in front of me. I got on and handed the driver the 100 franc note. He gave me a handful of change and smaller notes and I walked to the back of the bus, which had a number of people on it, and sat down. I rode for maybe an hour or so. The bus made many stops. People getting on and off. The bus was gas-driven and had a gas generator burner on the back. Quite often the driver would stop and add charcoal or wood or whatever generated gas. They had no petroleum fuel.

Finally, we came to a village. The bus pulled up beside another of the same kind and all the people started to get off. I followed. They got on the other bus. I followed. We started off on another one-hour ride toward Bordeaux. The bus finally stopped in Bordeaux at what I took to be a bus terminal, as there were other buses parked nearby. All the people got off. I followed and walked on down the street in a southerly direction. I hadn't spoken a word and nobody spoke to me. I don't know whether they knew who I was or just considered me another Frenchman.

Bordeaux is a large city. I had previously looked at my evasion kit map and knew the number of the main highway leading to the south and east toward Spain. My map had shown this highway running southwest through the city and parallel to a large river which also flowed from the southwest to the northeast. I walked the streets, but could not see a highway sign. At one point, as I walked through a narrow back alley, I met a Frenchman at the back of a shop. We were the only people on the street so I approached him with my map to see if he would point out on the map my location. As soon as he found out who I was he became very excited and put out his hand indicating "go away!" He didn't want to be seen helping me or associating with me by the Germans or pro-German people. I walked away very rapidly and got out of the area because I was afraid he might call the police. I kept walking in a southerly direction. It was about midday. I knew I would eventually reach the river and the highway that paralleled it.

Walking the streets of Bordeaux, I brushed shoulders with many German soldiers and sailors. They paid no attention to me because they thought I was a Frenchman. I was worried that I might be spotted by a French policeman who was pro-German. I kept telling myself that the worst that could happen to me was to be taken prisoner of war, so I just kept on walking the streets, keeping as inconspicuous as possible by following the crowd. I finally reached the river and the main street, which was parallel to the river, and was the highway I was looking for. At one point it turned into a wide boulevard, a sort of intersection and square which I knew was the center of the city. On the side opposite the river was a large building with Nazi flags, military vehicles and automobiles and many German uniforms in front. I assumed it was the German Headquarters for the city. I crossed to the left side—the river side of the square away from this Headquarters building—and walked on down the highway. Finally, after a couple of hours, I was out of the city and into the country south and west of Bordeaux.

That morning, before I left the farmer's house, his wife had given me a liter bottle of wine and a large chunk of dark French bread which I carried in the large pockets of my coat. It was late afternoon. I ate a little bread and drank a little wine as I walked. There wasn't much traffic, mostly French people walking or riding bicycles. Once in awhile a German military vehicle or truck with German soldiers would go by. I had seen signs, so I knew I was on the right highway which led to the south and east of France toward Marseilles. So far, so good. I had been very lucky. I guess I must have really looked like a Frenchman with my black beret and black, worn, baggy coat. I began to think that maybe I really could make it into Spain, but I was still at least 100 miles from the border and still in the densely occupied zone of France, within 10 miles of the coast. The weather this 7th of January, 1944 had been really nice; cloudy and cool, but no rain. It had been a very eventful day and a long day. I had to find some place to stay and rest.

During that day I must have traveled about 25 miles on the bus and walked 15 to 20 miles. I was very tired. It was beginning to get dark. We had been instructed in a situation like this to not try to travel at night because there was a curfew and it looked too suspicious; the German and French police were constantly patrolling the highway.

French farms, vineyards and villages were close together along the highway. They seemed to almost run from one into the other. I selected a farm house that was a little isolated from the rest and decided to seek help. I knocked on the door. A woman answered. I showed her my U.S. collar insignia to indicate who I was. She couldn't understand any English. She became very excited and afraid, jabbered in French, which I knew to mean "go, hit the road, get lost." She slammed the door in my face and I moved on, hoping she would not call the police. She evidently did not. I couldn't blame her for being afraid because, if seen helping me, she could have been shot by the Germans. I felt that the worst that could happen to me was that I could be taken POW. I did not realize that the German Gestapo could shoot me as a spy if I were caught in civilian clothes.

I moved on down the highway about a mile. It was now nearly dark and I had to get off the highway. I picked another farm house near the edge of a village and again knocked on the door. This time a man answered. He seemed to understand immediately who I was. He looked out to make sure we weren't being observed by neighbors, and pulled me inside. They fed me heavy, dark bread, cheese, wine and the roasted barley coffee. That night I slept in a feather bed again. I left the next morning, early, just as it was getting light. I went back to the highway and continued walking south.

The following few days were a repeat of that experience. In the evening, when I would look for a place to stay, sometimes the French farmers would take me in, other times they would reject me and send me on my way. I sometimes slept in feather beds, sometimes in the barn. I would walk the edge of the right side of the road. I was passed many times by German trucks and patrols but they seemed to pay little attention to me because I looked like a ragged, poor Frenchman. Most places I stopped I got my wine bottle filled with wine or coffee and milk and received a chunk of dark bread. No water. The French do not drink water. I became very thirsty several times. I dipped up water from the ditches along the road in the rubber bag from my evasion kit and put the purification tablets (halogen) in and let it stand for several hours. Then I would drink it.

I wanted to get farther into the interior of France—Vichy France— where the German occupation was less intense and where I thought the French people would be more friendly and more likely to help me. According to the map, I had to cross the large river that ran parallel to the highway. On the other side of the river I would be in Vichy France.

However, I knew that the large bridge at Agen, where I had to cross, would be a German checkpoint and closely guarded.

The night before I reached Agen I could not find a place to stop. I finally found myself in a farmer's yard away from the highway. The house was dark; evidently they had retired. There were a couple of hay stacks in the yard. It was cold and I was tired. I dug a hole in the side of one, covered myself with hay and tried to get some sleep. The next morning at the break of day I heard some stirring in the house. I went to the door and knocked. An old man answered. When he recognized who I was (he could speak a few words of English) he took me in and gave me a hot cup of roasted barley coffee with a big shot of cognac in it (new raw cognac). I was very cold and hungry; the temperature was freezing. There was frost on the haystack I had slept in. The drink really warmed me up.

The old man turned out to be a disabled World War I veteran with one arm. He was the agent at the nearby village railway station. He was, of course, a very pro-Ally sympathizer. He evidently lived alone. He prepared me a fried egg with a chunk of dark bread and more coffee and cognac. He also called in his friend and neighbor and I knew they were discussing what to do with me. I showed them my map and how I wanted to get across the river into Vichy France at Agen. They were very concerned about me going across that bridge because they indicated that the Germans check papers, passes and identification. I got the impression from them through a few words and sign language that the best time to try to cross the bridge would be late afternoon when many French people—workers and farmers— would be crossing, going home from work or fields.

Most of that morning the French railway agent and his friend were showing me their wine-making cellars or barns. I was asked to sample many kinds of wine from the large wooden barrels which were in the process of aging. By the time I left the place in the middle of the morning I was loaded and trudged off across the vineyard to the highway without a care in the world.

The French station master had also refilled my wine bottle and had given me a large chunk of dark bread, which I carried in the pocket of my coat. During the afternoon I got very thirsty and again filled my rubber bag with water from the puddles along the road, added a couple of halogen tablets and let it mix for an hour or so before drinking. I came to the Agen bridge about the right time, about 5 o'clock, just before dark, when there seemed to be a lot of French people crossing into the town. I mixed with a large group of French—some pushing bicycles, others walking. There were a few carts. I stayed on the opposite side of the roadway from the German guards who were posted at the east end of the bridge. The Germans didn't seem to be checking anyone, only watching people going across. I felt they were especially looking at me but I guess they only saw me as another ragged, decrepit Frenchman. I was also limping because walking along the side of the road with one leg off the higher pavement had caused my left leg to become very painful. I walked on past the German guards and followed the highway through the town of Agen.

At last I was in Vichy France, where there were supposedly fewer German patrols. Out on the edge of town I found another isolated farm house and a place to stay for the night. It seemed that people in the area were less afraid to take me in and somewhat less afraid of being caught for aiding me. I had sort of lost track of the days and time. I guessed I had walked about 25 miles a day for about five days in the direction of Toulouse and parallel to the Garonne River, which I had crossed at Agen. This night, on the edge of the village, I crept into a farmer's barn and slept in a pile of straw. The house and barn of the French farmers are one building, one half being barn and the other half they lived in. I was so tired and cold I didn't care where I slept. The house was dark and I didn't hear anybody stirring. Early the next morning I awoke. I was so thirsty and all I had was a little red wine left in the bottle. I drank the wine and got very sick. I was upchucking in the manure gutter behind the cows. Evidently the noise awoke the farmer and his family. He came out and, when he found out who I was, he took me in to feed me and gave me some milk to settle my stomach. They could not speak English. However, they indicated they could bring somebody who could. One of the boys went after the English-speaking person and I understood I was to remain there with them until the person arrived. About the middle of the morning a middle aged woman and the boy arrived in a horse drawn, two wheeled cart.

She spoke English well. She said that she had lived in southern Illinois until she was 13 years old. They were an Italian family living near the town of Castlesarssin. This Italian woman took me to her farm home, which was about five miles away. It was in a rather isolated area and the ride in the horse drawn cart took a couple of hours. For the next week or so I stayed with the Italian family—the woman, her husband, Dominic Bozotta, and their small son. During that time they made contact with the French underground. My long walk had at last ended.

I believe it was on Sunday that we went to visit her father. The old man was quite a character. He had worked in the coal mines of Southern Illinois years before. The only English words he could remember were "Goddamn sone-a-bitch" and he would repeat that and then say "Englise?" Then he would laugh. His daughter was embarrassed; he thought it was funny.

This farm family was very poor. Their farm was isolated in a hilly, rocky, wooded area. The house was quite primitive. They cooked in a fireplace and their only transportation and farm equipment was the horse drawn cart. After about a week, they told me that someone was coming to take me to the nearest large town, Montauban, which was a few miles farther to the southeast of the village of Castlesarssin. The man who came to pick me up was a short, stocky Frenchman and I remember he wore a leather coat which was an indication of wealth, high position or a government official. I assumed he was high up in the underground. They were very reluctant with the use of names and, of course, I couldn't keep any written notes even if I had something to write on because, if I were caught by the Germans, it would be disastrous for them. The man came in a small car, an Austin or Renault or Fiat. He could only speak a few words of English. For a Frenchman to have a car at that time was an extreme luxury and an indication of wealth and position. That afternoon he took me to the upstairs apartment of an old Frenchwoman where I waited for several hours. Montauban was a fairly large industrial town and railroad center. I never saw the Frenchman with the car again. After waiting several hours at the apartment in Montauban, a small, slight Frenchman in his mid thirties came and took me to a farm home on the outskirts of the city. Here I was told I would stay for an indefinite period. During that day I had been passed from one to another through five people and I knew for sure I had made contact with, and was under the care of, the French underground.

The farm family I lived with on the outskirts of Montauban was named LaPlace. They consisted of the 30 to 35-year-old, slightly built man; his wife, who had a crippled leg (probably polio); a daughter about five years old and his father, an old man who was well into his 70s. They must have been a fairly wealthy farm family. They produced mainly grapes for wine and I would guess had approximately 10 or 15 acres of land, which I believe was a fairly large grape orchard for that area. Their house was stone, two story, with no inside plumbing. The toilet was an outhouse with a hole in the floor (the usual rural facilities for a farm family). There were several long out-buildings; barns, and storage areas. They didn't have a car or any powered farm equipment. I believe they had a horse and maybe a cow or two. Their transportation was by bicycle. The house was heated by fireplace and a kitchen stove. I don't recall seeing all of the house or out-buildings.

I stayed with the family for four or five weeks. I could not speak a word of French. They could not speak English, but somehow with sign language and a few common Latin-related words we communicated and got along. The five-year-old girl was studying English in school and would sometimes help her mother with a few basic words. I had an opportunity to learn French; however, every day I thought I would be leaving and therefore didn't make the effort or take advantage of the situation. Day after day I spent in an upstairs attic bedroom, always out of sight of the neighbors or anyone who might come to visit. The neighbors on either side never knew I was staying there. Only at night, after dark, could I go outside and walk through the grape arbors to get a little exercise. The LaPlace family treated me royally.

They had so little. Food was hard to get. Most meals consisted of potatoes or onion soup with wine and, of course, dark, coarse bread, which was very tasty. They gave me a pocket knife. It was common practice for each person at meals to use his own knife to cut off a chunk of bread from the large long loaves that were passed around the table. Black French bread was the predominant food at every meal. One Sunday they had relatives in and served 1915 white wine. After I had been there a few days, they gave me a nice safety razor, which I still have. I had not shaved or had a bath for about three or four weeks and was getting very rancid. In January, the south of France is cold, sometimes getting down to freezing. I still had my two pair of longjohns and heavy wool socks. They were real lifesavers. The French don't believe in bathing very much, only washing their feet. There wasn't any bathroom or bath tub in the house. After I had been there a week or two, Mrs. LaPlace brought a pan of water to my attic room so I could shave and take a sponge bath, my first in about a month. The only thing they had to drink was wine and roasted grain coffee. I became so thirsty for a drink, I would go to the kitchen where they had a water pump next to the sink and would drink a glass of water. The old father would shake his head and say, "No, no," but I just had to have a drink of water.

One evening, Mr. LaPlace took me out to one of the remote storage barns on the farm, where I met about a half-dozen of the underground. They were having a meeting and making plans to sabotage the railroad yards in Montauban. They showed me the plastic explosives and a number of submachine guns. They were preparing bombs to blow up locomotives in the railroad yards. Early the next morning I heard a number of explosions. LaPlace said that several German locomotives had been blown up.

During my stay with the LaPlace family, there was nothing to do during the day but stay in my attic room. Mrs. LaPlace had a number of old *Lady's Home Journal* magazines in English which I read over and over.

Finally, one Sunday, LaPlace said I should follow him on a bicycle. We pedaled along a country road for maybe a couple of miles to another fairly large farm. He took me into the house to meet a couple of Americans, Lt. Bigler and Sgt. Jim Dyson, who had been hidden there for much longer than I. They had been shot down near Paris and had been in France for six or seven months. They were both in bed at midday and complained about having to wait so long for the French underground to get them out of France. A few days later, just before dark, two Frenchmen in a very small Renault convertible came by with Bigler and Dyson to move us all closer to the Spanish border. I said goodbye to the LaPlace family and thanked them for taking care of me. The old man hugged me and kissed me on each cheek, said, "*bon voyage*," and off we went in the little Renault with three Americans jammed into the back seat, which was hardly bigger than a baggage compartment.

The two French underground men were in the front seat, one with a submachine gun across his lap. They looked like a couple of Chicago gangsters. They were ready to mow down anything that got in their way. We drove for three or four hours over what seemed like back roads. Sometimes, they would stop and the man with the machine gun would walk ahead to check for German patrols at intersections. Finally, we entered a town and drove into the courtyard of a small inn or hotel. I believe the town was Tarbes. That evening the French underground gave me identification papers, similar to a passport, with my picture on them. The papers said I was a deaf and dumb mute, the result of bombing. They told us to hide in the kitchen cabinets if the Germans came. We met several Frenchmen who would accompany us to the Pyrenees Mountains and the Spanish border. Neither Bigler, Tyson, nor myself could speak any French, so they paired each of us with a Frenchman for the next day's train travel.

Early the next morning, at about daybreak, we left the hotel two at a time to go to the train station. I walked with Jim Dyson, he and I being the tallest. During the walk to the station we had to pass through the town square where the local French police patrolled. Dyson was a big, loudmouth Texan, always talking and very excitable. As we walked across the square, Jim would keep saying, "He sees us!" He almost panicked. At the station we joined the Frenchmen. We were paired with them and scattered throughout the train. After several hours riding, we got off the train at the town of Pau. We had to wait several hours for the next connecting train. The Frenchmen I was with took me to a huge Catholic church. It was like a cathedral. There he talked to the priest. I knew he was telling him I was a deaf mute because the priest was showing great sympathy for my handicap. He probably knew the situation. We again took the train from Pau to Lourdes at the foot of the Pyrenees. Only once did a conductor look at our IDs.

From Lourdes we walked into the foothills of the mountains. It was now dark and our group increased to three Americans, 10 Frenchmen, two Belgians and two Basque guides. One of the Belgians was a little pudgy fellow near 50. It was indicated that he was a VIP, a Belgian government official. No names were ever disclosed since if you were caught, the less you knew, the better off you were. The Frenchmen were going to North Africa to join DeGaulle. We walked single file in pitch black darkness; no moon. I wondered how the guides could find their way up the mountain. Sometimes we would tie a white handkerchief on the man ahead to see our way.

Many times we stopped and waited at the road crossings to allow the guides to check for German patrols. We walked all night until early morning. We came to a small farmhouse up on the side of the mountain. They fed us thin potato soup and a chunk of black bread. Then we slept in the hayloft of the barn all day until it was dark enough to continue up the mountain. All travel over the mountain was at night until we were very close to the border. One day we slept in a barn that had no roof. We dug into the hay to keep warm. Our Basque guides brought us goat bones which had a few shreds of meat on them. Everyone was so hungry they stripped them clean in no time. Another morning, we stopped at a farm house high in the mountains. They gave us thin potato soup and a chunk of black bread. It was warm and delicious. We slept that day in the hay mow adjoining the house. It was so cold that Bigler and I slept together with our coats on and with all the hay and feed bags we could find piled on top of us. One night, after having walked most of the night, we were very tired. We had stopped for a short rest. For something to drink the guides would give us small sips of wine diluted with water from a goatskin bag. At this stop they didn't have anything. I had been saving a bottle of Scotch that the LaPlace family had given me. I brought it out and passed it to Bigler and Dyson. Bigler and I each took a small sip. Dyson, however, tried to drink the whole bottle. That was a mistake on my part for allowing him to drink that much. We walked on a few hundred yards farther and he was out cold. We had to carry him a little farther to a barn near where we were going to stay for the night. We covered him with hay and he slept the day there.

That night, we walked up near the tree line, always climbing up higher. At one point, Dyson got so tired he sat down and said he could go no further and asked us to leave him. After much arguing, I finally threatened him with a court martial when we got back. Being the good, conscientious soldier that he was, he took that to heart. He got up and kept going. Later, when I met him in California, he thanked me for making him keep moving and not letting him give up.

The last day before crossing the border into Spain, we walked during the day. We were high above the tree line near the top of the mountain walking in three feet of snow—and it was snowing. Visibility was zero and there were no landmarks to go by. The guides were not sure of their direction. They found out that I had a small compass from my evasion kit. They came back to look at it to get their bearings.

Late that afternoon it had stopped snowing. The guides brought us to a cliff-like ridge overlooking a deep valley. We seemed to be high up near the top of the mountain. The snow was deep and you could see where avalanches had broken off the ridge and run down into the valley. The guides pointed down the valley and said, "There is Spain." They could go no farther. Good Luck! You're on your own…

Far down the valley, maybe two or three miles away, we could see a building. We worked our way down the ridge and, just before dark, we reached what turned out to be a sheep herder's hut that was only occupied during the summer. A few hundred yards before we got to the hut, one of the big French boys in the group got so tired he could hardly take another step. He kept calling, "Norman, help me." So I went back and helped him into the hut. He was about to fall down. He was about twice my size and I thought he would be the last to play out. He was probably a city boy. The hut had a fireplace. We built a fire and all collapsed. I had a small piece of hard French sausage, which I had saved in the lining of my coat. It was only a piece about the size of my thumb. I ate it, skin, coat ravelings and all. It was the best piece of food I believe I had ever tasted. We hadn't eaten a substantial meal for nearly 10 days. The next morning, early at first light, we started down the valley which led deeper into Spain and away from the border. Just the Americans of the group—Bigler, Dyson, and myself—left early, ahead of the French, because we had heard that the Spanish were throwing people who illegally crossed the border into jail. We felt that if we were not associated with or part of the group of French we might receive better treatment from the Spanish police. That assumption turned out to be correct.

We followed the river valley a mile or so downstream until we came to a road which, according to our handkerchief map, would lead us to the Spanish village of Isaba, about 10 or 15 kilometers. We reached the village about noon on the 23rd of February, 1944. We turned ourselves into the Spanish police. They put us in a small Spanish village inn, fed us, and—after identifying us as Americans—contacted the U.S. Counsel. We slept in a bed for the first time in about 10 days. We were correct in separating ourselves from the French, because they *were* treated differently. They were trying to go to North Africa to join the French Forces under DeGaulle. We never saw them again. At last we were free of the threat of imprisonment and under American government control. What a big relief!

The next day we were taken by bus to the city of Pamplona, where a man from the U.S. Embassy's Military Attaché Office took over caring for us. We were housed in a small hotel near the central square. The U.S. Attaché representative supplied us with $10 a week in Spanish pesetas and civilian clothing, including tailor-made suits. The weather was warm and dry. We were free to walk about the town. There were about 15 Americans and one French airman interned at the Pamplona hotel, located near the city square or plaza. It was the first opportunity in nearly two months for a hot bath. The hotel had no bathing facilities. It was necessary to go to the public bath which was located near the hotel and pay to use a bathing facility. For the 10 days that we stayed in Pamplona we experience many of the strange—for us—customs of the Spanish, such as midday siestas. During this time, all shops and businesses were closed. In the evening they would promenade about the plaza. We would spend much time drinking café con leche, a half coffee-half milk drink in the cafes about the plaza. We had the freedom to walk about the very old, feudal walled city. Several times, for exercise, I walked to the bullfight stadium where they have the famous Pamplona running of the bulls. The representative of the American Counsel supplied us with spending money, cigarettes and civilian clothing. In our group, no one could speak or understand Spanish, but we managed okay and at last we could enjoy eating our fill of potatoes, onions, eggs, fruit and bread. The hotel served two meals a day, breakfast and dinner. We could write letters which were carried out through the U.S. Military Attaché Office of the U.S. Embassy in Madrid.

I still have the letter which I sent to Dad announcing my safe survival and return to U.S. military control.

I had been listed as missing in action for about two months.

# THE BLOCKBUSTER

10 March 1945, Vol. 3, No. 1
Articles from the Station 136 newsletter

## Meet your Boss

It's a long haul from Superior, Wisconsin to Knettishall, Suffolk. If you don't believe it ask your Commanding Officer, Lt. Col. Chester C. Cox, whose residence is in the aforementioned city.

In February 1942, Captain Chester Cox joined the new 388th Bomb Group on the Wendover salt flats as her first Operations Officer. At this job he quickly established himself as a fine pilot, a capable department head and an all-round excellent officer.

As some of us know, the Group leading the 8th AF over the Normandy beaches on D-Day was none other than the 388th, with its Air Executive, Lt. Col. Cox, riding the Command Pilot's seat of the Lead aircraft.

*Lt. Col. Chester Cox*

Today, nine months after the invasion, Group Commander Cox is a veteran of five months as the Commanding Officer of Knettishall. During the comparatively short administration, the Wisconsin Wizard has achieved success that commands the admiration of every individual on the station. Hampered by losses in staff personnel and experienced crews, by miserable flying weather and I-Day pressure, the CO put his shoulder to the wheel and has emerged from a seemingly impossible winter into a spring which promises even more accomplishments.

Results of his winter campaign speak for themselves. During February, the Group shacked six targets, had six near hits and dumped 1,336 tons of bombs on the target.

To complete February successes, the Commanding General pronounced Station 136 superior and added the ultimate in Army compliments when he said, "Cox, your troops are well turned out."

These well-turned-out troops have a lot to say about their personable young CO. But one remark epitomizes them all. Colonel Cox—yeah, swell fellow!

### 388th Drops Record Load of Bombs During 8th's Feb. Blitz on Nazis

Joining the other units of the 8th AF in the record February attack on German industries and rail centers, the 388th dropped its largest month's total when 1,336 tons were released in 18 missions. This compares with the previous record month of June, 1944, when 1,248 tons were dropped, and with the first month of operations, when the Group's bombers dropped only 177 tons.

A breakdown of the bombing shows that three of the missions were visual, six were "visual assists" and six were entirely "pathfinder" operations.

The visual missions were the attacks on Hamm, Aunsbach, and Ulm, and the nine squadrons participating in those missions obtained six "shacks," verified by strike photos.

All the "visual assist" missions, in which some visual aid was to be had in attacking the targets, produced very good results and considerable damage was done.

PRU Evaluation of the Leipzig mission, entirely PFF, revealed excellent bombing results. Capt. Les Baum, the Group bombardier, says mickey operator-bombardier coordination is adding to the Group's bombing efficiency: February tends to prove it.

—

We begin this enterprise with very few illusions, no staff, with nothing much, really, other than a desire to keep you informed. *The Blockbuster* will again appear at odd intervals, perhaps every 10 days or so. Paper being the screech stuff it is, you will not all be able to have a copy. The copies that do exist are meant to be shared. In the old days, in Wendover, when there was more time, it was little or no trouble to knock out an edition. A good many fellows were connected with the project then. Now, some two years later, in Knettishall, that garden spot of the old world, our staff has been reduced to one part-time clerk who will staple pages, edit, type, gather news and sweep out the office more or less regularly. Should you care to contribute to these pages, by all means feel free to do so. Your notes, comments or stray bits of news can either be written out, preferably in English, and dropped off at the S. & I. Services Office, in the S-1 section at headquarters, or be delivered vocally, ext. 82. Public Relations is also prepared to handle your contributions. Suggestions, whether acted upon or not, will be most welcome. We have no policy, we have no choice of candidates; it isn't even established, at this point, what our deadline will be. We hope to continue, in spite of these handicaps, simply telling you things you might not otherwise know. In a town of this size it is impossible for a person, even an editor, to know everything that goes on around him. So, if you will share your news items with us, we will try to give you a little insight into operations, people, coming events and local happenings. One thing we may as well clear up at the outset: As harmless as the paper certainly is, it nevertheless reveals operational facts. *It cannot therefore be transmitted through the mails or carried away from the station.* Please remember.

—Ed

## People

Capt. Richard G. Oswald, 563rd pilot, has made four trips to London recently for radio broadcasts, describing his experiences as Lead Pilot for the 8th Air Force on its first shuttle mission to Russia last summer. Capt. Oswald broadcast to the Continent, did programs for BBC and also appeared on AFN's Combat Classroom.

Capts. Tolmer S. McKinley and Charles M. Pierce, Jr, of the 562nd, flew their first ETO mission 2 March 1944, and each completed his tour of operations with 30 missions exactly a year later, 2 Mar 1945.

S/Sgt. Joe B. Osborne, formerly of the 563rd, one of the lucky few to be sent back to the States under the rotation program, is now permanent party at the Greenville (Miss.) Army Air Base and liking it very much, despite having to stand retreat and all that sort of thing.

T/Sgt. Fred O. Meehan, formerly on Lt. Thayer's crew in the 561st, is now at Randolph Field, Texas, learning remote-control firing on the B-29 Superforts.

Sgt. Wilbur W. Curry, 561st mechanic severely injured when hit by a prop as he rushed to help put out an engine fire, is improving at the 65th General Hospital, and should be able to get out soon.

1st/Lt. Carl M. Fick and 1st/Lt. Carl J. Guerrein, formerly on Capt. Johnson's crew in the 562nd, are now Squadron Navigator and Bombardier, respectively, in the 560th.

## In case you didn't know:

Capt. John M. Flor is taking Maj. Leif A. Egaas' place as Group Navigator.

If you used five gallons of gas a week in your car back home (saying that you were on friendly terms with your rationing board) it would take you *five years* to consume the amount of gas used by each B-17 on an average mission.

A 563rd pilot was the *third* Air Force pilot to fly a P-47.

There are only two Command Pilots with the 45th Combat Wing, and one of them is stationed here.

Easter Sunday this year is also April Fools Day.

Our troops on the continent are closer to Berlin than they are to London.

## Goldwyn Here

Sam Goldwyn, one of Hollywood's most famous movie producers, visited the 388th recently on a tour of inspection of Lend-Lease equipment on the base.

Mr. Goldwyn, who arrived in London last month, was accompanied here by several 3rd Division officers. It was his first visit to an operational base. During his whirl-wind tour, he attended an interrogation and chatted with both flyers and ground crew on the line to learn first-hand how operational missions are conducted. He also inspected the 560th living site, the motor pool, the theater and mess halls, in order to get an overall picture of Lend-Lease.

So impressed was Mr. Goldwyn with what he saw and heard here, he promised to send us one of his latest pictures, *"The Princess and the Pirate,"* to be shown at this station before being released to the public over here. These arrangements have already been completed and the film will be shown one day, 20 March.

## Jerry Revisits England

Increased German air activity over England caused some action in the 388th area during the past week.

German planes were in the vicinity on four consecutive nights, at the time *The Blockbuster* went to press, although their main activity was concentrated on the first night of their visit. Jerry planes buzzed around for two hours that night, and one Nazi intruder shot down a RAF plane which crashed a few miles from the base. Four members of the crew bailed out over the field, and sentries on the line fired on at least two who floated down suddenly out of the darkness.

Capt. Walter C. Button, 563rd pilot and Station Air Inspector, had a narrow escape. Returning home from the 65th General Hospital, he was stopped by a policeman who advised him to seek shelter in a doorway. A few minutes later a strafing German plane hit the town, sending several rounds of cannon shells into buildings only a few feet away from Capt. Button.

It was reported 27 German planes were over England that night, in what was interpreted to be a last desperate gesture by the German Air Force.

## Coming Events:

11 March—Officers' St. Patrick's Dance
13 March—*"Hullabaloo"* USO Show
20 March—*"The Princess and the Pirate"* Bob Hope's latest
22 March—Gerald Riley, a seaman who escaped from the Nazis, speaks at Aero Club
23 March—Aero Club dance
24 March—Rocker Club Jam Session
25 March—Officers' Club Dance
30 March—Aero Club Jam Session
31 March—Rocker Club Jam Session

## Hospital To Duty

The doctors on the hill took one look at us, shook their heads, consulted briefly, then ordered one of the medics to admit us to the ward. Our experience with Army hospitals being limited, we permitted ourself to be led off to the sick bay with many a qualm. It was about the same as being admitted to an old abattoir for observation, our imagination being the fertile thing it is.

The ward turned out to be a surprisingly cheerful place; lights were on, the radio was on. Four patients were already enjoying clean sheets and pillowcases, propped up reading, and enduring their various agonies with truly Spartan calm. So wrapped up were they in the luxury of illness, they gave us not a glance. We joined them, picking out the best situated bed in the place, undressed and changed into pajamas. It felt rather like home.

Now, we thought, the door will open and someone will stalk in with disagreeable news, or possibly a needle. A bum foot was all we could boast of; still, amputation loomed as a possibility. It hurt like hell, if you want the truth. But no, the door opened and in came a medic with dinner. It was a good meal, and what made it better was having it served. We revised some presupposed conceptions of Army hospitals. That evening there wasn't much to do but read and listen to the radio. We slept like a pine knot and ate a good breakfast next morning.

The doctors made their rounds in the forenoon. Temperature? Headache? No, we had nothing but a game leg; they were solicitous and friendly. Others came and went; we stayed on. The days and nights more or less ran together, they were so pleasant and undisturbed.

After five days it happened, the worst thing that can happen to a person who is bent on enjoying bad health: We were discharged. Yes, the Morning Report probably said cryptically "from hospital to duty." To us, who had never so much as been on sick-call before, it meant returning to the old grind, the old chow hall; it meant rough blankets to sleep between and an old cast-iron bed to drape the body on. No more reading and listening to the radio, no more wallowing deep in the torment of idleness. It was, among other things, the roughest part of illness.

—Cpl. Schlaupitz

## While You Sweat Out The Trip Home

When the school bell rang on 26th February, over 700 enlisted men and officers began studies in 37 courses ranging from Mechanical Drawing to Poultry Production.

Classes run from 19:00 to 20:00 hours on Mondays, Tuesdays and Fridays. Briefing rooms, mess halls, the theater, Combat Crew Library and offices serve as classrooms for eager soldiers.

Any Tuesday night, if you walk into the Combat Crew Library, you may find Major D.C. Samuel or Capt. Bernard Frick giving an interesting discourse on international relations. Bombardiers, walking unexpectedly into their briefing room in the early hours, may find Capt. L.G. Conover instructing 40 interested persons in the fundamentals of Mechanical Drawing. Meandering into the Aero Lounge, one may hear S/Sgt. Sam Dreizen, ex-lawyer, ex-radar specialist, adroitly conducting the discussion of the GI Bill of Rights.

Discussion groups on the station have increased to 18, with over 300 members. At last we are making a real approach to why we fight.

Are you participating in any phase of the Education program? If you are not, you are missing the finest opportunity the Army has ever presented for building to meet the postwar world, or simply for worthwhile diversion.

—

Lt. George Oscar Puig's now world-famous Gremlins rolled back to Knettishall on March 1st after a series of broadcasts and one-night stands, and are now the toast of London. On February 22nd, the Gremlins played an hour broadcast on a direct short-wave transmission to good old USA. Other London stands included the famous Rainbow Corner, the South London Hospital and the Queensbury Club. Highlighting the entire string of engagements was the premiere of *"Winged Victory,"* held in London's new State Theatre. A jammed house of 5,000 paid tribute to the Knettishall music-makers.

When asked who was the most receptive audience they had ever played for, Maestro Tom Frank immediately shot back, "the boys at the Knettishall Aero, naturally."

# LITTLE *WILLIE'S* FIRST CREW

James B. Warner, co-pilot
Obenschain crew, *Little Willie*, 563rd Squadron

In February 1944, Lt. Dick Obenschain's crew finished its 25th mission in the 388th Bomb Group and breathed a collective sigh of relief. But, the anticipated orders for reassignment stateside were not to be for Obenschain, myself—the co-pilot—navigator Jim Ostler and Sgts. John Lopes and Gordon Pingicer. We had been reassigned to a composite squadron and would fly a B-17 with the RAF through July 1944.

Our aircraft during our bombing tour in the 388th BG was a B-17G we named *Little Willie*. During the RAF assignment we continued to read articles in the Stars and Stripes newspaper about the exploits of this aircraft and its new crew. Edward Jablonski, in his excellent book *Flying Fortress* (1965), highlighted the aircraft's pilot, Bernard M. Dopko, and his crew on a Berlin mission and the very close call they experienced. Later, the painting, *"Little Willie Coming Home,"* was used on the cover of the 388th Bomb Group newsletter. I do not wish to detract in any way from the magnificent flying of Bernard Dopko and the excellent publicity and news coverage afforded him and his crew for the Berlin mission and low level return to Knettishall. However, it has bothered me for over half a century that 24 missions for the Obenschain crew and one to Bordeaux, France for Col. David, all in *Little Willie,* go basically unnoticed. In the following comments I would like to provide some background and history for our crew and our aircraft.

In early September 1943, three replacement crews, among others, arrived at the 388th Bomb Group. The three particular crews were the Richard Obenschain, Arthur Pack and John Mouat crews. They were the product of crew training in the Martin Provisional Group. This unit, commanded by Maj. Glen Martin (later a Lt./Gen.-SAC), formed, guided and trained 33 replacement B-17 crews for the USAAF 8th Air Force in England. After a questionable beginning at Moses Lake, Washington (before the base was completed or equipped for training) the Group provided a thorough and comprehensive crew training program at Walla Walla AAFB, Washington. From May through July 30, 1943 these crews flew together, trained together, socialized together when possible and bonded as crews and families.

On August 1, 1943 the Martin Provisional Group departed Walla Walla AAFB at night on a "special" train, pulled by a coal-burning steam locomotive. The engineer had to be a direct descendent of Casey Jones. I do not remember ever being more tense, uncomfortable or concerned about high speed and rough travel than on the trip to Topeka AAFB, Kansas. What made the train "special" was that we went full speed ahead with only fuel and water stops, and if they changed crews I don't have a clue as to where or when.

The stop at Topeka was a welcome relief, and after about four days we were equipped with all kinds of personal flying equipment, including our own Colt .45 automatics, and declared equipped for whatever. The next leg of our travels, smoother and less nerve racking, took us to Camp Patrick Henry, brand new, in a pine forest in Virginia. It was not too many miles from Newport News and being so close to an ocean port city cast doubts on any possibility that we would fly anywhere. Sure enough, in about one week we were loaded on trucks and buses and departed for the Port of Newport News where we boarded a troop transport, the S.S. Cristobal. I think it had been a Caribbean cruise ship at one time with a capacity of possibly 500 luxury passengers. When we departed Newport News there were in excess of 5,000 troops on board.

We traveled up the East Coast to Newfoundland and became part of a pretty large convoy, including other transports, several freighters and several tankers. The tankers were slow, and 16 days elapsed before we landed in Greenock, Scotland. Canadian Corvettes gave us escort in the early part of the voyage, no escort for quite awhile, then U.S. Navy destroyers and finally RAF Coastal Patrol aircraft. There seemed to be continuous submarine alerts—sometimes as stressful as the train ride.

Upon arrival in Scotland, we were transported to a redistribution center named "Stoney" or "Stoneman." It apparently was not too far from Liverpool because John Wenzell and I hitched rides from the camp to the city in the daytime. We really got in trouble trying to get back to camp late that night in the blackout. After miles of walking we were rescued by an observant British lorry driver who recognized our uniforms and our obvious stupidity. Mind you, blackout lights on wartime lorries were not as bright as the night lights we now have for our cats by the litter box.

John Wenzell was the co-pilot on Arthur Pack's crew. They were assigned to the 562nd Squadron. John and I shared quarters at Kelly Field, Texas in August and September 1942 for pre-flight. There were 15,000 cadets at Kelly Field at that time and President Roosevelt visited, and we stood at attention in winter uniforms during his review. We were assigned the same primary flying school at Victory Field, Vernon, Texas, but did not have the same instructor. We went from primary to basic at Waco, Texas and did have the same instructor in BT-13s. We finally got to advanced at Ellington Field, Houston, Texas and again had the same instructor in AT-10s and AT-9s. We were together in the Martin Provisional Group and finally in the 388th BG.

From the redistribution center, crews were sent on their separate journeys to fill the combat-generated vacancies in the various Bomb Groups. Upon arrival at the 388th BG, the Obenschain crew was assigned to the 563rd Bomb Squadron with Major Francis (Hank) Henggeler commanding. When we entered the barracks for the aircrew officers, there were several empty bunks with luggage and possessions to be shipped to next of kin. The only crew that we were able to determine as operational was *Joho's Jokers* and they were on a three-day pass (probably because there wasn't anyone to fly with). Within one week, additional crews and aircraft arrived to bring the Squadron to strength.

In the first week of our arrival in the 563rd Squadron, our crew was assigned a B-17G model with the radical new chin turret. This was the first G model in the group and we were very proud and pleased. Within 48 hours, our engineer had located a source of steel, had it cut to his specifications, conned manpower into helping install half-inch armor plating for the pilot and co-pilot seats, a strip in the radio position, and two additional strips—one each for the waist gunners. I have no idea as to the weight, the effect upon lift and balance, but the added weight probably equated to at least one-and-a-half 500-pound bombs. Only the forgiving nature of the B-17 would allow this sort of life-saving luxury.

Our crew, after many discussions, settled on *Little Willie* as a good name for our new possession. The name was based upon a wartime military character of that time. The crew composition throughout our tour was:

| | |
|---|---|
| Lt. Richard Obenschain | Pilot |
| Lt. James Warner | Co-Pilot |
| Lt. James Ostler | Navigator |
| Lt. David Withrow | Bombardier |
| Sgt. Fredrick Austin | Engineer |
| Sgt. John Lopes | Waist |
| Sgt. Gordon Pingicer | Waist |
| Sgt. John Raney | Tail |
| Sgt. Harold Quick | Radio |
| Sgt. Frank Pasbrig | Ball |

I recall that Dick and I were from Virginia, Dave Withrow and Sgt. Fredrick Austin were from West Virginia, Jim Ostler from Chicago, Illinois, Sgt. John Raney from Texas, Sgt. Frank Pasbrig from Iowa, Sgt. John Lopes, Fall River, Massachusetts, Sgt. Gordon Pingicer, Perth Amboy, New Jersey, and Sgt. Harold Quick from Tennessee. Seemed to be a pretty good cross-section.

Dick Obenschain was an excellent pilot and aircraft commander. Regardless of the situation, he always remained calm and in control. These qualities radiated throughout the crew and provided the adhesive that bonded us together. We respected and supported each other throughout our tour and I felt fortunate and truly blessed to have been a part of it.

After about 10 days orientation practice in tight formation flying and area familiarization, we flew our first mission to Rheims, France on September 26, 1943. The mission was at medium altitude and the target was the launching ramps for the V-1 or Buzz Bomb. There was minimal fighter action and anti-aircraft activity. We thought the mission was a milk run, but the next two or three missions more than convinced us that bombing without fighter escort all the way could be very stressful and deadly. A list of our missions by number, date, target, and time per mission, is provided below:

| 1 | 9/26/43 | Rheims, France | 5:20 |
|---|---------|----------------|------|
| 2 | 9/27/43 | Emden, Germany | 5:20 |
| 3 | 10/2/43 | Emden, Germany | 6:10 |
| 4 | 10/4/43 | Frankfurt, Germany | 7:00 |
| 5 | 10/9/43 | Gdynia, Poland | 9:45 |
| 6 | 10/10/43 | Munster, Germany | 5:30 |
| 7 | 10/13/43 | Schweinfurt, Germany | 8:45 |
| 8 | 11/3/43 | Wilhelmshaven, Germany | 6:20 |
| 9 | 11/5/43 | Gelsenkirken, Germany | 6:00 |
| 10 | 11/13/43 | Bremen, Germany | 7:00 |
| 11 | 11/16/43 | Rjuken, Norway | 9:42 |
| 12 | 11/26/43 | Bremen, Germany | 7:00 |
| 13 | 12/5/43 | Bordeaux, France | 9:00 |
| 14 | 12/12/43 | Kiel, Germany | 7:30 |
| 15 | 12/22/43 | Munster, Germany | 6:20 |
| 16 | 1/4/44 | Munster, Germany | 5:30 |
| 17 | 1/5/44 | Bordeaux, France | 8:20 |

| 18 | 1/7/44 | Ludwigshaven, Germany | 7:00 |
| 19 | 1/11/44 | Bielefeld, Germany | 6:30 |
| 20 | 1/14/44 | Installations in France | 4:30 |
| 21 | 1/29/44 | Frankfurt, Germany | 6:45 |
| 22 | 1/30/44 | Brunswick, Germany | 6:30 |
| 23 | 2/3/44 | Wilhelmshaven, Germany | 7:00 |
| 24 | 2/4/44 | Frankfurt, Germany | 7:10 |
| 25 | 2/5/44 | Paris, France | 7:20 |

Reviewing the missions for our crew brings back many memories. I distinctly remember that all these missions were a mixture of prayer, terror and excitement, with either anti-aircraft fire or Luftwaffe fighters. If you add to that almost-guaranteed questionable weather, very early morning take-offs (particularly after General Doolittle assumed command) and forming a group in the dark with only flares as identification, the stress really builds up.

I note that we had a number of repeat targets and it tends to point up the early strategic bombing concept that almost lost out to political pressure from Churchill. The repeat targets were not necessarily the result of bad bombing, but the ability of the German military and industry to recover.

Some examples: Bremen, FW-190 plant bombed twice in two weeks; Munster, important rail junction bombed three times in two months; Emden, port city bombed twice in one week; Wilhelmshaven, naval installations bombed twice in three months; and Frankfurt, chemical factories bombed three times in four months.

We had some fighter escort on the medium-time missions, but the longer ones were a different story. Gdynia, Poland was almost a 10-hour mission with most of it over the North Sea, but in some areas close enough to the coast to get fighter attacks.

The mission to Schweinfurt on October 13, 1943 is a real contrast between official reports and my memory of what happened.

We were briefed that we could expect 10/10 cloud cover for most of the route which would provide some flak and fighter protection. Near the target area the cloud cover would drop to 5/10 cover and almost clear over the target. I remember the scene as heavy clouds while we assembled. When we reached our altitude the cloud cover had disappeared and it seemed we could see Schweinfurt from the English Channel. The 388th was the last group in the bomber force and we could see fighters well in front of us rising to attack. There were ground-to-air missiles, air-to-air missiles and flak. Luftwaffe fighters were extremely aggressive and the loss of B-17s was all too obvious. When we arrived over the target the attacks let up and we dropped our bombs and started our return leg. We sustained no battle damage and the group lost no aircraft directly from enemy action, except for one aircraft that ditched in the channel on the return leg. We think we got by while most of the fighters were refueling and rearming.

Rjuken, Norway was another almost 10-hour mission. I remember it because Col. David had used *Little Willie* on a mission to Bordeaux, France and our aircraft had been badly damaged. On the Rjuken mission we used another aircraft without a name but it did have bullet proof glass in the cockpit. Unfortunately, the heaters in the cockpit did not work, so we took turns going down to the nose and using the bombsight's electrically heated blanket to warm our legs. The target was a heavy water plant related to German atomic research.

Our two missions to Bordeaux, France, hit the long-range Luftwaffe aircraft that attacked and harassed ocean shipping in the Bay of Biscay. These missions were long and hectic with significant fighter attacks both to and from the target and at the target area itself.

One other mission I remember well is Bielefeld. This location was a secondary target and I'm not sure any of the aircrews were ever briefed that it was a school for advanced anti-aircraft gunners. It was a surprise.

Throughout our tour there were no Purple Hearts awarded to any member of our crew. We had minimal aircraft damage during our flying and we missed only one scheduled mission. We aborted for an engine failure shortly after take-off. On this abort we had a load of 500-pound bombs, but were not allowed to drop them in The Wash (the usual procedure). We flew around East Anglia with one engine out for three hours to use up fuel before landing at Knettishall with a full bomb load.

The Obenschain crew and *Little Willie* flew and fought efficiently for 25 missions. I am still amazed when I remember flying through walls and boxes of flak and returning to base without battle damage. I will be continually grateful that we were blessed with guidance, strength and protection during this period.

# Bringing *Little Willie* Home

By Bernard Dopko, pilot, 561st Squadron

*Little Willie's flight home from combat was immortalized in a famous painting by Keith Ferris titled "Little Willie Coming Home." This is the story of that March 6, 1944 flight, told on audio tape by Bernie Dopko, the pilot who brought Little Willie back. Dopko died in 1991.*

The mission started off badly. When they took us out to the plane, the first thing I noticed was that the de-icer boots were missing. I asked the crew chief what the problem was and he said that they had been replacing them, but since this was a maximum effort, they hadn't had a chance to put them back on, and the plane was going to go anyway.

I contacted the engineering officer—rather I contacted his tent—and he was gone, so I called the tower. The CO, who was Col. David, happened to be there. He asked me if I'd been to briefing and I told him yes.

"Well," he said, "didn't you hear that the weather is going to be unlimited visibility and it will be cloudless? The upper air temperature and conditions are not expected to cause any icing." He suggested that take-off was going to be in about 25 minutes and I had best get with it.

Being a 2nd Lieutenant, I said, "yes sir," and hung up the phone.

We took off without incident, formed up and I think we had about 21 planes from the 388th. We formed up with the 96th. We crossed the coast of France and continued on into the border of Germany. There was very little flak, and, it was true, it was cloudless; the visibility was just unlimited. In fact, the mission went without a hitch.

We had P-51s for escorts. That was the first time that they had escorted us, and it was very comforting to see them circling high overhead; they were in a group way, way off to our right. There was no problem; we made the bomb run. But just coming off the target there was heavy flak and we

216

took a jolt right underneath. It was hard enough that there was this whoomph and the right wing just lifted up. The co-pilot yelled that Number 3 was losing oil pressure and in Number 4 the manifold pressure was dropping. So I told him to feather both of them. He hit both buttons and, by gosh, they feathered quick. Number 3 we could see had thrown oil all over the wing and all over the elevator.

The tail gunner called back and said, "are we still with it?" or, "what's wrong?" I told everybody to hang in, we were trying to get back in formation. But it was impossible on just two engines. We were falling behind rapidly. About that time fighters hit the group ahead of us. They swept through the group, attacking head-on, and came right back by us. They didn't attack us at that point, but instead wound beyond, about four of them, wheeled up in a loop, and the tail gunner called up that they were coming in dead level at 6 o'clock. Just about the second I heard him, the upper turret and both waist gunners cut loose. Just a few seconds later, the airplane shuddered about three times, and I knew we'd been hit again. The waist gunner called out that the tail gunner had been hit, and that we had a pretty big hole in the tail, right over the waist. I told him to go back to the tail gunner and get him out of there. About that time the tail gunner called back and said that he was "pretty good," and that he was going to stay. And he called out again—he said, "here they come again"—and I could hear him cut loose; the top turret and the tail, and the ball turret—all of them were firing.

Well, the tail gunner got one of the fighters. He whipped right on his back and went straight down, trailing heavy smoke. Then they broke off. I told the guys that we were under control, that we had two engines out and that I was just going to hang on because, I thought to myself, "I'm going to take this thing down to the ground." I put her in a very steep spiral, a bank; about that same time, two fighters passed right over the cockpit. What had happened was, just when I put her in a steep bank they were lining up on us, and I turned right out of their line of fire.

Anyway, we got down to the deck. It was low clouds, about 2,000 feet, and a thin haze down there. We broke out of that, and we were still over Berlin. The navigator called out several landmarks. He picked up the main autobahn that was heading west and gave me a heading for England and we just followed that at about 100 feet. We were sailing down that and, I don't know how we lost the autobahn, but all of a sudden this church steeple was right ahead of us and I had to lift the wing to get over it. I told the co-pilot to give a little more boost and—we talked about this later— we were probably about 38-40 inches; I figured that was about as much as we could do, and I got it up about 200-250 feet.

I told the co-pilot to start fiddling with Number 4, because we didn't know what was wrong with it. Number 3 was gone, but, "try and restart Number 4." In the meantime, we continued almost straight west. We were out over farmland. There was occasional ground fire. We could see one truck in particular stopped and there were some infantry men who raised their rifles at us as we went by. The bombardier got right out in the nose with a pair of binoculars and he was sweeping the horizon continually; that's one of the things that helped us get home. To avoid towns and to avoid what looked like trucks and military things, we would go out around them as best we could. In fact, we went out around a little village and we could see some tanks outside that little village. In the meantime, the co-pilot, by gosh, he got Number 4 going. We learned later what had happened is that we took a piece of flak right through the intercooler and it wrecked the turbo induction. That's why we lost our boost, and at down low she worked fine.

Well, heck, with three engines, we kept her right down on the deck anyway because things were just going too good. If we got up high, some fighter might find us. And we got clear into Belgium, and were going into Holland, when all of a sudden in Number 4, the cylinder head temperature went way off the scale and we started to lose oil pressure, so we had to feather it. We kind of regretted that we didn't get as much altitude as we could when we had three engines, but anyway…

Then we really started to sink low and, by the time we got to the Dutch coast, we really were at 100 feet. And right up ahead there was a gun emplacement at a military encampment of some kind and 40mms cut loose. We could see their tracers arcing right back towards us. Well, they gave us enough time. I flipped that thing to the power side on the left and we actually were low enough that we put a sand dune between the guns and ourselves and sailed out over the Channel.

We got down to as low as 50 feet over the Channel, but I mentioned to the co-pilot, "I think we can take what's left," and we just agreed. So we put her up there almost full boost. We were pulling about 40-42 inches. At that time, you know, 45-46 was supposedly maximum for no more than five minutes. We'd been pulling almost full boost for almost two-and-a-half hours now; maybe three hours. That just shows you what those old engines would do for us.

Anyhow, we got over England. You know, it's a straight shot in over that flat land there—down from The Wash and Kings Lynn, down through there—and we were going right towards Honington, which was a big repair depot. We almost decided to go in there, but Knettishall was just a few minutes more and all of a sudden there it was. I just made one sweep of the field, came in straight on, fired a couple of flares telling them we had this wounded tail gunner on board. By the way, he was hurt pretty bad. He later got a Silver Star for that. He was wounded and stayed in the tail, and we really credit him for helping to chase the fighters off.

But we landed without incident. Golly, we got to checking the plane over and we had the elevator surface—we had a hole in there as big as two basketballs; just enormous—and holes in the rudder, and in the nacelles of Numbers 3 and 4, which caused the damage. They weren't very big holes there, but the flak just went right straight in and cut the oil line, cut the turbo intercoolers and cut the turbo boost pipe. We had a great big chunk out of the tire on the right hand side. We had a pretty good-sized hole back of the radio room.

Many, many B-17s came home on two engines, but they didn't happen to be written up like ours was. But you know, the real story of this is, the 388th lost six or seven planes that day; and the ground crews of those planes had really nothing to do. And the ground crew right next to *Little Willie* had lost their plane. So they set to work repairing *Little Willie*. In fact, we weren't on the ground a half-hour and they had the cowlings off and were stripping down and taking those engines off. They replaced all four engines, they replaced the rudder, the elevator on that side, the turbos and the intercoolers on 3 and 4. The rudder cable and the elevator cable were replaced. You see, I came back with full left rudder and full trim. And they got in there when they were replacing the elevator, which a piece of flak had gone right through the rudder hinge, and so they started to adjust her up with light tension and they couldn't get it, I guess. It had just been pulled out. Anyway, they replaced it. I betcha they worked 36 hours straight, those two crews, spelling each other.

Well, when you put new engines on, of course, they're slow-timed, as they were called then. You put about four or five hours time on them. The new crews in the group usually do that, and the new crew flew it for that length of time, about a day-and-a-half afterwards. I asked the pilot how she was and he said, "She just flies pretty sweet," so, hmmm, that's the last thing in the world I wanted to hear. But anyway…

On the third day, we flew again and this time it was back to Berlin. Only this time we were not as lucky. Again, just after the target, there was a burst right nearby. It didn't seem like it was that close. But it caught an oil line, I think, and part of the gas tank, because all of a sudden we had flames pouring out behind Number 3. We were trailing flames clear back to the elevator. Gosh, the co-pilot yelled that out and I hit the bail-out bell, and the bombardier opened the bomb bays, and all the guys left.

I stayed for just a few seconds longer; I took it down 2,000-3,000 feet, thinking I could put the fire out, because sometimes that happened. I put it on auto and got back to the bomb bay, and the flames were already burning there and boy, I jumped—I just got out of that baby.

My chute opened at about 2,000 feet. I wasn't picked up immediately; I walked for about a day-and-a-half before I was captured while the rest of the fellows were captured right away.

We were POWs for about a year-and-a-half—let's see, March through May of the following year. But everybody survived. Nobody was injured.

And we did spend a little time as guests of the Luftwaffe.

# A View From the Tower

By James Flynn, controller

Eighty of us were sent off on a secret mission to England early in the war.

The only thing we had in common was that we were all washed-out cadets—washed out for all sorts of reasons, from physicals to advance training. And, we all had applied for OCS and had been accepted.

The ranks were corporal to master sergeant. We were sent to RAF bases for a couple of weeks' orientation in operating a Control Tower, then off to a remote RAF school in the boondocks. It was a tough program; Morse Code, weather, navigation, lots of night flying, etc. Fifty percent flunked the courses and got reassigned. We used the RAF radio control and language. When we passed, we were made second lieutenants and sent to an RAF base.

Their officers lived well—bat women, chits, waited on at table, beds made, etc. The ironic thing was, they had "flying pilots" (no co-pilots in their bombers) who were sergeants (didn't attend the "right" school). Often their bombardiers and navigators weren't officers. We really needled the RAF on this score. We enjoyed the experience.

There was some resentment of us. An American corporal made as much as a British captain.

Their brass often questioned me about the effect of the Yanks' daylight bombing effort. In later years they were considerably impressed. When a few old RAF friends came to visit at Knettishall in later years they commented on how we flew twice as many missions as they did in a given month regardless of weather, and on the overall efficiency of our operation.

We were released to the 8th Air Force after a couple of months. They were short of controllers.

Knettishall was somewhat chaotic in the first month it opened, but the energy and general smarts of the personnel got us functioning efficiently very soon. There was a lieutenant colonel in charge of ground operations who got things done. He improved the food, improved the roads, built NCO and officer clubs, organized the Gremlin Band for dances—they were good—found a way to get black market booze in London, brought in girls with a special truck brigade from the nearby towns for dances—he knew what the guys wanted.

The tower was a special place. All the brass from Division and Headquarters would come there as the planes would be returning from a mission. We usually knew the extent of losses and damage from radio reports. We had to have the crash crews ready, ambulances, etc. One could see the pressure from the Operations people.

Early in the war, we lost more than two-thirds of our planes on one mission. They flew on a milk run the next day with another bomb group, then stood down until we got replacements in a few days. At one time those in the tower, early in the war, were reluctant to make friends with the air crews, so many of them were lost.

It was tough on the nerves. We operated 24 hours a day, seven days a week. Four crews. The GIs where sharp, dedicated to their jobs.

I remember one senior officer who was doing circuits and bumps (landings and take-offs) when my runway van gave him a red light as he was landing, requiring him to go around again. The pilot got me on the RT Control and demanded to know why I shot a small flare up and used the flashing red light at the beginning of the runway.

I said, "Your wheels were not down."

"Roger! Roger, meckul control!" was his response.

Later, he ran over to me at the Officers' Club and said, "Please, please keep this quiet."

We always did, and we got along famously with the air crews. These guys were doing the real job.

# The Year I Can't Forget

By James E. O'Connor, co-pilot
*La-Dee-Doo* crew, 560th Squadron

*The following is excerpted from the author's work, "The Year I Can't Forget."*

## March 2, 1944

The B-17 crew of Lauren D. Porter, later also to be known as the *La-Dee-Doo,* first met formally on a Sunday afternoon shortly after arriving at Ardmore Army Air Force Base, Oklahoma. It was a warm, sunny, early spring day, a welcome change from the Rocky Mountain snow squalls. We met and shook hands outside of a tarpaper barracks near the flightline. We were all dressed in our Class A uniforms with ties, insignia, wings, etc., but without blouses or coats due to the unseasonably warm weather. Fortunately, one of the crew members brought a camera and took several snapshots of the crew. These are the only known photos of the entire group together.

• Pilot L.D. Porter was from Canby, Oregon, age 22, married with a child named Kenny; tall, wiry, amiable. He worked at Boeing Aircraft in Seattle early in the war making B-17 Flying Fortresses, the ship he was destined to fly.

• Me, Co-Pilot Jim O'Connor, a.k.a. "Big Jim" for my small stature; hometown, Oak Park, Illinois. One of four crew members who were 19 years old at the time. I was attending De Paul University in Chicago before entering the Army Air Force.

• Navigator Bill Moell, a.k.a. "Snuffy," was a native of Elko, Nevada, recently married, attended the University of Utah and moonlighted by driving a big semi-truck on weekends between Salt Lake City and Denver.

He transferred to the Air Force from a mule-pack gunnery outfit, and hence was also known as "The Mule Skinner." He became a Group Lead Navigator, but hung out and went on pass with our crew.

• Bombardier Wally Koseluk was of Russian-Polish background, a high school teacher from Oswego, New York. At about 6' 3" and 225 pounds, he was the tallest member of the crew and maybe the biggest bombardier in the 8th Air Force. Familiarly know as "Koz," he was single with lots of girlfriends.

• Engineer Nick DiMartino was a native of Pittsburgh and had previous combat duty in the Pacific before joining our crew. Slight of stature, agile, friendly, polite and smiling, Nick knew every inch of the B-17 with all its functions and possible malfunctions. Constantly active and alert in the air, his knowledge and experience saved us on more than one occasion.

• Radio operator Larry Hildebrecht was a high school music teacher from North Dakota. He was handsome and neat in appearance with a dapper Clark Gable mustache. He was well-built and a physical fitness buff, holding the record for the most sit-ups at a large Air Force training base. Like the pilot and navigator, Harry was recently married.

• Ball turret gunner Bill Malley was from Providence, Rhode Island. At age 25, he was the senior member of the crew, and had been a sergeant in the Army before transferring to the Army Air Force. Thus, he was given some respect and was a stabilizing influence on the younger gunners. He had some previous navigational training and ended up as the crew's navigator when Bill Moell became a Group Navigator.

• Harvey Cohen was one of our two waist gunners and one of the four 19-year-old crew members. A native of Philadelphia, he had a cheerful, upbeat, friendly personality. In later life he became Deputy Chief of Detectives in Philadelphia.

• The other waist gunner was Wally Blumenthal, also age 19, and a native of Chicago. After a few missions, Wally was assigned to ground duties when the 8th Air Force decided to drop one of the two waist gunners. However, he remained associated with the crew, going on monthly pass with us to London, as did Bill Moell.

• B A Webb, age 19, was the tail gunner and was a native of Columbus, Mississippi, the only Southerner on the crew. He was good-natured and had a drawl as thick as molasses. Like some Southerners, he had no names other than his surname and two initials. He answered to B A, which didn't stand for anything in particular.

And that was the original crew of the *La-Dee-Doo.*

*Lt. James O'Connor*

## May 18, 1944

On this date our crew left Ardmore, Oklahoma on a troop train bound for the 271st Staging Base, Kearney, Nebraska. We arrived at the flattest piece of land on the face of the earth, perfect for an air base. We spent about a week there getting last minute combat orientation lectures and being assigned a brand new silver B-17G. We were to fly it across the wide Atlantic to an unknown destiny somewhere in the skies over Europe. The drama and significance of the step we were about to take was mounting in our young lives. A grizzled U.S. Air Force officer, a veteran of the ill-fated Polish Air Force and the RAF during the Battle of Britain, tried to inject some serious reality into us 19 and 20-year-old buoyant Americans. In a thick Polish accent, he addressed the auditorium of combat-bound airmen.

"You young kids just thinking of having a smoke and a coke! Look to yer right and look to yer left. Only one out of the three of you is coming back alive. War is hell. I know, because I haf been dere!"

We laughed and nudged our friends to left and right, but the fact of the matter was that by mid-summer 1944, only one out of three 8th Air Force crewmen survived.

## May 28, 1944

It was just at sunset that our crew took off from Newfoundland and headed out over the vast Atlantic. Darkness was already falling in the east, and it seemed symbolic of the dark unknown world and uncertain future into which we were entering. A pleasant feminine voice came from Gander air tower, that of a young Canadian WAAF (Women's Auxiliary Air Force) presenting the customary departing information—air temperature, altimeter setting, wind direction, etc. She ended with a warm friendly touch not common among our American tower personnel: "Goodbye and good luck." And at that moment of leaving our homeland and flying into the dark unknown, it felt as though somebody cared.

As Lauren put the ship on automatic pilot, and we checked all the gauges and dimmed the cockpit lights, I switched over to the crew intercom with a somewhat lonely feeling.

"Where the hell are the candy bars?"

"Hey, guys; Wally's sacked out already!"

And I realized we were all together in this thing, and that we would live or die together. It was a comforting feeling.

Most of the crew soon settled down into their individual warm cocoons and drifted off to sleep. The pilot, co-pilot, navigator and engineer, however, were to stand guard duty all through the night. Also, Bill Malley, our ball turret gunner with navigational training, was to keep company with navigator Bill Moell in the nose throughout the whole voyage. Little did we realize that he would soon be our regular navigator for our complete combat tour, a most unusual situation. Koz, the bombardier, who also had some navigational training, came down with a painful migraine sinus problem. He spent the whole trip bundled up and sleeping on top of the crews' baggage stowed in the bomb bay.

The night gradually wore on, and Lauren and I kept silent vigil, lulled by the constant droning of the engine. Occasionally, Nick, the engineer, would hand up a candy bar as he kept close track of the fuel level in the tanks. About the only occasional intercom talk now was between the navigator and the pilot. The weather had closed in from above and below, and Snuffy was unable to get a celestial navigational fix on his sextant to verify our position. Dead reckoning was his only option, and a switch in the winds could play some strange tricks. In the meantime, the weather turned foul, and we passed through several rain, snow and sleet squalls. Apparently the controls felt a bit mushy to Lauren, and he switched on the bright landing lights. Sure enough, ice was forming on the wings, a potentially dangerous situation adding to both the weight of the ship and the distortion of the airflow over the leading edges of the wings. Fortunately, Lauren was able to activate the de-icers in the wings. Rubber boots or tubes began to expand and contract, and the ice began to crack up. In earlier days, those de-icers were removed in the States before flight to the ETO because they could be a hazard in combat. However, when some ships disappeared over the stormy Atlantic, the de-icers were retained.

When the 388th Bomb Group, our future combat unit, was transferring to the ETO, a ship was lost, probably due to icing conditions.

We eventually flew through the weather and about 600 miles out at sea we picked up the Allied radio homing beacon from Derneycross, North Ireland. It was a friendly, welcoming sound, and we could safely home into our destination, right? Wrong! We had been strongly warned that the Germans often "bent" or deflected the beam, luring, like an enticing mermaid, unsuspecting crews to an icy fate in the waters north of the British Isles.

However, as the brilliant morning sun flashed into our eyes, we looked down on the greenest, most lush and beautiful land we had ever seen. Just then our Irishman, Bill Malley, popped his head up from the nose passageway and shouted, "There it is, Holy Ireland!"

Home was the sailor, home from the sea. And the cares of the long stormy flight disappeared like a dream in the night.

## June 6, 1944, D-Day

On this day, perhaps one of the most fateful in World War II, if not in the modern history of the world, we were awakened by the roar of hundreds of aircraft flying low overhead. The time was about 5:30 a.m. They were all heading south beneath a ragged overcast. The heavy bombers were undoubtedly above the overcast with their fighter support. But the ships we saw, which we could almost reach up and touch, were the ones that riveted our attention. These were the endless multitude of C-46s and C-47s, flying singly or towing large gliders filled with airborne or paratroopers. Wave after wave swept over as we glanced at our watches to ascertain zero hour. Immediately, we knew that this was the long-anticipated invasion of France, the opening of the second front, the Big Dance that the world was waiting for. We also knew that the lads flying a few hundred feet above us would in a few minutes be in the thick of it. And for many, D-Day would be their last day.

June 6, 1944 was also my 20th birthday.

That evening my buddies had to hoist a few to commemorate the two major events. They all inscribed their names on my tie along with the fateful D-Day date. Also, that night we were introduced to another phenomenon of war, the V-1 or Buzz Bomb.

We were at a base near Bovington undergoing training prior to assignment to a bombardment group. Around midnight, a few hours into our sleep following an eventful day, the air raid sirens began to wail. To this day, I find it the most haunting of sounds and memorable of the war. We threw on our clothes and jackets and were herded into nearby air raid shelters. We soon learned that it was more of a precautionary measure than the possibility of a direct bombing attack. The military authorities were somewhat jumpy, weighing the possibility of a German counter-attack by air. Earlier that day we were all issued .45-caliber automatics that we carried at all times. After awhile of cautious appraisal, we climbed up on top of the bomb shelters and surveyed the night sky. Off in the distance toward London we could see the prowling searchlight beams and the bursts of anti-aircraft shells. The low rumble of flak guns rolled over the countryside. We were to learn that it was not a raid by conventional German bombers, but an entirely new weapon, the Buzz Bomb or V-1. The V-1 was a pilot-less robot; a 1,000-pound bomb powered by a conventional engine and targeted toward cities and installations in southern England, especially London. It was more of a terror weapon than one of strategic military value, but with Hitler and his constant threats of a "secret weapon" one was never sure. Our government leaders also knew that the world race was on for an awesome super weapon, the atomic bomb, though the ordinary citizen and soldier were mercifully unaware.

So, our remaining few nights at Bovington were spent trying to catch a little sleep on mattresses spread on the cold concrete bomb shelter floor. But several miles east of us, English families were huddled together in basements and air raid shelters, while less than 100 miles to the south, men were dying on the beaches and along the hedgerows of Normandy. So, we didn't complain.

## June 10, 1944

Our week at Bovington was up, and we again boarded a small but efficient English train and headed north into East Anglia. Our destination was the 388th Bomb Group. We had a short layover at the university city of Cambridge, so we walked through the picturesque town. The summer break was underway, but even if classes were in session, the wartime enrollment must have been quite small. Like us young American college kids, the British lads were far from their classrooms and cricket fields, fighting the war all over the world. It was for a noble cause, and it was simply our destiny, our karma.

Ultimately our crew got off the train at a city named Thetford, the closest station to our air base. We boarded GI trucks with our luggage and raced through the five miles of countryside to the 388th. Our familiar training companions from the States were now reduced to but two 10-men crews, L.D. Porter's crew (ours) and Paulsen's crew. Paulsen was a young, good-natured Scandinavian farm lad from North Dakota, who grew up during the Dust Bowl days and, for two years, survived on little but turnips. There was a suave Bostonian bombardier we called "Boston Blackie" and a navigator named Alan Goldman, a.k.a. "Goldie," a native of Far Rockaway, New York. Goldie was probably the biggest joker I ever knew in the service. It was a fun crew, and we were glad to have them along as buddies.

Knettishall, after which the base was named, was perhaps a thriving farm village several centuries ago. However, it was now but a remote crossroads and a heath or wasteland with patches of woods here and there. The village had a row of stone cottages whose housewives did our laundry for a few shillings and a bar of soap. It also had a deserted medieval church and one pub, which had a couple of wooden benches and one keg of nut brown ale.

The squadron's Quonset barracks and bomb shelters were dispersed around the base for camouflage purposes. The 560th, our unit, was flush next to the village, and we had but to climb over a stone wall to be on Main Street. From the air, it looked like part of the town. The local farmers farmed the land all around us, and a haystack with a herd of Holstein milk cows was right outside our barracks door. A field of beautiful red poppies carpeted the pastureland during the summer and early autumn.

When our humble, rookie, *La-Dee-Doo* Purple Heart Corner crew settled into the 388th Bomb Group at Knettishall, we started once again at the bottom rung of the ladder. The four officers were assigned two double-decked bunks at the far end of the barracks. We were informed that the empty bunks we were taking over belonged to a crew shot down a couple of days before. The enlisted men, our six gunners, were assigned to a similar Quonset hut adjacent to us. The quarters were separate but equal as regards lack of facilities. We soon found out there was an invisible but real pecking order among the barracks' inmates. It revolved around the number of missions each person and crew had flown. Lt. Bonacelli's crew was finishing up their tour of duty about the time we arrived. His navigator, Bill Kruger from Milwaukee, later became a good friend of mine as he stayed on as an intelligence debriefer following missions. I can still see Bonacelli's elated face as he prepared to celebrate the completion of his last mission with his crew. "San Francisco will never be the same after I get back," he chortled. And I believed him. He and his crew were survivors.

If a certain crew had one more mission than another, the former got respect. The standard good-natured putdown of disdain was, "Get some (missions) in, Rookie!"

To put our crew in perspective, at its peak in mid-summer 1944, the 8th Air Force had over 200,000 men, with 40 bomb groups and 15 fighter groups. One of those heavy bomb groups was the 388th, a self-sufficient unit of some 3,000 men. Our group was comprised of four squadrons of

12 crews each. Each bomb group usually put up 36 ships in a normal maximum effort mission.

A typical mission in 1944 consisted of over 1,400 bombers, B-17s and B-24s; and 800 fighters, mostly P-51s and P-47s. By late December of 1944, a maximum effort consisted of 2,000 four-engine bombers. From 1943 to April 1945, the end of the war in the ETO, the 8th Air Force suffered 40,456 casualties, with 30,000 killed and 26,000 prisoners of war. These were America's best and finest.

Of the 450 combat crews to pass through the 388th Bomb Group, 138 were missing in action, over 200 completed their tour, and some 100 rookie crews returned to the States following the end of the war in Europe.

At the time, however, as we stowed our barracks bags at the foot of our bunks, our destiny as regards the above statistics had not yet been fulfilled. So we looked forward to a cloudy, ominous future with a curious mixture of reasonably high morale, sense of doing our duty and resignation to our fate. It simply was our karma to defend our people and confront a great evil engulfing the world. Yes, Virginia, it was all worth it, and the human family survived as it is because of the sacrifices of these forgotten nameless ones. "Greater love than this no one has, that he lay down his life for his friends."

## June 12, 1944

Gradually, the crew settled in and became accustomed to the life and daily routine of the 388th Bomb Group. The 388th was probably a typical example of the 40 bomb groups comprising the 8th Air Force. We began daily training flights, long hours of formation flying with other rookie crews under the guidance of former combat pilots. One of them was a happy-go-lucky captain from Florida named Ken Pentent, with whom I became good friends. He had a Limey girlfriend who was a school teacher in a nearby town. After a long monotonous afternoon of practice flying, he would reward us by flying down the town's main street and letting the girl know he was still thinking of her.

The night before he left to return to the States, we had a last drink together at the Officers' Club bar. We tore a ten-shilling note in two and each of us wrote a message on a half, which we exchanged. I wrote the lines of a World War II ballad: "We'll meet again; don't know where, don't know when…" And he wrote on his half: "Be sure and get there before the bar closes." However, our paths were never to cross again.

We attended various ground school classes, including the Link Trainer instrument flying sessions designed especially for the pilots. The reality was that the majority of crews who were lost in combat went down during their first five or eight missions. Thus, experience and training were of the utmost importance.

The chow at the big consolidated mess hall, while nothing fancy, was substantial and sufficient. We were, after all, in a combat zone and all of our food had to be shipped over from the States. A typical dinner consisted of canned stew, white rice and stewed tomatoes, sopped up with homemade bread. There was also plenty of Spam, orange marmalade, tomato juice, powdered milk and powdered eggs.

We also familiarized ourselves with the recreational facilities of the base, including a bona fide movie theater showing nightly films or hosting traveling USO shows. The rose-colored felt seats came from a bombed out cinema in London, and I think our supply of Scotch came from the same place. It was inevitably Johnny Walker Red Label. The 388th Officers' Club was proud of having the longest bar in the ETO—42 feet. It was a rough-hewn, western-style log bar extending the length of one wall of a large Quonset hut. A large oil painting of a reclining nude, tastefully done, plus three mounted deer heads, provided the decor. A sign identified it as "Commanche Joe's Saloon." The entire club, two Quonset huts in the form of a T, was unpretentious but cozy and functional. A couple of pool tables and some big, well-worn stuffed chairs before a large open fireplace helped to while away a rainy day. A big painting of B-17s and the

Statue of Liberty over the hearth carried the motto of the 388th—
"Fortress for Freedom."

The enlisted men and noncoms, of course, had their own watering
holes with which they were happy. All in all, it was a busy, efficient little
town, where everyone happily went about his business doing his particular
job. Everyone had an essential function to perform, from the cooks to the
combat crews to the long-suffering ground crews who worked day and
night, sleeping in tents on the flightline with their particular beloved
bomber. The latter were the unsung heroes of the war.

As with all front-line combat units, military discipline was reasonably
relaxed, morale was high, flying efficient and everyone was gung ho to win
the war, survive and return home.

## July 4, 1944—Independence Day—Mission Number One

After months of flight training, ground school, travel and anticipation,
the opening day of the World Series, the Super Bowl, the Big Dance, had
finally arrived for L.D. Porter's crew, a.k.a. *The La-Dee-Doo*. It began like
most of our 35 missions were to begin. At approximately midnight the duty
sergeant, a big pleasant former gunner from North Carolina, quietly entered
the barracks and shone a flashlight on a roster in his hand. He spoke softly
as he aimed the flashlight beam into the face of each crew member scheduled to fly that day. "Loo-tenant, wake up. Y'all are flying today."

He slowly worked his way the length of the Quonset hut, skipping a
relieved crew here and there who were getting the day off. He finally
arrived at our corner, and we were up, into our long underwear, woolen
uniforms, flight suits and A-2 leather jackets in a couple of minutes.

We rode swiftly down the hill from our 560th Squadron site on bicycles, with the cool damp night air clearing our brains. But always there
was a coldness in our bones, even in summer. Into the chow line at the
mess hall ambled sleepy-eyed aircrew in all manner of uniform and flight

gear. The big deal before a mission was two real eggs for breakfast, instead of the mushy powdered eggs. They were cold storage eggs from the States and of some antiquity. Occasionally a sleepy-eyed chick would look up at you. After breakfast, we loaded into GI trucks which raced through the darkness and disgorged us in front of the briefing room on the flightline. Usually, 36 crews, 360 airmen plus the CO, a few intelligence, weather and auxiliary officers, looked up at a stage containing a covered, wall-sized map of England and northern Europe. A cord was pulled, and the chart, route and destination of the day's mission were unveiled. A low murmur of anticipation would arise from the audience. If it were a deep penetration mission, e.g. to Berlin, Leipzig or Schweinfurt, there would be a groan of wonderment, plus some graveyard humor. The briefing officer would proceed to give the necessary information, routes in and out, nature of the target, German opposition, rendezvous times, etc. The weather officer gave his meteorology report, and the briefing would end with the synchronization of watches.

On this, our first mission, we were assigned to aircraft 42-37787-R, #787. The target was a railroad bridge southeast of Paris, at Sully-Sur-Roine, France. The object was to cut off rail supplies and reinforcements to the enemy troops fighting in Normandy. We carried two 2,000-pound bombs, the largest the B-17 could handle. We were one of 12 aircraft in our squadron that was to lead the 45th Combat Wing (three groups with a total of around 110 bombers). Altogether, the 8th Air Force put up 600 bombers this day. The Lead Pilot was Lt. Col. Chester Cox, the Deputy CO of the 388th, and his back-up was Lt. Bonacelli from our barracks, probably on his last mission. As a rookie crew, we were flying Tail End Charlie. Take-off time was 4 a.m., the crack of dawn.

At approximately 2 a.m., the main briefing with total personnel present concluded. There followed individual specialized briefings for the pilots, navigators and bombardiers. The gunners headed out to the ships to install their .50-caliber guns. At around 3 a.m., the briefings all ended, and each crew member had a particular duty to perform. The co-pilot's job was to procure the crew's parachutes and escape kits. Between times, the Catholic group stopped off at a makeshift chapel on the flightline where the chaplain administered the sacraments and gave a farewell blessing. The Protestant and Jewish flyers probably had similar arrangements. After the tasks were all completed and the ship checked over, there was usually a wait of a half-hour or more before take-off time. The crew gathered around the stove in the ground crew tent and either dozed off on the cots or had a last smoke. Everyone was usually alone with their own thoughts.

At 4 a.m., as the first streaks of dawn appeared in the eastern sky, a green flare shot up from the control tower: Start engines. A tremendous roar filled the night from 134 powerful 1,200 hp engines. Then, a second flare to start taxing out to the runway for take-off. One by one, the heavily laden ships waddled up to take-off position. After the magnetos were checked and tail wheel locked, Lauren and I looked at one another and at Nick DiMartino, propped between us with his hands on the throttles full forward. The pilot gave the nod, released the brakes, and we roared down the runway. The excitement of that moment of take-off never diminished.

On a maximum effort mission, it would take some two hours for the 8th Air Force to form over England. We would fly in a big lazy climbing circle until the last ship, squadron, group and wing were in position in the bomber stream, around 1,400 B-17s and 24s in the summer of 1944. Finally, we'd head out over the North Sea or toward the continent and climb to altitude. The gunners practice-fired their guns, and we got on oxygen and put on steel flak helmets at 10,000 feet. Every 10 minutes or so we had an oxygen check with each crew member reporting in to the co-pilot.

On this, our first mission, we crossed the French coast at Dieppe and waist gunner Harvey Cohen reported the first flak coming up from the German anti-aircraft batteries. We were all curious to see what it looked like up close.

As we approached the target area, the weather unexpectedly closed in, 10/10 complete cloud coverage. Hence, we had to return to England with our bombs. It was disappointing not to have accomplished our mission, but we had received our baptism of fire and got credit for Mission Number One. Only 34 more to go.

At the debriefing by an intelligence officer, the crew hunched around a table with a smoke, a cup of hot cocoa and a good shot of bourbon supplied by the medics. None of us had ever celebrated the Fourth of July like this before.

## July 10, 1944

Our crew had been in the ETO for six weeks now, and we had our baptism of fire, completing three combat missions. So the time came for our first pass, leave or furlough. The custom in the 388th was for each crew to get a 48-hour pass once a month, a break from the seven-day-a-week combat grind. And almost inevitably, they would head for bombed-out, war-weary, shabby London—like lemmings head for the sea. That was where the crews unwound, forgot the war for a couple of days, bolstered their morale and cemented their camaraderie.

There was little if any distinction between officers and enlisted men on the crew of the *La-Dee-Doo*. There was a mutual respect, and we were on a first name basis. Each man had an essential job to perform for the good of all, and our lives depended upon it. In the air, especially in combat, the pilot's word was law and there was no disputing it like in the Hollywood movies.

Altogether, most of our crew went on pass to London about four times. The first thing we did on our initial trip was to engage two ancient but meticulously preserved World War I-vintage taxis to take us on a tour of London Town. Two jovial Limey taxi drivers honked their way through the London traffic and confusion and gave us a poor man's historical tour of a city that was old before America was discovered. The sites included Westminster Abbey, Christopher Wren's magnificent St. Paul's Cathedral (about the only building left standing in the bombed-out center of London), the famous London Bridge and the prestigious government buildings. And all the while we kept our eyes and ears pealed for the V-1 robot bombs which came over at irregular intervals night and day. We usually stayed at the Regent Palace Hotel overlooking Picadilly Circus in the heart of London. All the windows had been blown out of one side of the building and were replaced by wooden shutters. However, the main ritual on each pass was the gathering of the crew for a sumptuous (for wartime England) spaghetti dinner at an Italian restaurant on Charlotte Street in the industrial area. Berterelli's was the best-kept secret of 388th bomber crews in World War II. Our 10-man crew would file into the restaurant to the curiosity of the Limey patrons, put three tables together, place a bottle of Chianti on each table, then systematically attack a five course meal or so, as smiling Italian waiters in frayed tuxedos flitted around filling glasses.

Another vivid memory of London consisted of the evenings we took the tube (or underground subway), to the enormous dance hall known as Covent Garden, an opera house dating back to 1732. There, on the concrete subway floors in full view of passersby, whole families spread out their blankets in preparation for a night's sleep. These were the bombed out poor of London and they had been living like this in the subway for several years since the London Blitz.

The train rides from Thetford to London enabled us to view the quaint beauty of the small towns and rural countryside of England. The deep-green hedgerows, rolling fields and slow-flowing streams of East Anglia were scenes out of 18th Century pastoral paintings.

All too soon our two-day vacation from the war would come to an end. We would return to combat somewhat hung over, but dedicated to our rendezvous with our duty and our destiny.

## July 19, 1944—Mission Number Seven

This was a "maximum effort" day for the 8th Air Force Some 1,200 heavy bombers, B-17s and 24s, operating in five forces, attacked targets in south central Germany. The 388th Bomb Group was assigned to strike Schweinfurt, a heavily defended target producing most of the ball bearings for the entire German military.

On a previous Schweinfurt raid, October 13, 1943, "Black Thursday," 60 American bombers were shot down in the target area out of a total force of 291, a loss of 600 highly trained airmen. Altogether, 82 bombers were lost that day, 28% of the total force. Today, however, out of the 731 escort fighter planes, we had a number of long-range P-51 Mustangs accompanying us all the way into Schweinfurt, some 500 miles from home. The 388th put up 36 ships, with our crew assigned to aircraft 42-32030, #030. Take-off time: 05:00 hours.

The mission got underway ominously when, while forming over England, Lt. Malaniak's ship #851, *Little Boy Blue,* was involved in a mid-air collision over Bury St. Edmunds. (*Blue* was originally my friend Capt. Ken Pentent's ship, which had survived 66 missions.) At 15,000 feet, the ship was cut in two by the props of the ship below, just forward of the waist windows. The forward section spun into the ground killing Malaniak and seven other crewmen. The tail section fluttered to earth allowing the right waist and tail gunners to parachute out safely. Five 1,000-pound bombs blew up on impact leaving not a trace of the bodies of the pilot, co-pilot and engineer. Their names are inscribed on the Memorial Wall of the Missing, along with 5,122 others, at the Cambridge American Military Cemetery.

Patchy clouds covered the entire route in, but it was clear over the target. Bombs away at 09:36 hours from 25,000 feet. The lead ship of our group was hit by flak on the bomb run and the formation was somewhat dispersed, causing many of the bombs to miss the MPI. The crew of the *La-Dee-Doo* was in the last Wing (100+ ships), the last Group (36), the last Squadron (12) and the last Element (three), flying in so-called Purple Heart Corner, the most vulnerable position in the formation. We were flying off Lt. Sherman's wing, whose co-pilot, Harry Davis, became my best friend for the rest of the war. Out of the hundreds of bombers hitting Schweinfurt, our ship was the very last one over the target. The sky was black with flak, the worst we had ever seen. And being at the tail end of the bomber stream, the German gunners by then had the exact range. Bursts of flak were exploding right below and around our ship, bouncing it up and down and sending jagged pieces of shrapnel through the fuselage. Usually unexcitable tail gunner B A Webb got on the intercom and yelled out, "Loo-tenant, the flak is right on us! Let's get the hell *out* of heah!"

The flak was so devastating that immediately after bombs away, the Group Leader made an abrupt 45-degree right diving turn off the target to get out of the range of gunfire. Our crew being the last ship on the outside of the formation, the speed and angle of turn was greatly exaggerated for us. The plane was practically standing on its wing at a 90-degree angle to the ground as the air speed rapidly increased. Being off the left wing of Sherman, the pilot could not see, so I, the co-pilot, had to do the best I could and handle the plane alone. By now there was both a gray undercast and a gray overcast, absolutely nothing visible by which to gauge our flight attitude. Vertigo (the loss of balance and perspective) took over and all I had to hang onto was the ship alongside. Eventually, the Group stabilized and we rejoined the bomber stream for the long haul home.

The crew started breathing again and assessed the battle damage. The flak had taken out rudder and trim cables and an oxygen bottle in the radio room. The engineer, Nick DiMartino, counted more than 20 large holes in the ship. Tail gunner Webb and radio operator Harry Hildebrecht had close calls. Navigator Bill Malley was grazed by a piece of flak that tore his flight jacket and pierced the bombardier's equipment bag.

At 12:58 hours, 32 aircraft out of the original 36 limped back to Knettishall. As the wheels touched down on the runway and the crew was about to utter a collective sigh of relief, a traumatic bouncing and vibration informed us that we had a tire shot out. The pilot, Lauren Porter, yelled over to me to quickly unlock the tail wheel. He then gunned the engines, pulling the ship off the runway into the muddy infield, thus keeping the landing strip clear for the other incoming aircraft, many with battle damage or wounded on board. As Lauren cut the engines, the silence was deafening and we sat there for some moments completely whacked out. A truck came out to pick up our weary crew, and we had really earned our cup of cocoa and shot of bourbon at the debriefing that day.

The 8th Air Force lost seven fighters and 15 bombers, four of which were from our Group.

## July 20, 1944—Mission Number Eight

Following yesterday's fatiguing mission to Schweinfurt, we were trucked to the mess hall after debriefing about 3 p.m. or so. The stew and rice went down pretty nice—our breakfast, dinner and supper. Then, we rode our bikes to the barracks to crash on our bunks and lapsed into unconsciousness before the heads touched the pillows.

For the third straight night, the flashlight beam shone in our face sometime after midnight. There followed the soft apologetic southern drawl, "Wake up Loo-tenant. Y'all is flying *again* today."

On this day, more than 1,200 8th Air Force heavy bombers were scheduled to strike numerous objectives in the Frankfurt, Leipzig and Mainz areas of central Germany. Some 727 fighters flew support and also strafed ground targets. Nineteen of our bombers and eight fighters were lost in aerial combat. The 388th was briefed to bomb Lutzkendorf, an oil refinery near Merseburg. Our crew flew in ship #154, one of 28 planes put up by our Group. Take-off time was 06:30 hours. However, because of haze and effective German smoke screen at target area, the secondary target was attacked, an optical factory at Welzler north of Frankfurt. Bombs away at 12:04 hours from 23,000 feet. Meager to heavy flak was encountered along the way, with 12 aircraft receiving minor flak damage.

Our crew flew in the High Group of the 45th Combat Wing, composed of the 96th, 388th and 452nd Groups. There were three 36-ship Groups to a Wing, usually a single formation of over 100 bombers, separated from other Wings fore and aft in the long bomber stream being patrolled by

U.S. fighters, mostly P-51 Mustangs and P-47 Thunderbolts. We flew in the six-ship Element led by Lt. Fitzpatrick's soft-spoken pilot from New Orleans who bunked at the far end of our barracks. The crews of Ong (a Chinese-American), Sherman (whose co-pilot was my good friend Harry Davis), Olson (a former glider pilot) and Paulson (whose navigator was Goldie the Joker) surrounded us. We had come to know these peer airmen, and if we all returned safely each mission and didn't have to fly the next day, we would have a beer together at the Club. A budding artist in the group painted the name and a B-17 on the back of our leather A-2 jackets for four English pounds ($16 U.S.).

The Catholic group would attend a 5 p.m. Mass and sometimes convince the chaplain, Father Carmody, a tall, easy-going young priest from Hartford, Connecticut, to have a drink with us afterwards. Living from day-to-day on the edge of life, it felt good to talk to a priest who might be anointing you the next day.

## July 24, 1944—Mission Number Nine

The target for today was the St. Lo area in northern France in support of the U.S. First Army. The whole 8th Air Force was assigned to bomb German forces to aid an offensive of our troops (Operation COBRA). The 388th Bomb Group sent up 35 aircraft between 09:10 and 09:40 hours, joining up with the 4th Combat Wing. Our crew was flying in ship #286, *Skipper an' the Kids.*

It was one of our rare missions to northern France, rather than east to Germany. We crossed the Channel at about 12,000 feet and thus could observe the land and seascape more closely than usual. The sea was blue-green, and the German-occupied Channel Islands of Jersey and Guernsey were skirted as the enemy flak crews started putting up a barrage. I remember seeing one American aircraft go down because its formation had ventured just a bit too close. I believe we had 250-pound or

500-pound anti-personnel or general-purpose bombs, but we also carried a 1,000-pounder on the underside of each wing, a total of 8,000 pounds of bombs. Weather in the target area was marginal; hazy with broken skies. Hence, the Wing had to make four bomb runs before dropping bombs at 13:11 hours from 15,000 feet, 10,000 feet lower than usual. Due to the obscured target area, ours was the only Wing in the Third Air Division of the 8th to drop its bombs. The others could not chance bombing our own troops; 1,102 heavy bombers aborted with their bombs, and hence Operation COBRA was postponed for a day.

The flak was relatively light but accurate, with about a dozen rockets being lobbed into the formation. Battle damage was mostly minor, with our ship receiving but three holes. Nick DiMartino informed us that his nephew was somewhere in the trenches down below.

This was our first mission in #286, aircraft 42-97286-L, *Skipper an' the Kids*. We were to fly another 13 missions in the same ship during the remainder of our tour, plus three aborted missions due to loss of engines. It served us well, taking much battle damage while returning us safely through thick and thin. We considered it our ship, and often called it the *La-Dee-Doo*, the name selected by our crew. However, *Skipper* ultimately had a tragic ending that I will describe later.

The ships became almost human at times, and their loss was deeply felt by both the flight crews and especially the ground crews who lived and slept with the planes. Part of the camaraderie of being the member of a band of 10 men, deeply bonded together and daily sharing in life and death situations in defense of our country, was the custom of selecting a name for the crew. Lauren left it up to the six enlisted men to decide—a thoughtful gesture. The name selected was the *La-Dee-Doo*, the result of an in-joke among the crew members. Pappy Yokum, a character in the comic strip *Lil Abner*, used to hum these meaningless but cheering words to himself when in danger or trouble, like walking past a graveyard at midnight. So, occasionally upon beginning a bomb run or under a flak attack, one of the crew would defuse a tense situation by getting on the intercom and humming, "La-Dee-Doo."

## August 6, 1944—Mission Number 15

The target for today was generally conceded to be the ultimate: Berlin (a.k.a. Big B). Berlin was the cultural center, the pride and joy of Hitler's Third Reich. And, as expected, it was a very heavily defended fortress. When the target was first announced, a spontaneous groan erupted from the assembled bomber crews, and everyone lit up another cigarette. Legends had arisen around the tenacious German defense of their capital.

Looking around the room, I knew that several crews would probably not make it back, especially our own. We were flying ship #849, *Red Cross Darling*, an old, patched-up, war-weary relic. To top it off, we were assigned to fly in our not-unfamiliar position of Purple Heart Corner, the most vulnerable spot in the whole formation.

On this memorable day, the 8th Air Force put up 953 heavy bombers to hit seven oil refineries, five aircraft and engine factories and other targets in the Berlin and Hamburg-Kiel areas. The specific target of the 388th Bomb Group was the Tiger Tank factory in the heart of Berlin. Our bombers were escorted by relief shifts of 554 fighters. Some 25 bombers failed to return, and six U.S. fighters were lost. The Americans claimed 34 German aircraft.

The 388th Group put up 22 ships for the 45th Wing, and we made our usual rendezvous circles over England. The lead ships continually fired distinctive colored flares identifying their respective units. Some two hours later we headed out over the North Sea and began the slow climb to our bombing altitude of 25,000 feet. The adrenaline began to flow as the gunners test fired their .50-caliber guns, and the suspense began to build up as we put on our oxygen masks and donned our steel flak helmets. Curiously, it wasn't with fear or great apprehension that we approached the German coast, but with a heady feeling of exhilaration. It must have been like this down through the centuries as men headed into battle, knowing that the ultimate gamble was at hand, the throw of the dice that would determine life or death. It must have felt like this as the knights began their charge at the battles of Hastings or Agincourt in the Middle

Ages, with horns blowing and banners flying. It must have felt like this before Pickett's charge at Gettysburg.

German radar and patrol planes had long since picked us up and the Luftwaffe fighter pilots would be ready to scramble. In the coastal towns and cities, the air raid sirens had begun to wail. The first pilot and I had to resort constantly to emergency RPMs to keep old *Red Cross Darling* up with the formation. She creaked and groaned as we gradually climbed into the morning sun. We gingerly made our path between islands of black flak as we passed over various German cities and military installations. Over Berlin the sky was as clear as a sheet of light blue glass. The only clouds to be seen were the puffs of black flak that seemed to come up from a ring of guns surrounding the city. We hunkered down and began the bomb run, some 10 minutes of straight and level flying as the Lead Bombardier focused in on the Tiger Tank factory. All 36 ships in the Group dropped their bombs simultaneously off the Lead ship. Strike photos later showed a perfect concentrated pattern, a shack.

Just after bombs away, Lt. Kluth's ship, #088, *Fortress Nine,* was hit by a flak burst in the area of the flight deck. The oxygen tanks exploded, and the pilot gave the signal to bail out. The crew evacuated safely and spent that night and the rest of the war in a German Prisoner of War camp. It was their 24th mission.

We had done our work for the government, and now were on our own to get back home as best we could. Our "little friends," the long-range P-51 Mustangs, must have fended off the German fighters, and we were relieved to see the blue-green waters of the North Sea once again. The spirits of our crew noticeably lightened as we headed for home with nothing worse than a handful of flak holes. Exhilaration replaced our fatigue, as *Red Cross Darling* touched down safely on the runway. She brought us some 600 miles to Berlin and back. She gave us all she had. We had passed the test and were now no longer rookies, but a veteran crew.

## August 11, 12, 13, 1944—Mission Number 17 (attempted)

Halfway through our tour of 35 missions, our crew ran into a streak of bad luck. For three missions in a row, we had to abort or turn back on the way to our target because of the mechanical failure of an engine. The engine was the Number 2, the ship was our old faithful #286, *Skipper an' the Kids*. Each time, we lost oil pressure, had to feather the prop, leave formation and return to base without getting credit for a mission. Each time, the pilot wrote up the defect, and each time the ground crew apparently remedied the situation. The second time, when we returned with a full load of bombs, some 7,000 pounds, and over 2,000 gallons of high octane in the tanks, we almost stalled out upon landing.

It was one of those close brushes with death that happens in an instant, and is just as soon forgotten. As we felt the ship begin to stall out, Lauren yelled for the landing gear to be retracted, gave it full emergency throttle and the remaining three engines had just enough power to pull us up and around. He called the tower and got permission to dump the bombs in a designated area off the English coast.

The crew's frustration was at the boiling point when the same engine acted up the following day. Lauren had had it. He pushed the throttle full forward on Number 2 to make or break the recalcitrant engine. The engine blew up, caught fire and trailed flames the length of the ship. I pressed the fire extinguisher button, feathered the prop, and we headed for home. The next day, voila, a brand new engine for *Skipper.*

## August 16, 1944—Mission Number 18

Today, the whole 8th Air Force, some 1,000 four-engine bombers plus fighter escort, attacked 11 oil refineries in the heavily industrialized and heavily defended Magdeburg-Leipzig area. Once again it manifested the necessity of cutting off fuel supplies to the German armies. And it was a day to be remembered by the crew of the *La-Dee-Doo*. We were almost listed on the casualty board along with the 24 bombers shot down.

The specific target of the 388ᵗʰ Bomb Group was a synthetic oil plant at Zeitz. The Group supplied 26 aircraft, but two had to abort. Take-off time was 06:25 hours. Bombs away at 11:35 hours from 21,500 feet. Good results.

On the bomb run, Lt. Sarten's crew flying just off our right wing was involved in a mid-air collision, a constant potential danger in close formation flying. The ship above them dropped down and sheared off the tail with its props. I still have a picture in my mind of the tail gunner's face as he looked up into the propellers just above his head. The ship went down out of control. The pilot, with 31 missions in, and the rest of the crew with 30, were all killed.

The flak was intense and accurate over the target area. Practically every ship in the group received battle damage, while five crew members were wounded. Our ship lost the Number 2 engine from a flak hit, and we were unable to feather the prop. The propeller windmilled, so we had to evacuate the bombardier and navigator from the nose due to the probability of the prop breaking off from its shaft and flying through the side of the aircraft. We were forced to drop out of formation some 500 miles deep in the heart of Germany and try to make it back alone. The Number 1 engine also apparently picked up a flak hit, as it began to throw oil and lose pressure. The pilot cut back to half power. We began losing altitude in order to maintain air speed, while the 388ᵗʰ Bomb Group was disappearing in the distance. There seemed little hope of survival, and a very dark, lonesome feeling settled over the crew. The pilot ordered all gunners to check their guns and to be alert at their positions. We knew German fighters lurked in the area like sharks stalking stray, wounded whales. But we were determined to go down fighting.

There wasn't a cloud in the bright noon-day summer sky in which to take refuge as we anxiously made our way across western Germany. Near the border of German-occupied Holland, the tail gunner, B A Webb, reported an unidentified fighter in attack position closing in on the tail. We braced ourselves for the encounter. Then, lo and behold, an American P-51 Mustang with a checkered nose came alongside and waved his wings in greeting. A couple of other P-51s and P-47s joined in and escorted our wounded ship safely to the Channel. We finally crossed the English Channel at about 1,000 feet, still trading altitude for air speed. To see once again the white cliffs, hedgerows and green fields of England was a beautiful sight. We were down to our last few hundred feet as we arrived at Knettishall, some 45 minutes late and presumed lost. At the intelligence debriefing everyone drank a double shot of bourbon doled out by the medics. How sweet it was to be alive.

## August 25, 1944

On this date the popular bandleader and celebrity Glenn Miller visited the 388th Bomb Group. Together with his 50-man U.S. Air Force Band, he put on a concert in a big hangar on the flightline for 3,000 men of Knettishall.

Major Miller toured the airfields of the 8th Air Force, bolstering morale, giving the boys a vicarious sentimental journey back to their hometowns, their girlfriends and neighborhood soda fountains in the States. In the afternoon, he christened a shiny new silver B-17, naming it *Moonlight Serenade* after his theme song. In the evening, the base personnel crowded into the mammoth hangar, sitting on the floor, hanging from the rafters and every other conceivable perch.

However, for many of the combat crews, the red flag or card went up in the clubs, bars and lounges. The message was that there was a mission on for the next morning; head back to the barracks and get whatever sleep you can. So our crew missed the concert.

But, as we filed into the Mess Hall at around midnight for our pre-mission breakfast, there was Glenn sitting at the CO's table, having a post-concert snack with a handful of upper eschalon officers. There were a couple bottles of Scotch on the table, and the conversation flowed freely as the bandleader and the officers unwound.

Our crew, dressed in flight clothes and A-2 leather jackets, sat several yards away, quietly eating our oatmeal and scrambled eggs. We were aware of the celebrity, but we were far more preoccupied with the day's mission and our destiny within the next several hours. However, one humorous little scrap of conversation remains in my mind after more than 50 years. Glenn Miller, ever the loyal PR man for the Air Force, ventured the statement, "The 8th Air Force could win the war in the ETO all by itself, without the assistance of the ground forces." A red-faced colonel present from an Army unit responded, "Miller, you stick to playing your violin, and let us fight the war."

Of all the men present in that room, especially the air crews about to enter into combat over Germany, the last man one would expect to die would be Glenn Miller—tall, handsome, a trim 40 years old, the symbol of immortal American youth, dancing and the good life. And yet, within a few months, he mysteriously went down in the sea without a trace on a routine flight to Paris. His bones still lie somewhere beneath the icy waters of the English Channel, a long way from his hometown of Clarinda, Iowa.

Rest in peace, Glenn Miller, along with the other 32,000 8th Air Force lads who never went home again.

## September 5, 1944

On this day the 388th bombed an aircraft engine plant at Stuttgart in southwest Germany, some 75 miles from the Swiss border. However, our crew had the day off, so we slept in that morning for a change. Over the target, the bombardier on Olson's crew, Lt. David Rosenthal, who bunked next to us in our barracks, was struck in the throat by a piece of flak. He must have died instantly. Rest in peace. Four members of other crews were wounded.

Also, the new ship christened by Glenn Miller on August 25, #43-37599, *Moonlight Serenade,* was hit by flak over the target and lost two engines. The pilot left formation and was escorted by a few of our fighters. However, a third engine caught fire and the crew had to bail out over the Vosges Mountains west of the Rhine River in occupied France. Four crewmen escaped via the French underground, while five were taken prisoners, one of whom was later killed by the Germans. It was only their second mission. Usually, American flyers were safe if captured by the German military. But it was not unknown for German civilians to kill airmen out of hand, using pitchforks or whatever weapons were available.

Thus, *Moonlight Serenade* went on its last "Sentimental Journey" less than two weeks after it was christened. It was not a good omen for Glenn Miller.

## September 10, 1944—The 200 Mission Party

On Sunday, September 10, at 14:00 hours, all official activity came to a halt in order to celebrate the upcoming 200th mission of the 388th Bomb Group. Following a mission to Nuremburg, which returned at 13:00 hours Sunday afternoon, all duties were cancelled until Monday, September 11, 12:00 hours.

Practically a 24-hour program began with a baseball game between a Knettishall Base team and the Canadian All-Stars. This was followed by all kinds of organized sporting and social events, culminating in a fabulous barbecue and copious free beer. In the evening, a dance for the enlisted men was held at the main hangar, while a smaller-scale party was held at the Officers' Club. Four bands supplied the music. A chartered train brought 400 girls from London, along with numerous guests from neighboring cities and villages. Some 1,400 guests joined in the festivities. The guest of honor was popular Gen. Jimmy Doolittle, the CO of the 8th Air Force. He shared the podium with Gen. Earl E. Partridge, CO of the 3rd

Bomb Division, and the beloved Col. William B. David, CO of the 388ᵗʰ. Three finer COs were not to be found.

It was a day to be remembered, especially for the permanent party and ground personnel who had spent many months in England, performing the day-to-day tasks necessary to keep the combat crews flying.

## September 17, 1944—Mission Number 25

Today, a shuttle mission to the USSR-Italy-UK, comprised of 72 B-17s and 59 P-51s was completed. However, the main focus was on Arnheim in the Netherlands where some 20,000 British and American paratroopers and glider troops were to be dropped behind German lines. The operation, code named Market-Garden, was described in detail in *A Bridge Too Far* by military historian Cornelius Ryan. It was not a great Allied success. The 8ᵗʰ Air Force put up over 800 B-17s escorted by three fighter groups to bomb 117 flak batteries and installations. This was to soften up the enemy in preparation for the drop. The *La-Dee-Doo* crew once again flew in #286, *Skipper an' the Kids.* We carried anti-personnel fragmentation bombs. The 388ᵗʰ put up a maximum effort of 39 aircraft. Take-off time: 06:30 hours.

Weather over Holland was hazy, but all elements attacked their objectives visually with very good results. Six-ship squadrons bombed some targets. Flak was light to intense, depending upon where you were.

One of our bombs got hung up and did not drop at the target site. Coming back over the Channel after dropping down from altitude, Wally Koseluk, the bombardier, went back to assess the situation. The bomb suddenly let go and crashed right through the closed bomb bay doors, narrowly missing a ship flying in formation beneath us. It was another scare for *Skipper an' the Kids,* and triggered a cussing out from the pilot below.

All aircraft returned to base by 12:11 hours. Upon our return, the American C-46s and 47s were going out with the airborne troops for the invasion. Hundreds flew over our field, an awesome sight.

## September 18, 1944—Receiving the DFC

It was probably the afternoon following our 25th mission that our crew, along with another, was hastily summoned to base headquarters. We were told to wear Class A uniforms. We were loaded on a GI truck and whisked off, probably to Wing or 3rd Division Headquarters, or wherever. Upon disembarking, we lined up at attention outside a hut, seven officers and 10 noncoms. The only absentees from our original crew were Snuffy Moell, our former navigator, and waist gunner Wally Blumenthal, now assigned to ground duties. The rest of us had just completed 25 missions. Our reward: The Distinguished Flying Cross. Originally, the tour of duty in the 8th Air Force for heavy bomber crews was 25 missions. Then, as the chances of survival increased, the number was increased to 30. When we flew our tour in 1944, it was up to 35. But still the DFC was awarded at 25 missions.

I believe it was Col. Olds, the 45th Wing CO, who presented the medal to us and gave us an official handshake. I have a photo of him pinning the DFC on the last man in line, our deserving little engineer Nick DiMartino. And the last shall be first…

Thus our *La-Dee-Doo* crew members were entitled to wear the European Theater of Operations ribbon with three battle stars, having participated in the campaigns of Normandy, Northern France and Germany. Secondly, we were awarded the Air Medal for, I believe, the first seven missions. This was followed by an oak leaf cluster for each additional seven missions, for a total of an Air Medal with four clusters. And, thirdly, we received the Distinguished Flying Cross. Since the awards were more or less automatic, we accepted them with a kind of nonchalance, knowing it was simply a matter of doing your job and surviving, like most everyone else in combat. However, after 50 years of reflecting upon the young lads who gave their lives, just doing their jobs so that their nation and the human race could survive in one of its darkest hours, I have a deeper respect for those awards and the men who received them.

Each dawn was a new battle, another invasion. By noon, we were often some 500 miles deep into enemy territory, completely on our own, surrounded by hostile forces. Each evening, we knew, we would either be dead, a prisoner of war in Germany, or back in our bunks in England getting a little sleep before the next day's mission and a new battle all over again. The airmen never turned back in the face of adversity; they played out the hand of cards that fate and divine providence dealt them as best they could. Like our old ship *Skipper an' the Kids,* always back in the pack, straining its guts to keep up with the group, knowing that nothing but trouble awaited her, they gave everything they had simply because it was their duty.

## September 21, 1994—Mission Number 26

Today was the actual 200ᵗʰ mission of the 388ᵗʰ Bomb Group. We celebrated it at the I.G. Farben Industry synthetic oil plant at Ludwigshaven, Germany. The 388ᵗʰ put up 39 ships, one of which was our crew in old #286, *Skipper an' the Kids.* We carried five 500-pound general-purpose bombs, and five 500-pound M-17 bombs. There was nearly complete cloud cover over the target, so we bombed by radar. Bombs were away at 13:56 hours from 26,000 feet. Flak was moderate and inaccurate. Upon returning to England, what was presumed to be a happy conclusion to a routine mission suddenly turned into a crisis situation.

A combination of heavy autumn haze and English fog rapidly closed in, diminishing visibility to near zero. To complicate matters, either a wind shift or miscalculation on the amount of fuel to be consumed for the mission found the ships dangerously low on gas. The Group Leader sent out an emergency mayday message: The whole formation was to disband and land at any airfield possible, every crew for itself.

Then began a very harrowing and tense situation of perhaps hundreds of aircraft coming down blind through overcast and fog, running out of fuel and fighting for landing position anywhere. The pilot was flying on instruments, tuned into any airbase tower. There were scores of yelling, panicking pilots. The rest of the crew peered from their individual positions, straining to see any ship on a possible collision course.

Fortunately, we managed to survive and land at an RAF base in southern England. Lauren just muscled his way into the traffic pattern in a situation of pure chaos. Several other ships made it in with us, and the English were quite overwhelmed. They did feed us some powdered scrambled eggs and warmed over fried potatoes, our first food in perhaps 18 hours. The crew collapsed on cots, dressed in their flying clothes. After borrowing some fuel from the Limeys the next morning, we flew back to Knettishall, haggard, but still happy to be numbered among the living. The luck of *Skipper an' the Kids* was holding out.

## September 28, 1944—Mission Number 28

Today, the entire 8ᵗʰ Air Force sought to deliver a mortal blow to the German oil industry, thus crippling the German armies. The 1ˢᵗ Division bombed oil refineries at Merseburg, the 2ⁿᵈ at Kassel, while the whole 3ʳᵈ Division attacked the I.G. Farbin plant at Merseburg. Hence, the target of the 388th was Merseburg, a name to be forever remembered by our crew. Our ship was old faithful #286, *Skipper an' the Kids*. The 388th put up three squadrons of 12 ships each, comprising the 45ᵗʰ A Wing. Take-off time was 07:00 hours. We were flying off Sherman's wing in the Lead Squadron, while Frawley's crew in #878, *Millie K,* was off to our right. Another squad was stacked above us, and a third below. A route was followed across Belgium into Germany, picking our way between islands of flak here and there. The primary target was 8/10 cloud covered, so the secondary target was bombed by radar methods. Strike photos showed poor results.

The flak was extremely heavy and very accurate. While performing evasive action following bombs away, Lt. Heimendinger in the Low Squadron lead ship hit and cut Lt. Lord's aircraft in two. The latter went into a spin out of control, killing eight of the crew. Heimendinger, with 26 missions, and Lt. Maring, the command pilot with 21, were killed, along with 10 other crewmen. Rest in peace. Frawley's crew in *Millie K* was hit by flak and lost two engines. The crew bailed out near Cologne and were taken prisoners. It was their seventh mission. Lt. Gierach in #434, *Panhandle Kid,* was hit by flak, lost a couple of engines and the crew had to bail out near Liege, Belgium. Fortunately, the area was in the hands of American forces, so they all made it safely back to England, including my beer-drinking buddy Harry Hobbs, navigator from Chicago and Princeton University. We were to meet again in Texas. Lt. Michael in #520, *GI Jane,* was shot down at 14:00 hours east of Aachen. The crew was taken POW. Olson's crew from our barracks, flying in #219, *Rebel's Revenge,* received a direct hit between Number 1 and Number 2 engines and spun out of formation. Lt. V.R. Olson, a good natured Scandinavian, finally ran out of luck on his 25th mission and was killed. Rest in peace. The rest of the crew survived and were taken prisoners.

That fateful day, the 388th Bomb Group lost six or seven ships, 17 aircraft had major battle damage, and among the returning airmen,10 were wounded.

By 05:42 hours, 25 ships returned to base, not including #286. We got back sometime later. *Skipper an' the Kids* did not escape the intense flak barrage. Tail gunner Webb was slightly wounded in the leg. The ship was riddled with between 75 and 100 flak holes. The Number 2 engine was shot out and feathered; another engine lost half power. Upon landing sometime after the main bedraggled group, we discovered our hydraulic system had been shot out, losing brakes. Lauren cut power and we simply coasted to a stop off the end of the runway. The *Skipper* ground crew rode up frantically to administer to their baby. They stood there wide eyed, with mouths hanging open, assessing the damage. They couldn't understand why the Number 2 engine didn't fall right off the wing and the whole ship collapse.

One of our consolations crossing the Channel was the assurance that we could ditch in the sea and eventually get picked up by RAF rescue ships. But after landing, we observed that a piece of flak as big as a softball had perforated our inflatable dinghies.

Along with mission Number 18 on August 16, it was our longest day. It took more than a week to repair the ship in order to fly again, and I don't think it was ever the same. More than 30 of our 8ᵗʰ Air Force bombers failed to return home on that fateful day.

## October 6, 1944

On this day, it was announced that the commanding officer of the 388ᵗʰ Bomb Group, the beloved Col. William B. David, age 32, was being transferred to another theater of operations. Col. David had been CO of the 388ᵗʰ ever since it originated at Wendover Field, Utah. He supervised its establishment at Knettishall, England, in June 1943 and led the group on its first mission to Amsterdam on July 17, 1943. Over the next 15 months, Col. David saw his share of combat, having flown 25 missions, including stints as Command Pilot. His decorations consisted of the Silver Star, two Purple Hearts (having been wounded twice) three DFCs and four Air Medals. On one mission, he was burned about the face and neck due to enemy action, and hence seldom wore a tie, adding to the informal spirit of the group. He was warm and friendly, returning every salute with a smile and a wave. A native of Calhoun, Georgia, he was a graduate of the University of Georgia, receiving a degree in electrical engineering. He was also an outstanding athlete, being named All-American tackle on the Georgia football team in the early '30s. He joined the U.S. Army Air Corps in 1934.

According to the recollection of our navigator Bill Malley, Col. David approached our crew at the debriefing session following a very difficult mission. We were the last ship in, and he probably noticed our badly shot up #286, *Skipper,* landing precariously after Mission Number 28 to Merseburg.

"How many German fighters hit you?" he inquired concernedly, as we sipped our cocoa and bourbon. We responded that all the damage was simply due to enemy flak. And he smiled and shook his head incredulously.

It was a sad day when Col. David departed Knettishall. Fortunately, a popular officer who had been with the 388th from the very beginning and was the deputy CO, Lt. Col. Chester C. Cox, replaced him. He was 28 years of age, a native of Wisconsin, married with one son. He joined the Army Air Corps in 1939. Like Col. David, Lt. Col. Cox was a Command Pilot and flew 25 missions. On D-Day, June 6, 1944, he led the 8th Air Force in bombing German positions in Normandy. He continued the fine traditions initiated by Col. David, and served as the CO for the 388th for the remainder of the war in Europe.

## October 7, 1944—Mission Number 30

Despite the events on the base, the life and struggle of each rank and file combat crew continued. We had a job to do, and if we survived our 35 missions, a return to the States and a 30-day leave awaited us. Right now, it was our only goal in life.

On this autumn day, the 8th Air Force put up over 1,300 heavy bombers in four forces to attack once again the vital German oil and transportation centers. We also struck a variety of other targets in the central and northeast sections of the country. The 1st Division went to Ruhland and Zwickau, the 2nd to Kassel and Magdeburg and the 3rd to Merseburg, Lutzkendorf and Bohlen (near Leipzig). The 388th was invited to Bohlen.

Our crew was flying in #286, *Skipper,* once again. She just got out of the hospital after the Merseburg catastrophe and had a couple of new engines, as well as beaucoup patches and Band-Aids to plug up the flak holes and hold her together.

The 388th put up a full deck of 36 ships, and zero hour for take-off was 06:30. However, on take-off, Lt. Resch in #195, *Blind Date,* lost power and crash-landed in a field near the town of Walpole. All the crew got out before the ship caught fire and the occupants of eight houses were evacuated before the bomb load exploded. It was an ominous beginning for another long day.

Our Lead and High Squadrons bombed the primary target visually at 12:30 hours from 26,000 feet. The Low Squadron bombed the secondary target, the Nordhausen Airfield, at 13:40 hours from 23,400 feet. The bombs fell in the hangar area. Flak was moderate with damage to 17 of our aircraft. Just before the bomb run at 12:10 hours, between 30 to 50 fighters in a curious, unorganized formation like a swarm of angry bees appeared off to our left. They were about 500 feet above us and in the glare of the noonday sun. The navigator, who kept the ship's log, informed us that we were supposed to be getting a relief escort of P-47 Thunderbolts at that precise time. But the gunners were suspicious; something was not right. The ships appeared to be black with one light blue aircraft, probably the group leader. Suddenly, the fighters queued up and began an attack on the formation in front of us from the tail position, 6 o'clock high, like sharks in a feeding frenzy. Tracer bullets and 20mm cannon shells lit up the doomed B-17 squadron like lights on a Christmas tree. Within a matter of seconds, 12 bombers were blown up or sent spinning down. Also, an occasional German ME-109 or FW-190 spiraled down trailing smoke. Our group could do absolutely nothing but throttle back and hold our breaths to see what the Germans were going to do. Four P-47s also throttled back and crept alongside our formation. To enter into that chaotic shootout would have been suicide.

The crew of the *La-Dee-Doo* fell into a dead silence, almost shock. I remember thinking that men were dying and being judged right before our eyes. A voice on the intercom, as if in a trance, quietly began counting parachutes opening up, according to procedure.

But then it suddenly ended just as rapidly as it began. The Luftwaffe fighters scampered off after just one pass, the skies gradually cleared of debris and became calm once again as we began to receive the first flak from the target area. However, a whole squadron of B-17s, 12 ships containing 120 men, had completely disappeared. The whole show lasted but a few minutes, and it was an awesome and solemn moment. On this day the 8th Air Force lost 52 bombers and 15 fighters.

## October 8, 1944—The Countdown

Our crew now had 30 missions in, with five more big ones to go, and they weren't getting any easier. Each mission became more important and each day the tension increased. Crews had been known to be shot down on their very last trip, rendering useless in a sense all the blood, sweat and tears of the 34 missions which went before.

Also about this time, an incident occurred which increased the drama for me. It was late afternoon on a golden autumn day. The red poppies on the hill leading down to the airfield were fading, and the leaves were turning in the nearby woods. The weather was fair over England, but a storm front hung over Germany, so we had the day off. The air crews just fiddled around, throwing a football, writing a letter or playing cards on the double-decked bunks. Suddenly, there was a jarring crash and an oily plume of smoke arose up into the sky from a forest about a mile off the runway. A pilot with whom I was playing cards—a lad from Milwaukee—and I jumped on our bikes and headed toward the scene of the accident. About 20 minutes of furious pedaling brought us to an open field where we parked our bikes and entered the woods. Members of the fire department from the nearby town were scattered about putting out the fire started by flaming pieces of wreckage. A P-51 Mustang from a neighboring base had spun into the ground from some 10,000 feet or so.

Two doctors from the base had a GI blanket, and they were looking for the remains of the pilot, so my buddy and I offered to help. The first thing I found was a GI shoe with a foot still in it, and I placed it on the blanket. The others contributed a piece here and there. At the base of a huge smoking tree, one of the doctors lifted up a pile of intestines like a string of steaming links of sausage, and carefully placed it on the blanket. He said we have 29 feet of them inside us. Looking up the tree, we saw the victim's skull, rib cage and spinal column wrapped around the trunk about 25 feet in the air. Just about all the flesh had been blown off the bones. Rooting around a small pile of wreckage, I found the pilot's dog tags. The next of kin stamped on the plates was a woman from Columbia, South Carolina, probably his wife or mother.

In my mind's eye, I saw a telegram from the War Department with red stars on it being delivered to a little house on a quiet, shady street. It was that way a few months ago when my brother was shot down in Burma.

Having done what we could, we waved goodbye to the doctors and walked to our bikes. It was about sundown when we passed through the little village near our base. We stopped at the local pub and had a pint of ale. The ale was drunk mostly in silence.

## October 16, 1944—The Last Mission, Number 35

This was to be the last mission for the crew of L.D. Porter, a.k.a. the *La-Dee-Doo.* The target was a heavy gun factory at Hannover, Germany. The 8th Air Force put up more than 1,100 bombers, striking various objectives in the industrial heart of Germany. The 388th Bomb Group contributed 39 aircraft that were airborne between 09:55 and 10:24 hours. The command pilot was Major Beach. It was fitting that we were flying in ship

#286, *Skipper an' the Kids,* with whom we shared so much blood, sweat, tears and flak. She was faithful to the end, and now just one more time!

The target area had 10/10 cloud cover, so we bombed by radar. The bombs coming down from the High Squadron above us very narrowly missed our formation; however, we were not home safely as yet. An overcast had moved over southern England and the group had to drop down beneath it upon approaching the coast. As a consequence, the cockpit windows began to frost up rapidly due to the change in altitude, temperature and dew point. Our ship was pinned in the middle of the formation like a hot dog in a bun, just a few hundred feet off the ground. In case of a collision, bailing out was not an option. Suddenly, it was panic time once again as it was impossible to see out the windows.

Since we were flying off the left wing of our Element Lead, I, the co-pilot, had the only chance of seeing the nearby ship. And my only chance of seeing out the window was the fact that our little engineer, Nick DiMartino, squeezed in between my seat and the window. Taking a little screwdriver out of his pocket, he furiously kept scraping a hole in the heavily frosted window about the size of a silver dollar, our only visual contact with the outer world. Gradually Lauren was able to ease the ship out of the formation, and we left the group. There was too much at stake. Flying alone over the treetops and hedgerows, we began to breathe once again. An RAF Spitfire on coastal patrol gingerly drew along side of us apparently to determine if we were friend or foe. In a short time, our wheels touched down on the runway at Knettishall.

## December 10, 1944—The Last Mission of Skipper an' the Kids

As the crew of the *La-Dee-Doo* said their last good-byes and returned to the States and their hometowns to live out their lives, one old battle-scarred friend was left behind, #42-97286, *Skipper an' the Kids.*

We had shared so much and so deeply that our destinies had permanently bonded. Our crew had flown some 15 missions in #286, plus three aborted missions in which we lost engines. She had been shot up time and again, yet she never failed to bring us back. *Skipper* faithfully remained on duty that autumn, leading into the cold bleak British winter. Then, one day in December 1944, she was taken up on a mission to Prestwick, Scotland, under the command of veteran Lead Pilot Capt. Littlejohn. The weather closed in, and while feeling their way through the overcast, the ship lost contact with the tower and disappeared. The date was December 10, 1944.

The following March, *Skipper* was found in a remote valley on the rugged, barren Isle of Arran in Prestwick Bay. All 11 men on board were killed, including Major Doc Bell, a flight surgeon from the 388th. *Skipper* had flown her last mission and died with her crew. Rest in peace.

*After the war, James O'Connor entered a monastery in Iowa. Father O'Connor still lives there today.*

# JUST THREE CAME BACK

By Sid Golden, combat photographer and waist gunner
563rd Squadron

While the taste of my first mission is still fresh, I want to record what I consider a very important phase in my life. But rather than attempt to write of all that has or will happen, I shall limit this record to actual combat experiences. Yet, frankly, where or how to start is my main problem. So much has happened in the past 24 hours that it is hard to believe, let alone write about it.

Yesterday, I was green. Green, untried and curious. Today, although a veteran of the Battle of Berlin, I'm still curious. How many more like that will I survive? Perhaps this seems a bit on the pessimistic side. If so, there's good reason. For this day I have seen Life and Death walk hand in hand. Never before was I so conscious of my Maker.

This morning at 02:00 hours, 33 of us left this hut and, tonight, three of us came home. Now, as I write this, our hut is quiet. Very quiet. They're collecting the personal belongings of those who went down. Just a little cardboard box to next of kin. Across from me, Sam Catalano is writing a letter. I'm writing this. And Feener is gloriously drunk (his last raid).

Three out of 33.

At 01:30 hours this morning I was awakened by the Charge of Quarters: "Briefing in one hour." This was the day. Although I dressed rather hurriedly, my mind dwelled on different thoughts. I wasn't exactly scared. Not yet, anyway, for I was too new for that. Just curious. So I can say, curiosity prompted my thoughts and actions. I left the hut after the traditional "See you tonight," and I made my way to chow. Around me, in the cold, damp English air, shaded flashlights flickered on and off as crews groped their ways to the mess hall. Inside, I got my chow and sat down with some of the boys. We shot the breeze in general, and filled up on fresh eggs, fruit juice and hot coffee. After that, I hightailed for briefing, after which I went to the photo lab.

As I went out the door, I asked the Boss Man for a furlough when I returned. Granted. Hell, I could have asked for anything and probably would have had it granted—when I returned.

I climbed into the Jeep and Joe Puster took me out to the ship. I left him at the ship with the "See you tonight," and went to meet the crew. I was flying with Lt. Oswald and crew in the *Wizard of Oz*. Our position in the formation was Second Element Lead, Lead Squadron, Lead Group. A very choice position in case of fighters. In that position, the ship is tucked in with ships all around it. No good for flak, though, for it's like a bullseye.

After the introductions, Oswald remarked, "This is your first; maybe it will be our lucky one." It was.

I guess we all had the same thoughts in mind, and it's strange as to what omens a man will cling to for support.

The time for take-off grew near and, finally, we all got aboard. Oswald warmed the engines awhile, then taxied to the runway. In the faint light of dawn, I could see the rest of the ships strung out in back of us, nose-to-tail like elephants in a circus. Finally, the green light from Ops, and we were next. Engines were revved up to their maximum and the ship shook as both pilots stood on the brakes. She strained like a horse at the barrier. Then brakes released and down the runway we went.

As we went upstairs, the sky around us became alight with flares. Each group leader was signaling to the ships that were to make up the various element of that particular formation. This jockeying for position lasted quite awhile, and we kept circling the base until the formation began to stack up. It's quite a job with all those ships in the air. But at last we were in formation and went on oxygen, then headed to the point to form the Combat Wing. After forming the Combat Wing, we headed for the pre-determined position where we would form the Air Division, but when we arrived, we were late, and the Air Division had already been formed and gone. So our Combat Wing headed eastward toward *Festung Europa*.

Since we had plenty of time before we reached the enemy coast, we just took it easy. Each man, after checking his position and guns, just sat down to wait. The radio op was busy, so I checked the gun in the radio room, after which I checked my own gear.

But before long, the navigator brought us back to reality. We were making landfall. So, on went the flak gear. During that time we had crossed the enemy coast and then hit our first bad luck. Being an hour late, we missed our escort, and that meant a fight in and out again. All we could do is hope some of the escort would come back for us.

Then the first of the flak opened up, and I took a quick look at it. About eight bursts off the right wing and I decided my curiosity was satisfied, so I buckled on my chute.

Suddenly, it seemed as though I was inside a boiler factory; all hell had broken loose. Our gunners started firing and it wasn't for testing purposes, either. Looking out of the radio hatch I saw the reason—Jerries. This party was on and Jerry was escorting us right in. Those damn FWs were coming in all around the clock. You just couldn't keep up with them. No sooner did one peel off and come in, another was right behind it. Then one jolly bastard came in from 1 o'clock low. I spotted him and called it out. Our ball turret got on him, but instead of going after us, he caught our right wing man. One minute we had a right wing ship and the next it was a ball of flame.

Calling the left waist, I asked him to swap positions with me, for these fighter attacks were what I was supposed to photograph. So we swapped. I might add, at that temperature, which was approximately -45 degrees centigrade, it's damn cold, but under the circumstances a Turkish bath had nothing on us. You get so damn tense that after a few minutes all your clothes are soaking wet. I was no exception to that.

After awhile the FWs left us and we didn't know why, and cared less, until it came over the intercom: JU-88s at 9 o'clock level, about 1,800 yards out. The lousy square heads sat out there, out of range of our guns, and started to lob rockets in on us broadside. All you could see was a trail of smoke and whoosh, right through the formation. It wasn't accurate shooting, and we lost no one to it, but it sure was a boost for religion.

Then, after disposing of their rockets, they came in on us. They didn't do too much damage, but they certainly left a few of their number behind—in a blaze. That .50-caliber isn't exactly an egg beater. And so we went on. In all that time, I still wasn't able to get a picture of fighter attacks. Every time I'd get set, I had to drop the camera and grab the gun.

During all that time, we were getting closer to The B, and the rest of the trip in was without enemy action. Finally, the navigator told us we were on the IP. This is where we really expected to catch hell.

Well, I left the waist and went back to the radio room to get in the camera hatch. I opened the hatch, and, in between the flak bursts, there was the city of Berlin. The flak was so thick around us you could walk on it; it was just solid, above, behind, below and on all sides. The radio op told me to look out toward 1 o'clock. Vapor trails at 1 o'clock high—ME-109s, and coming in like a swarm of hornets. I didn't think they'd come through their own flak, but they did. Jerry was out to try and stop us. Well, there wasn't much use in my just looking. I had pictures to take; I could worry just as well in the hatch.

Some groups had already dropped their load and I could see the bombs bursting in the city, and took shots of it. But Jerry, in the meantime, was charging a damn steep price of admission. We had lost our original wing ships and now their replacements were gone. Every now and then I'd see a Fort going in down under us, some to flak and some to fighters. Some got out and some just had the deck stacked against them. There were plenty of chutes to be seen, of both sides. At least Jerry was taking a beating also.

Finally, they found a target and bombs away. I tracked our bombs down and saw them explode smack in the middle of this factory. It was a perfect shack job and flame and smoke rose to testify to our accuracy. It was a picture that cannot be described except through the camera. I kept grinding away at the mess and saw other buildings around blow up one by one. Those bombardiers sure wrecked that place. Now, *let's get the hell out of here!*

Up to this point we were working for the Government of the United States of America and 130 million people. Now, we were in business for ourselves. By this time Jerry must have really been PO'd, for the flak seemed to be getting worse, if possible, and those MEs just came ripping in on us. To add to our troubles, the bomb bay doors wouldn't close, so the engineer had to crank them up manually. At that altitude, that's a damn hard job, as is any exertion. It's hard to breathe. His oxygen mask was restricting his movements, so the engineer ripped it off and proceeded to crank up the doors. I kept an eye on him in the meantime with an oxygen bottle handy, just in case. But after awhile all was okay, and now all we had to do was get home.

Jerry had other ideas on that subject. Once again, I swapped positions with the waist gunner, still out to get pictures of fighter attacks. Jerry came up on our tail and his lead blew part of our intercom system out, but the tail gunner blew him out—just like a candle. This wasn't exactly kosher, and put us in a hell of a spot with that system out. But we managed, somehow. Well, this went on, and no sooner did we get through with one bunch of those bastards and a new bunch would take over. Hell, there was every kind of ship and marking that the Luftwaffe had up there, all getting their licks in. Those "bandits" kept after us until we could see the Channel, then our luck broke with us. A squadron of P-47s came out after us and went after those Jerries, chasing them back. Those little friends sure looked mighty good to us as they took up positions on all sides of the remaining groups. Then, the Channel was under us and we let down out of altitude.

It had been a long, hard and hectic day, and we were pooped. We circled our base, and—after the ships firing the red flares for casualties—we landed. At the revetment we looked over the ship and it was a mess. Like a fresh slice of Swiss cheese. But, in spite of it all, we suffered no casualties. The bombardier had a piece of flak hit him in the chest, but the flak suit took the impact; just knocked the wind out of him. One 20mm cannon shell exploded across the navigator's table and blew half his clothes off his back, but he wasn't even scratched. We picked up four 20mms in the bomb bay, one through the tail and the entire ship was riddled with flak and machine gun holes. Close.

At interrogation we all got a shot of good American whisky and sure needed it. That damn place was like a wake. We had lost 13 ships—130 men, approximately, and 30 were out of our hut. Only Sam Catalano, Feener and myself left out of the 33 that went out this morning.

I'm not particularly hungry tonight, so instead of chow I'm writing this before I forget all the gory details. But I'm sure glad I'm going on leave tomorrow. This hut is too damn quiet.

So ends Mission Number One. Only 24 more to go.

*Sid Golden, combat photographer*

*388ᵗʰ planes bomb St. Lo in support of U.S. ground troops on June 22, 1944 (Photo by Sid Golden)*

## No. 87, 27 March 1944

The following letter Hq. ETOUSA, is quoted for information and guidance of all personnel this station:

1. At the direction of the Secretary of War, instructions will be issued to all personnel, both military and civilian, under your command:

All personnel will refrain from discussion or speculating on, privately or for publication, information concerning secret weapons, secret equipment, and troop or ship movements, before such information has been officially released.

Furthermore, unless authorized to do so, no person will engage in discussion or speculation, private or public, regarding current or future military plans or operations.

When the above-mentioned subjects bear any relation to international conferences, nothing about them will be passed, discussed or published at any time without the specific authorization of the Executive Office of the President of the United States.

2. The Secretary of War emphasizes that these instructions apply equally to military personnel and to civilians. You are directed to see that all such under your command or jurisdiction are acquainted with the quoted instructions and that any infractions are promptly dealt with.

By direction of the Theater Commander: /s/ John C.H. Lee
Major General, US
Deputy Theater Commander

—

Effective now, the A.P.O. is changed from 634 to 559 for this organization. The letters previously addressed to the old A.P.O. number will reach the individual without delay; however, all correspondents should be notified of this change.

—

MOVIES:
Today—Double Feature, *"Off the Beaten Track"* and *"Broadway."*
Tues.—*"Madam Curie,"* Greer Garson and Walter Pidgeon.
Wed.—*"Hitler's Children,"* Bonita Granville.
Thurs.—*"Dangerous Blonde."*

—

AERO CLUB:
Tonight—Bingo at 19:30 hrs.
Tuesday—Drawing lessons at 19:00 hrs. by T/Sgt. Wright and S/Sgt. Alegre.
Wed.—G.I. Board of Governors' meeting at 19:30 hrs.
Thurs.—Rhumba dancing lessons at 19:30 hrs.
Friday—Dance for lower four graders.

—

SOCIAL:
Photographers will be here from the Rainbow Club all this week to take photographs.

—

LOST:
22-jewel Bulova wrist watch with brown leather band. Finder please return to Base Sgt. Major's office.

## No. 88, 28 March 1944

DETAILS FOR TOMORROW:
    Officer of the Day: 2nd Lt. Elmer T. Poppendieck, HQ 388th
    Staff Duty Officer: Lt. Hilton, 562nd Bomb Sq.
    Rocker Club C.Q.: S/Sgt. Frederick Hipp, 562nd Bomb Sqd.
    (S.Q. will report to Club Manager at 17:45 hrs for instructions)

—

BLACKOUT:
Blackout time is 19:58. All lights will be blacked out at that time. This blackout time will be strictly complied with by all personnel.

—

To expedite telephone service at this station, now that directories have been distributed, all personnel will place their calls by number only.

—

Various organizations on the post are fixing up day rooms for the men. There are still a few plush bottom chairs in some officers' quarters. It is requested that all officers that have these chairs in the quarters turn the same into Quartermaster immediately.

—

It seems ridiculous to have to caution grown men to stay off newly-laid cement, but the Utilities Officer has informed this Headquarters that when some new cement is laid, almost invariably, some big-footed GI walks through it or attempts to draw some fool picture in the cement. Kindly refrain from both of these practices. If you must indulge in such, make mud pies.

—

Arrangements have been made by Quartermaster to furnish additional coal and supplies, etc. and the Commanding Officer of the 562nd Bomb

Squadron has agreed that those men living in Site 8 may use the bathing facilities provided in Site 7; therefore all men living in Site 8 are free to use bathing facilities in Site 7.

—

UNIT AND SIMILAR FUNDS:
Accounts will be closed on the last day of each month. (Par 18a (5) AR 210-40). Council books with all supporting papers (deposit slips, vouchers and monthly bank statements) for the period subsequent to the last inspection to 31 March 1944 will be submitted to the office of the Air Inspector for inspection on or before 10 April 1944.

—

The Special Services Officer has arranged to have a Liberty Run to Bury St. Edmunds this evening. Transportation will leave from the Red Cross Picket Hut at 18:30 hrs and will leave Bury on the return trip at 23:15 hrs. Lt. William Sanderson, 561st Bomb Sqd., is designated to accompany the Liberty Run for this week and is charged with the conduct and safety of the men for the run. Further additional and specific instructions will be verbally issued by the Special Services Officer.

## No. 89, 29 March 1944

There will be a truck leaving the Red Cross picket hut at 18:00 hrs. tonight for the boxing matches at Rattlesden.

—

There will be a meeting of the Rocker Club Board of Governors tonight at 18:30 hrs. at the Club.

—

OVERDUE BOOKS:

The following named officers and enlisted men have books overdue at the Station Library: Capt. Roberts, two books; Col. Cox, one book; Capt. Samuels, three books; Maj. Egaas, three books; T/Sgt. Zaner Faust, one book; S/Sgt. William Helfrich, three books.

—

LOST:

Barracks bag containing cigarettes and cigars, picked up in front of Base Headquarters late the night of March 27 or early the morning of March 28. Will the person who picked this bag up please return it to the Station Adjutant.

—

BICYCLE LIGHTS:

The following is quoted from a letter Hq. ETOUSA, Subject "Maintenance and Operation of Motor Vehicles" File AG451/2 PubGC dtd 24 January 1944:

1. British law requires that each bicycle ridden on a road during black-out hours display a white headlight and a red taillight; that its rear mud-guard bear a white painted area of at least 12 square inches; and that such white area be maintained in a clean and unobscured condition.

2. Lights need not be shown when a bicycle is being wheeled by a person on foot or is stationary at the near (left hand) side of the road.

3. Violators of the law may be arrested by the military police or the British civilian police and are subject to disciplinary action.

*GIs gather around for coffee from the Red Cross*

# GLANCY'S BAG

By Roy Barry, ball turret gunner
Barwick's crew, *Lil' Miss Tammara,* 561st Squadron

*In 1995, a travel bag once belonging to Sgt. E. L. Glancy of the 388th was found in an attic in East Anglia, where it had apparently been stored for 50 years. The question of why Sgt. Glancy had left the bag was answered when his name was found on a casualty list. This is the story of Earl Glancy's last flight, as told by a crew member who survived it.*

On April 9, 1945, I was part of the B-17 heavy bomb crew whose mission and target that day was the railroad marshalling yards at Munich, Germany. My enlisted rank was staff sergeant and my crew position was Sperry lower ball turret operator.

Our ship's name was *Lil' Miss Tammara,* named after our commander's newly born daughter. Our commander, 1st Lt. Rex E. Barwick, was killed instantly on that Munich trip by a large chunk of flak which, upon exploding, hit him in the abdomen and literally cut him in half.

Because our regular bombardier had been assigned for that mission as a Lead Bombardier in our Group Commander's ship, we were assigned a fill-in—Togglier Sgt. Earl Glancy.

Leaving the target area over the railyard at Munich, as we banked away, we were hit with two direct flak bursts, large fragments of which tore open our Plexiglas nose and knocked out our Number 3 (right in-board) engine.

A large shell fragment entered our nose compartment, passing through Glancy's body and—according to our navigator, who was only a few feet away from Glancy when he was hit—Glancy was mortally wounded and was lucky to have gotten out of the ship.

277

Our navigator himself was trapped in the control cables up in the nose section and was finally sucked out by the slip stream from another hole blown in the engine side of the nose. Our navigator speculated that the flak fragment that traveled through Glancy's body also went on to go through our pilot's body, killing him, too.

The shell fragment that tore our Plexiglas nose apart created gaping holes in the fuselage, also severing gasoline lines leading from our wings to our engines; we caught fire when our electrical cables were severed by the flying flak fragments and short circuited, creating sparks. The fuel spewing about was ignited, along with oil and oxygen leaking from severed lines, to the extent that the heat that was generated caused fuselage structural members to melt.

Because our source of on-board electricity had been shut off by flak damage, my ball turret became inoperative from lack of power and I could not rotate it to remove myself from inside. I was trapped until I could dislodge the cranks that are used for just such loss-of-power emergencies, finally forcing my turret into such a position that I could partially open the escape and entry door and force my way into the ship's fuselage.

I attempted to go forward through the radio room and bomb bay, but all I saw was a solid wall of roaring flame; so I went to the waist exit door, which had already been removed by other crew members before they parachuted out. I leapt and made my jump earthwards from 24,000 feet. It is my understanding that our ship crash landed—a flaming, total wreck—about 15 miles west of Munich, with our pilot dead at the controls. His wallet was found by German soldiers and bore his name, embossed in gold. We were shown the wallet later at Luftwaffe Headquarters in Munich.

Upon landing, I was knocked unconscious for a time and fractured my right ankle. When I came to, a Luftwaffe major in dress blues was standing next to me with his pistol out. He was holding some civilians at bay and telling them I was a prisoner of war. It turned out they wanted to kill me, so I owed my life to that Luftwaffe pilot. As we walked together towards the center of Munich he explained to me that he was a jet fighter pilot who flew the new ME-262.

A similar escape took place on the outskirts of Munich when another Luftwaffe pilot found our co-pilot, 2nd Lt. Warren C. Perkins, lying on the ground unconscious, still strapped in his parachute harness and about to be shot by SS troopers. The Luftwaffe pilot outranked the SS and ordered them away, helped our co-pilot off with his chute harness and took him prisoner. He then commandeered a German army truck and had Perkins conveyed to a local hospital to be treated for his broken arm.

While the Luftwaffe major took me into custody and kept the civilians at bay with his pistol, I spotted, out of the corner of my eye, our radio man and waist gunner attempting to crawl from around a building about a half-block away. I was watching when, as the two of them rounded the corner two SS men armed with machine guns came from the back of the building and shot and killed them. I attempted to go to their aid, but the major restrained me, saying, "Nein, they ist kaput. Dead."

Shortly after returning home after the war, I received a letter of inquiry from Glancy's sister in New Jersey asking me what happened to her brother. She did not believe the war department that her brother was dead. I told her that he had indeed been killed, or at least mortally wounded, even if he did escape our flaming ship.

It is my understanding that Glancy was on his second tour of flying duty. We understood from him that he often lived off base and stayed with some civilian folks in Thetford.

# MISSION DIARY OF WILLIAM J. BRUNK

Pilot, *Patty Jo,* 563rd Squadron

**Mission One:** Chateaudun, March 28, 1944. Five hours and 30 minutes. Awakened at 01:00, and was pretty sure our first mission was in progress. We were scheduled to take off at 07:50 but due to instrument weather, take-off was two hours and 30 minutes late, still being an instrument assembly. One target was a series of airports deep in France. We were about 200 B-17s escorted at various points by P-47 Thunderbolts and P-51 Mustangs. I flew Number Two position (Low Right) in the Low Squadron of our 388th Bomb Group. No enemy fighters were either seen or engaged for the entire mission and as a "show" the trip was uneventful until we encountered a small area of deadly-accurate flak directly over the target. I saw two Forts brought down in flames directly ahead of my ship. The ball turret gunner said a number of parachutes emerged from one. I was impressed by the accuracy of the flak. We encountered no damage and landed in good order, unscathed. Our bombing was also accurate and our target was completely destroyed by direct hits.

**Mission Two:** French scrub, April 1, 1944. Three hours and 35 minutes. Originally intended for a DP and ME raid, this mission turned out as more of an April 1st effort. About 40 miles inside the French coast en route to darkest Germany we ran into instrument weather so bad that we couldn't contact our fighter support. We were forced to turn back. On the turn, the Jerry coastal anti-aircraft batteries threw a bit of flak into the lower group causing some battle damage. Hence, we were credited a mission. An easy one, but nothing accomplished except a little practice.

**Mission Three:** Osnabruck, April 8, 1944. Five hours and 50 minutes. Briefed on this mission yesterday but scrubbed due to weather. This morning we were to knock out the Achmer Air Field at Osnabruck. We did just that with excellent bombing results from 19,000 feet. Our fighter support was marvelous, so good that no enemy fighters came up. Flak came up in quantity though, and was good. We were hit twice, picking up quite a few holes, but none seriously. I flew Number Three position in the Lead Squadron. Saw no ships go down and our group lost none.

**Mission Four:** Charleroi, April 10, 1944. Six hours. Awakened at 02:43 and briefed to hit a German aircraft salvage and assembly plant near Brussels, Belgium. However, the target was cloud covered so we picked as a secondary an airfield nearby. Our results were as usual. There is no airfield anymore. Encountered moderate flak, but this time it was very inaccurate. No damage to anyone. Our fighter support was good and Jerry's planes stayed away. No losses in the group.

**Mission Five:** Rostock, April 11, 1944. Ten hours and 50 minutes. Rough. This one is one for the books. We took off at 06:25 and bombed Rostock, Germany. That is a concise report. In more words, they hit us with everything. We encountered flak first a couple of hours before the target and were fortunate in not getting hit. Shortly before the target we were hit by 22 ME-410s and they really checked us out. Over the target, we encountered heavy flak plus rockets and some new stuff that looked awfully pretty. Then, after the target, eight FW-190s flew through and ripped us some more. All in all, about 25 of us went down, five from our group and two, Ely and Osterkamp, from the squadron. Damage to my plane, *Patty Jo*, consisted of eight large flak holes.

*(The following is an account of this same mission taken from the diary of Brunk's tail gunner, Phillip Sullivan.)*

"Heavy flak along the coast. That flak scared the hell out of me. Arrived opposite target, made a right turn about 50 miles inland, bandits were reported at 11 o'clock. Twenty-two ME-410s pass on our right going to rear of line. They queue up for attack, form a line abreast about 1,600 yards out and start throwing rockets and 40mm cannon shells. They knock a few Forts out behind and Lt. Ely, our Number Two man. Fort in back with wing tip aflame and one with fire between Number 2 engine and fuselage. Eight fighters start in six-abreast and two behind come in to press attack. I open up at 800 yards. Ships (2) behind are already firing. ME-410 comes in to 200 yards. We shoot the hell out of him. Right engine afire, left prop windmilling. Pilot bails out. Two other ME-410s down. Lt. Elliot's upper gunner gets one of them. Jerries stay out of range and pick on stragglers. Two try and get Fort with wing fire. Gunners drive them off and he turns and heads for Sweden. Attack is over. Osterkamp and Elliot thrown out of formation by prop wash and join another formation. We are three ships alone, with us in tail-end position. Decision made to bomb Rostock, Germany. Get two of three important targets there. Start home. About 20 miles out, bandits reported at 12 o'clock. Ely's crew bails out. FW-190s make a pass. Seven on our squadron, below and up and one comes by us like a bat out of hell. They blow the vertical stabilizer off one Fort. Crew bails out. They seem afraid to make another pass at us. Didn't get a chance to shoot this time, which is all right with me. None of the crew like the idea of just three ships flying alone. We would have been cold meat. Leader will not join bigger formation. Damn him. Boy, I really sweated. The flak was heavy on target, too. P-38s pick us up at Danish coast. My God, did they look good. First breath I breathed in six hours. Flak again over Denmark. Finally arrived home. Flak hits in stabilizer, in Number 2 engine, big piece sticking out of cowl of Number 3 engine; right cockpit two holes; in nose, navigator and bombardier hit by flak but not hurt; and other flak holes. Target results good. Mission rough as hell. Osterkamp later reported to have made Sweden after he was knocked out of formation. *Patty Jo* #242, best in the ETO!"

*Pilot William Brunk and crew stand by as propellers are turned on* **Patty Jo**

**Mission Six:** Hazebrouck, April 20, 1944. Four hours and 50 minutes. Back from a pass to London and really ready to go again. We took off on this mission at 14:30, which is the first we have started a mission other than early morning. It was a target on the French coast; supposedly a rocket emplacement. We bombed by squadrons, making two runs on the target. Moderate flak was encountered. We picked up three small holes. The target was hit, though I don't know if it was destroyed. A very short and easy mission.

**Mission Seven:** Marshalling Yards at Hamm, April 22, 1944. Six hours and 43 minutes. This was probably one of the most beautiful raids ever flown. Pre-invasion tactics demanded that the marshalling yards at Hamm, the largest railroad center in Germany, be destroyed. The number of planes was immense, with plenty of fighter support. We skirted Happy Valley (the Ruhr) and, although the flak was terrific, our group never lost a ship, and my plane never had a scratch. The bombing, however, was the important thing, and it was terrific. We got direct hits with 500-pound demolition bombs and 100-pound incendiaries, completely destroying the yards and most of the town.

**Mission Eight:** Friedrichshaven, April 24, 1944. Nine hours and 45 minutes. Here we attacked a gear plant and for the first time we missed target. This was due to the terrific defense that was put up by Jerry at the target. The Group Lead ship was hit and it ruined the bomb run. We were also hit harder than we have ever been. *Patty Jo* was full of large holes and, worst of all, Steiner was hit in the arm by flak and will be laid up for from two to six weeks. We gave him first aid at the scene and then we were hit again and again. My instruments were knocked out. We saw some enemy fighters, too, but our escort took care of them and they never made a pass. Rough.

**Mission Nine:** Hannover, April 26, 1944. Eight hours and 50 minutes. This started out to be a raid on an aircraft assembly plant near Brunswick, but weather mixed conditions so badly that we were caught above a solid overcast with no PFF ship. We attempted to drop our bombs on the city of Hannover. Bombing results unknown. Later reconnaissance will determine it. We picked up only one burst of flak but it got an oxygen system and the interphone.

**Mission 10:** Berlin, April 29, 1944. Eight hours and 45 minutes. This morning had an early briefing and found that our "ambition target" had come up. Yes, it was Berlin! The weather was favorable and we went over en masse with plenty of escort. The mission wasn't too rough except over the target. However, we had flak all along the route. At target, however, the flak was terrific. We did lose only two ships, although we had two deaths and many wounded in the group. *Patty Jo* will be out for several days.

**Mission 11:** Metz, May 1, 1944. Seven hours. Today the group ran two missions. I did the afternoon one, going to Metz, Germany, to attack the marshalling yards. We completely knocked them out with some beautiful bombing. The entire mission was excellent. Flak was good and we got one large hole in Number 1 induction system and some smaller ones. The group lost no planes today.

**Mission 12:** Berlin, May 7, 1944. Nine hours and 15 minutes. Awakened at 02:00 and went to the worst briefing I've yet seen. Weather was doubtful and we had two targets arranged, the submarine base at Kiel; or Berlin, the latter being the primary target. We made it to Berlin, bombing from 24,000 feet through 10/10 coverage using PFF. The result must have been devastating, as the target was the city proper and I have never seen more planes at one place all carrying 1,000-pounders down to the MK-47 incendiaries that our 388th carried. The flak was terrific but our variety of bombing altitudes, courses and chaff apparently confused Jerry sufficiently as little damage was done. My *Patty Jo* didn't have a scratch.

**Mission 13:** Juvincourt, May 9, 1944. Five hours and 10 minutes. Today we had our first true milk run. The English have been recently suffering pretty heavy casualties by Jerry night fighters based in France. They asked us to help them out, so today we went in after the fields and planes on the ground. Our 388th group went after this field at Juvincourt. Our bombing could have been better, but we did quite a bit of damage. What made it a milk run was the shortness of the trip; five hours. No flak over the target and not too much elsewhere and no enemy fighters. Our support was wonderful.

**Mission 14:** Liege, May 11, 1944. Five hours and 45 minutes. An afternoon mission and an easy one, though flak was good and knocked down two planes in the group ahead. We were supposed to hit the marshalling yards here, but our bombs to an extent were short and we may have killed some innocent people. Sure hope not. We got one hole in *Patty Jo* knocking out Number 1 battery.

**Mission 15:** Osnabruck, May 13, 1944. Six hours and 45 minutes. The marshalling yard here was our target and we left it in a state of ruin. I was leading the Second Element of the High Squadron to start, but the Squadron leader aborted and I led the High. Flak was good, but we were fortunate and never got a scratch.

**Mission 16:** Caen, France. May 23, 1944. Six hours and 45 minutes. This was intended for a deeper raid, but near our original target we found adverse weather so we wiped out the bomber base at Caen on our return. A tedious but easy mission.

**Mission 17:** Liege, May 25, 1944. Five hours and 50 minutes. Had been here once before after the marshalling yards and found it an easy mission. Today, we went after the locomotive shops at the same place and found the mission quite rugged. Flak knocked down the Lead ship with Col. Chamberlain and the Deputy Lead with Lt. Hildebrand. Also would have gotten our Lt. Breed except for a heroic feat of flying. He lost five men as it was. My new ship, replacing the vanquished *Patty Jo*, was hit very hard. One of which came in the windshield directly in front of me taking a course that must have missed me by a hair's breadth and showering glass all over the cockpit. Bombing result: good.

**Mission 18:** Strasbourg, France, May 27, 1944. Eight hours and 10 minutes. Quite a long raid today and a beautiful one. The weather was marvelous and the snow-covered Alps really stood out. Our target was again marshalling yards and our bombing was perfect. We had more fighter support than I have ever seen. P-38s, 47s and Mustangs were all over the place.

**Mission 19:** Magdeburg, May 28, 1944. Eight hours and 50 minutes. This was a long DP with beautiful weather. The entire Air Force was over there and, as a whole, did shack or near shack bombing on all the various targets. Ours was the ordnance depot at Magdeburg, a tank and artillery works. We also shacked. Flak was good and hit our ship a number of times, but only minor damage. We lost Fjelsted today, which is the first entire crew our 563rd Squadron has lost since the April 11th Rostock raid. With the heavy losses during that time, our squadron had an enviable record. Codding was also lost from one of the other squadrons.

**Mission 20:** Troyes, May 30, 1944. Six hours and 45 minutes. This was the easiest mission I have had. We were to hit the locomotive repair shops here and we really shacked them, too. The nice part of the mission was the smallness of the amount of flak. I lost the supercharger on Number 2 engine and had not yet left the English coast. In spite of this, we went over and back.

**Mission 21:** Soest, Germany, May 31, 1944. Six hours and 30 minutes. There, just the other side of Happy Valley, we were to continue our destruction of transportation by erasing more marshalling yards said to control more cars than all but one of Germany's yards. Well, if it did, it doesn't anymore, as we shacked it but good. We also successfully dodged all the flak they threw up and never had a scratch on the plane.

**Mission 22:** French Coast, June 2, 1944. Four hours and 30 minutes. Today I finally got a Pas de Calais mission. Softening up the invasion coast, we hit coastal batteries near Boulogne. This is the first time an occupied country had ever been bombed by PFF methods and I believe we took Jerry by complete surprise as his flak was very poor, though he attempted to throw a lot of it up. Our carpet, and especially the chaff, took care of it beautifully. It was my turn to fly the Abortion Element and was fortunate in filling in.

**Mission 23:** Cape Gris Nez, June 4, 1944. Four hours and 30 minutes. Was glad to see another pre-invasion coastal pounding and, though we almost had to scrub it due to weather, it went very well. Flak was of the tracking variety and, with our 282 mph ground speed and evasive action, it never caught us.

**Mission 24:** Cape Gris Nez, June 5, 1944. Five hours and 10 minutes. Today we had intended to hit some emplacement inside the coast but ran into a front, so dropped our bombs along the Cape Gris Nez coast adding to the general destruction. The French coast surely is a mass of ruin.

**Mission 25:** Cross Channel, June 6, 1944. Six hours and 25 minutes. D-Day! Today it started! A huge show, and we were high in the cast. Every available plane in England was over and we pulverized a place for a beachhead. Paratroopers followed and then the landing barges. We are in!

**Mission 26:** Tours, June 8, 1944. Seven hours, even. Today we went over to knock out a bridge to prevent Jerry from bringing troops and supplies to the beachhead. Weather was wretched with contrails that were really bad. Had good flak over the target and picked up a few hits, but no major damage.

**Mission 27:** Pontaubaul, June 11, 1944. Seven hours and 30 minutes. Here we bombed a railroad bridge PFF. Results unobserved. Weather was terrible with solid soup from 4,000 to 18,000 feet. This is the first mission that I didn't see any flak. Did encounter four ground-to-air rockets, however, but they were inaccurate.

**Mission 28:** Bremen, June 18, 1944. Seven hours. Our first potentially rough mission since D-Day. Here we attempted to knock out an oil refinery, but as weather was PFF, results were unobserved. Flak was so heavy all the way from the IP to the RP that one could have tread lightly on it. We felt at least six bursts lift our ship, but received only one hit, which broke an aileron rib.

**Mission 29:** Cognac, June 19, 1944. Seven hours and 30 minutes. This was an airport job, but we ran into a front of very bad proportions and never got a chance to even see the target. Everyone in the Group had vertigo very badly and I was no exception. We had a very poor Group Lead and after we got above the front, instead of staying there, the leader brought us down through it for over 150 miles. Wow!

**Mission 30:** Ruhland, June 21, 1944. Eleven hours and 20 minutes. This was to be one of the biggest stories of the war that backfired tragically, making even a bigger story, one that can't be told until after the war, and may never be told. We took off at 04:45 and bombed an oil refinery at Ruhland, Germany, intending to go on to Russia, through to Italy and return. We shacked the target and landed at Poltava, Russia. We encountered moderate flak seven times and were hit by ME-109s en route. That evening in Russia, we were attacked on the ground by an estimated 200 German planes and completely wiped out. My plane, *Fairman Willie*, was hit directly and completely destroyed. Sullivan and Abernathy were guarding it at the time and both were hit, Sullivan quite badly. We left him in a field hospital at Poltava. Duration of the German raid, two hours and 20 minutes.

# Back For a Second Tour

By Dong "Swede" Ong, pilot, 562nd Squadron

I was one of the few who flew two combat tours in Europe.

A tour consisted of 25 sorties, or missions. The number of missions required for a tour was determined by the hazards encountered in each theater and type of aircraft and operations. The 8th Air Force bombardment operation of B-17s and B-24s flying out of England to the Continent was considered the most hazardous of all the areas during World War II. My unit, the 388th Bombardment Group, had 270 aircraft processed through and lost 179.

Our crew experienced the normal mishaps—battle damage to the aircraft, engine shut-downs, large holes due to shrapnel damage, gas leaks and one man wounded. Following one mission, the ground crew stopped counting after 300 holes.

When we had 25 missions, the tour limit was raised to 35. At that time, I was asked to return for a second tour and I consented only if the remainder of my crew was to be released. The colonel agreed, only if I and my co-pilot returned after a 30-day leave at home.

By procrastinating, I managed to stretch out my return, with travel by train and lengthy layovers in New York, Chicago and elsewhere.

On my return, I was processed in Atlantic City, a large processing center for air crews going and coming. Many of the people were there for months waiting for processing. Some only had eight missions and were sent back to the U.S. Because of this backlog, I thought that the war in Europe would be over before I could be processed and returned. At any rate, when my documents were reviewed, we who were returning for another tour were put at the head of the line!

During my physical examination, I encountered difficulty with an eye test. The doctor told me he would have to ground me; however, when he reviewed my papers he found, stamped in large letters, "Combat Returnee." He slapped me on the shoulder and said, "You are a borderline case," and passed me.

There was another humorous moment, and it involved Lt. John A. Dupree, a bombardier who was also returning for a second tour with the 388th. It followed that we two sort of teamed up together. John was a tall, handsome young man from Los Angeles. We each had two B-4 bags and, everywhere we were sent, we had to struggle with them. During processing, we were issued additional gear consisting of blankets, gas mask, canteen and eating things. We attempted to explain that these items were not required, since these were available at our unit. The authorities insisted, and we were required to handle an additional bag. We then put everything into one bag and, since John was able to handle the additional weight, he carried that third bag.

We were to travel by train from Atlantic City to the pier and board the Queen Elizabeth. Those of us returning were at the head of the column. Behind us were thousands of troops who gave us the raspberry every time we stopped to rest. When we got to the train, John and I decided to lose our third bag.

When we arrived at the pier and in formation, Lt. Dupree was called forward. He was chewed out for leaving the bag on the train! It seemed that he left something in the bag that identified him. I then stepped forward and told the authorities that it was mistakenly left behind.

"John thought I had the bag and I thought he had it," I explained.

I was ordered to stay put, was chewed out, too, and told in no uncertain terms that officers and enlisted men alike had to carry their own bags.

Meanwhile, boarding of the Queen Elizabeth continued. When all had boarded, I was then permitted up the gangplank. When I got up to the hatchway, the Marine attending would not let me board, but the Marine major at the base of the gangplank waved me on.

I stepped over the hatchway threshold and there was our third bag.

*Cpt. Dong "Swede" Ong*

After crossing the Atlantic Ocean, we arrived at the processing unit in England. Again, there was a large backlog and again we were placed at the head of the line. We were only there a few hours before being placed on a train for our unit.

I reported in late that night and went to the Officers' Club. I did not recognize most of the officers there since many had rotated home. I did see the colonel the instant he saw me. He was surprised and he hugged me and expressed glee. He said, "What are you doing here? We released you a month ago! But, since you are here, we can sure use you. I'll pick out a crew for you. You can choose your own missions."

At any rate, I flew another tour of 25 missions and did *not* get to choose my missions. In fact, I was sent on and led most of the deep penetrations into Germany.

# FROM BIG B TO V-E DAY

By Bob Slockett, tail gunner
Billy K. Faurot's crew, 561st Squadron

**Mission One:** Early in the morning of March 15, 1945, our crew and hundreds of other B-17 crews were awakened. It was about 2 a.m. We dressed quickly, went into the mess hall for a breakfast fit for a king (eggs anyway we wanted them, bacon, sausage, French toast, Cream of Wheat, toast, orange juice and strong Army-style coffee) and hurried over to the Mission Control Briefing Building. We were told we were to go on a seven-hour flight to Big B (Berlin) to knock out marshalling yards in suburban Orienburg.

After the briefing, all gunners went to the armorer shop and picked up their .50-caliber machine guns and ammunition for loading in their particular location on the plane. As tail gunner, I had two .50s to load into the tail.

At a specified time, Billy K., our pilot, taxied our B-17 out to the runway and took off with hundreds of other B-17 crews, one after the other. We climbed through thousands of feet of cloud cover in total darkness except for what could be seen from the lighting of our plane. There was an eeriness associated with the reflected light bouncing off the swirling clouds as we brushed through them. It was only about 3 am.

We rendezvoused at 10,000 feet over the English Channel, joined our position in the group formation, and climbed further to about 25,000 feet as we headed straight for Big B. We encountered some flak from German anti-aircraft guns after daylight near Hannover. The temperature was –32c at that altitude. As tail gunner, I sat on a bicycle-like seat and had placed four or five plates of steel armor, about 10 square inches and 1/2-inch thick, under my butt for protection. Small pieces of flak might bounce off

293

small sections of armor plate, but they would offer no protection against a direct hit by an 88mm shell that was normally fired from the German anti-aircraft guns.

After 3½ hours, our group arrived at Big B and turned on the bomb run (a period of constant altitude and air speed to allow the bombardier to sight the target and drop the bombs with precision). At the altitude of 21,000, feet we had to have our oxygen masks on. We also had to have our electric suits hooked up. We were on the bomb run just one second when I simultaneously vomited into my oxygen mask and defecated in my electric heated suit. It was completely involuntary and unexpected. I was apparently at a very high level of anxiety and then all of a sudden we were on the bomb run at Big B and all my control reflexes relaxed. The hundreds of huge black puffs of smoke (flak) from bursting 88mm German anti-aircraft shells surrounded us but none were closer than about 20 feet to our plane. There was no fighter opposition. We dropped our bombs on the marshalling yards with good accuracy. As soon as the bomb run was completed we dove away from the target and the anti-aircraft fire as rapidly as we could and headed back home to Bonnie England. Soon we arrived at the English Channel and then at our airfield near Thetford. We landed safely with a sense of accomplishment having completed our first combat mission. We took our guns off the plane, cleaned them at the armor shack and went to debriefing at the Briefing Headquarters Building. We were all given a shot of cognac, questioned about the mission by debriefing officers and then released to go to the mess hall. I went to my Quonset hut quarters first to clean up my "bomb run mess" and then to the mess hall. Several of the guys at the mess hall said, "Where did you go, Bob?" with sly, mischievous grins on their faces. They knew where I went, so I didn't answer them.

Jack Holt, our radio operator, threw chaff out of the open waist exit every time we flew over or near a populated area on our route to Berlin. Chaff is stripped aluminum sheet used to deceive the enemy radar by providing a false image on their screen. Jack did a good job; actually too good—by the time we arrived at the target there was none left to confuse the Berlin anti-aircraft gunners. We were not shot down so we forgave him.

**Mission Two:** Our next mission was two days later, on March 17, 1945. We had a good sense of what it was like now to go on a bombing mission over Nazi Germany. As a result, we weren't filled with as much apprehension as we were before our first mission.

There were, however, a couple members of other crews who went on sick call immediately after coming back from Mission Number One. We heard that they suffered battle fatigue and were subsequently removed from flying status. They never flew another mission and were returned to the States after a short R & R period.

Our March 17th mission was to Ruhland, Germany, about 40 miles from Poland where Russian troops were gathering for large scale assaults on the Germans. Ruhland is about 80 miles southeast of Berlin. Our Group's specific mission was to knock out the flak guns so the rest of the 8th Air Force could bomb synthetic oil refineries. Our crew was one of the six crews in the lead formation. We led the entire 8th Air Force on this mission. I believe General Doolittle and his staff liked the way our crew handled themselves, especially Billy K., our pilot. He was a "hot" pilot. That's the most laudatory thing you can say about a good combat pilot.

Bombing Ruhland's synthetic oil refineries was reminiscent of the 8th and 15th Air Force raids on the Ploesti, Romania oil fields earlier in the war. A war cannot be fought without oil, and the Nazis were well aware of that. They defended both Ploesti and Ruhland with an enormous number of anti-aircraft guns. When we reached the target at Ruhland and began the bomb run we determined it was too cloudy to drop our bombs with any degree of accuracy. Lt. Brown's crew, who was on our right wing, was shot down by anti-aircraft fire while we were on the bomb run. We then flew about 110 miles southwest to Plauen, our secondary target. Plauen is about 20 miles from the Czechoslovakian border. Anti-aircraft fire was moderate at Plauen in contrast to the heavy and accurate fire at Ruhland.

We carried 20 fragmentation bombs. We were on oxygen for five hours of an eight hour trip. I had some trouble with my oxygen mask freezing up. We were at 25,000 feet where it was -48C. Mighty cold. No enemy fighter opposition was seen by our crew; we expected them to come up in full force someday in the near future—flak from 88mm shells bursting all around us and the Luftwaffe firing at us at the same time is a good description of our expectations. I had no trouble with my stomach or bowels on this mission. Fear of the unknown causing our anxiety level to be excessively high was not as much of a problem as it was on our first mission.

Our mission to Plauen was calm compared to the next 8th Air Force trip to bomb marshalling yards at Plauen two days later on March 19, 1945. More than 100 Luftwaffe fighters, including 36 jets in formation, were encountered. This was the largest number of jet airplanes seen as a unit up to this time. U.S. fighter planes claimed 42 German fighters shot down, including three jets. Our crew was not assigned to go on the March 19th mission.

**Mission Three:** On March 21, 1945, preparatory air operations for the forthcoming crossing of the lower Rhine River by Allied ground forces began. The crossings, scheduled for March 23rd, included the bridgehead at the small town of Remagen. Our crew, plus 1,254 other heavy bombers, in conjunction with aircraft of the British Royal Air Force and the 9th Army Air Force, were briefed to bomb Ruhland again with six 1,000-pound demolition bombs on March 21st, our third mission. It was too cloudy again for accuracy so we bombed a Plauen tank factory instead. Anti-aircraft fire at Ruhland was very accurate again. Our plane was bounced around like a Piper Cub in violent up-and-down thermal drafts.

Our B-17 received seven flak holes in the waist and tail. One hole was less than two feet in back of me. It was from a live 88mm shell that went up through the tail leaving a hole the size of a football. The shell blew up above the tail of the plane. It must have been a timed shell, not one that would blow up on contact. Lucky for us. The whole tail would have been torn from the fuselage if the shell had exploded upon contact.

We dropped our bombs at 23,000 feet where the temperature was –38c. There was very little flak over Plauen, our secondary target. We encountered some on the way back to England. There was no damage to our plane over Plauen; black puffs of bursting 88s were too far away. I saw one of our B-17s, on our tail, burst into flames over Ruhland. There were no chutes as the parts of the plane fell into the clouds below.

We were on oxygen for five hours of an eight-hour mission. We had good P-51 fighter support. On the way back there were 16 ME-262 jets that looked over our formation. They flew parallel to us but just out of range of our .50-caliber guns. Then, suddenly, they turned our way and made a pass through our formation at near supersonic speed, without incident. When we arrived back safely at our field, we were met by ambulances and their para-medical crews. We were very happy to report that nobody was injured as the ambulance crew and debriefing officers personally examined the damage to our plane. We stripped the plane of our guns, cleaned them and reported for further debriefing after the usual shot of cognac.

We normally didn't hear of the total number of B-17s lost in our group during a mission. We learned more about our losses from a British newspaper a week or so later. It seemed that the American press normally reported less casualties than actually occurred and the British press results were closer to the actual.

There were British pubs nearby our airfield, just a short walk or bike ride through the beautiful, hedge-rowed countryside. Many evenings you would find us drinking warm British ale at one of the pubs. We went to the pubs mainly as a diversion. There were always a few of our comrades who stayed too long and came back to their Quonset hut all tanked up. On two occasions, a gunner came back late from a pub and woke us all up with a shot from his .45 through the ceiling. We all had .45-caliber pistols that we carried with us on our missions for security if our plane was shot down. There was another occasion where a gunner came home late after a night out at one of the pubs and puked in his upper bunkmate's shoe. You can visualize the argument that took place the next morning when the victim put his foot in the contaminated shoe.

Over a period of days, I noticed that the crew member in the bunk next to me always kept a box of crackers on the floor next to his bunk. My curiosity was aroused even more when I woke up one night to see him wide awake at about 2 a.m. eating those crackers. His explanation was that he had a tape worm that got very hungry at 2 am. It crawled up into his throat, he said, and descended back down to his stomach when fed.

New air crews go on short navigational missions over England before they begin flying missions. One of our B-17s mysteriously exploded in the air over central English farmland. The entire crew perished except the tail gunner. He was trapped in the tail which was blown free of the rest of the plane when it exploded. The free-falling tail structure, with its frightened passenger, swirled down erratically and landed in the middle of a huge haystack. The very fortunate survivor freed himself, walked to the nearby farmer's home to report the tragedy to our base headquarters and searched the area for the remains of his crew.

**Mission Four:** On March 22, 1945, we were briefed to bomb an airfield two miles south of Frankfurt in support of Allied troops that were preparing to cross the Rhine River. The Remagen Bridge was the only access left to cross the Rhine. The German troops destroyed all other bridges crossing the river in order to give them time to strengthen their defenses. The Remagen bridge was about 65 miles northwest of Frankfurt and was the location of a bitter battle of U.S. troops with the defending German Army. Our bombs seemed to all fall on the target leaving it a mass of black smoke and flames from the many Nazi planes in hangars and on runways. We must have surprised the Luftwaffe because none of their planes were seen to get off the ground. There was a lot of flak from the IP, along the bomb run and past the target. Their gunners did a good job of tracking us. We received three good-sized holes in the fuselage near the bomb bay doors. One hunk of an 88mm struck the Number 1 engine and knocked out a cylinder. Billy K feathered the engine for the return trip. The flight lasted six hours, with four hours on oxygen. We bombed at 26,000 feet, the shortest mission we have had so far.

**Mission Five:** On March 23, 1945, the Allied ground assault across the lower Rhine River began and we were briefed to bomb marshalling yards at Hengstey, a suburb of Dortmund, 45 miles northeast of Cologne (Koln) and about 50 miles southeast of the Dutch border. There was a moderate amount of flak, but it was very accurate. We were fortunate; we received minor battle damage. I reported back to Billy K. that I could see nothing out of order to the controls in the tail. Our wingman, Lt. Don Dennis' crew, was shot down over the target. I saw five chutes escape the plane just before it blew up; however, the entire crew did escape the plane and became POWs. Only Lt. Dennis lost his life at the hands of civilian captors. We dropped our bombs at 23,000 feet and were on oxygen only three hours. Mission 5 was completed satisfactorily. We hit the target and arrived back safely.

**Mission Six:** On March 24, 1945, in conjunction with General Montgomery's ground troop assault across the Rhine River, our crew was one of 1,033 heavy bombers of the 8th Air Force to strike 14 airfields in western Germany. Our target was an auxiliary air field near Rheine, Germany, about 15 miles due east of Amsterdam. We saw huge armadas of British Short Sterling bomber-drawn gliders loaded with troops and equipment. Today was our first milk run. The Jerries were too busy fighting Monty and his troops to worry about us. There was no flak over the target and only five burst at us as we passed over the Frisian Islands on our way back to the base. The Frisians are a group of islands off the north-westerly shore of the Netherlands. We bombed at 20,000 feet and were on oxygen for two-and-a-half hours of a four-hour flight. We shacked the target, leaving it a mass of billowing black smoke. The Jerries won't use that field again for a long time. There were 27 German FW-190s and ME-109s shot down during the mission, our sixth.

Our crew was given a three-day pass. We had flown on four missions in a row, and four of us—Jack Holt, radio operator/gunner; Roger Koenitzer, waist gunner; Steve Podolan, ball turret gunner, and myself, tail gunner—went into London. We had a good time and did a variety of things. We went to Covent Gardens, a magnificent dance hall that rivals the Palladium in Hollywood, USA. I met the cutest little redhead, danced a lot with her and took her home on a double-decker bus. Her father met us at the door and didn't allow her to invite me indoors. I promised to phone her but never did. Oh my, I don't know why I didn't; she was a very pretty, sweet 16-year-old. We rode one of London's famous double-decker buses on a sightseeing tour. I believe we enjoyed riding around 25 feet up in the air more than seeing the historical sights such as Big Ben and Churchill's residence at No. 10 Downing Street.

You have to realize we were just 19 to 21 years old and not very worldly wise nor intellectually oriented. After debarking the bus along the Thames River, we stopped and talked with a couple girls in one of the parks. There was talk of going with the girls to a party, but we decided not to. The park consisted of the usual lush green grass, shrubbery and a man standing on a soap box exhibiting his oratory wiles on our ascendancy from Neanderthal man and why we haven't progressed more satisfactorily civilization-wise. We left the park and went to Picadilly Circus. While walking along the main street we passed a couple of girls who hurried up to us from behind and goosed us. We looked back at them with a surprised smile and continued on our way at a faster pace. We came to an intersection and saw a man acting strangely down a hill under a lamp post. We decided that he was a "queer" trying to get us to go down the hill to meet him. We didn't succumb to his invitation. We threw some stones at him, instead. None found their mark. In the year 1945 people thought differently of homosexuals than they do now.

Another thing we did that I'm not very proud of occurred at a restaurant in London. The four of us ordered steak and enjoyed the meal. However, we learned from the waitress that the steak was from a horse, not from a cow. Can you guess what we young punks did? You guessed it. We walked briskly by the cashier without paying.

**Mission Seven:** Our next mission on March 28, 1945 was to Hannover which is located about 80 miles south of Hamburg and 150 miles west of Berlin. We were briefed to bomb Hannover's rail yards and to expect plenty of flak over the target, but Jerry must have sent most of his guns against Monty. We carried eight 500-pound bombs and four incendiaries. We assembled over France in dense clouds at about 7 am. We could hardly see our wingman, who was only about 30 feet off our right wing. We were proud of Billy K. for getting us safely off the ground, up to an altitude and in combat formation after a successful rendezvous and assembly. We bombed at 26,500 feet where the temperature was -41C. We saw only six bursts of anti-aircraft fire. Our lead ship had to abort because of flak damage so the deputy lead took over. We were on oxygen for four hours. We saw no enemy fighter opposition, unlike reports from other planes in our group. We dove off the bomb run and were homeward bound for good old Knettishall, happy to have survived.

**Mission Eight:** We ran into a lot of soup while assembling over France on March 30, 1945, our eighth mission, so we split up. We caught the rest of the formation halfway to the target. We were briefed to bomb submarine pens at Hamburg, but it was too cloudy so we hit the oil dumps close by. We made direct hits on the storage tanks as evidenced by the billowing masses of red flames and black smoke that rolled up to at least 10,000 feet. We dropped our bombs at 25,000 feet where the temperature was –38c. Their anti-aircraft gunners sent an awesome barrage of flak up at us. We had an escort P-51 pilot stop by and fly formation with us on our right side between the waist and the tail. He was so close I could see his features.

During the flak barrage I saw his jaw set in angry determination. He rolled his plane over into a vertical dive. I followed him all the way down as he pointed his nose toward the red flashes coming from the German anti-aircraft batteries. All of a sudden the German guns were silenced. There were no more red flashes from their guns. Our P-51 escort friend did a great job and undoubtedly saved some B-17 crew members' lives.

We received about 10 holes from flak. One piece missed Bombardier Byron Bland's foot by half-an-inch. Another hunk of flak missed Jack Holf's head by two inches. There was a hole in the right bomb bay door that a fat man could crawl through. And to top it off, we had two engines out of commission (feathered) and one on fire. I counted five planes in our formation with feathered propellers. Billy K. dove the plane down as we left the bomb run and fortunately the fire in the one engine blew out.

Billy K. called us over the intercom and said that if he and Chuck couldn't get one of the three inactive engines started we were going to try to get to Sweden, which was neutral and would detain us until the war ended. Sweden is only about 100 miles north of Hamburg and with some luck and expert piloting one engine might get us there in a controlled glide. Fortunately, Billy K. and Chuck, the co-pilot, got one of the three engines started so we could maintain altitude. We had one engine on each side operating. We threw out any excess material on board (such as metal flak protection pieces) to lighten the weight on the plane. Six of our 12 500-pound bombs were hung up on the bomb run. Byron, our bombardier, was able to correct the situation by climbing into the open bomb bay to repair the release mechanism. As a result of Byron's mechanical ability we, fortunately, were able to drop the bombs into the North Sea to further lighten our load.

Billy K. eased the plane down to 500 feet and flew at that low level all the way back to our English home base. We flew so low that the German Luftwaffe on the island of Heligoland in the North Sea were unable to detect us on their radar. If they saw us, we probably would have been dead ducks. We were a good crew but I don't believe we could have fought off a dozen FW-190s by ourselves.

Once again, emergency wagons met us after landing safely via Billy K.'s expertise. Fortunately, no one except the co-pilot was hurt. He had a small cut in his right thigh from flak but refused to tell anybody about it until days later. He didn't want a Purple Heart for such a minor injury. We were all very happy this mission was over.

**Mission Nine:** Our crew was briefed to bomb submarine pens at Kiel on Mission 9, April 3, 1945. Kiel is 30 miles south of Denmark and about 50 miles north of Hamburg, Germany. It is on an inlet to Kiel Bay which leads into the Baltic Sea. We hit Kiel visually at 25,000 feet.

It was –42c at that altitude. My heated boots went out on me and my feet froze. I kept kicking the bottom of the plane to try to thaw them out. There was a moderate amount of flak but it was very inaccurate. The closest bursts were about 50 feet on either side of us. There were no enemy fighters to attack near us. We observed what looked like the whole German Navy scamper away in all directions in the harbor of Kiel Bay. They wanted to distance themselves from the submarine pens as quickly as they possibly could. We were on oxygen for well over five hours. I had a bad cold which didn't help matters a bit. We flew back to the base mostly over the open waters of the North Sea.

**Mission 10:** On April 4, 1945 we hit the Kiel submarine pens at 25,000 feet where it was –38c. There wasn't much flak bursting near us; just a few barrages. There were a few German jet jobs nearby that our P-51s scared away. There were a lot of dense clouds up to about 20,000 feet that we had to climb up through to get to the target and then down through on our way back to Knettishall. Mission 10 was accomplished successfully. We were the Low Lead Element on this mission.

**Mission 11:** On April 5, 1945, we were briefed at about 3 a.m. for our 11th mission to bomb rail yards and an aircraft parts factory in Nuremberg. The targets at Nuremberg were about 75 miles from Czechoslovakia and due west of Pitzen. Nuremberg, of course, was the site for the post-war Allied war trials of Nazis who committed atrocities during the war.

This mission will always be remembered because I came very close to losing my life. My oxygen mask became disconnected. At an altitude of 25,000 feet, where only traces of oxygen are present, most humans become unconscious in three minutes and expire a few minutes later. The mission was routine until a few minutes before arriving at the point of the bomb run. At that time, Billy K. always had us call in to be sure everybody was okay. I didn't answer his call, so the waist gunner, Roger Koenitzer, and the radio operator/gunner, Jack Holt, began throwing empty shells back at me in the tail. I very slowly turned around to them each time a shell hit me, but I was nearly unconscious so couldn't respond to Billy K.'s plea on the intercom. I instinctively knew what my problem was, but lost the coordination necessary to re-connect the oxygen supply tube to the tube on the mask.

Billy K. then sent Roy Hurshey, engineer/top turret gunner, back in the tail to assess the situation. Roy was equipped with a portable oxygen cylinder and immediately realized that my mask was disconnected from the source of oxygen. He quickly connected my mask to the oxygen line and gave me a shot of pure oxygen. I recovered almost immediately.

Over the years I have questioned superficially if my occasional lapses of memory might have been caused by the loss of oxygen that occurred to me on this mission. I facetiously mentioned this at our 49th Anniversary Reunion in Savannah, Georgia in 1998. Our crew last saw each other when we were discharged in 1945. Byron Bland, our bombardier, spontaneously replied, "No, not so. I have memory lapses without ever having been without oxygen!"

I sincerely thank Billy K. for establishing the bomb run call-in rule, Roger and Jack for throwing empty shells at me in the tail to try to get my attention and Roy for crawling all the way from the top turret gun station to the tail with a portable oxygen cylinder and mask. They saved my life and I will always be proud of how effectively they handled the situation.

Once we began the bomb run at Nuremberg, we were met with a lot of flak and at least one FW-190. There was a short trail of smoke coming from his engine as he passed under us out of range. I fired at him once but he disappeared below before any further damage to his plane could be observed. We headed back safely to our base at Knettishall.

**Mission 12:** Our next mission was four days later, so we had some time off. We picked up sides and played softball during the day. At night, there were dances at the NCO club. I went to one of them and met a cute little brunette. We danced awhile and then took a walk out into the fields behind the club. It was a beautiful spring evening with the bright moon and stars shining down on us. We kissed, but nothing else. I must not have felt very romantic. I escorted her to the bus that brought the girls in from Thetford. The next night a buddy of mine told me that my "girl-friend" asked about me. She was at the NCO Club dance again. She wanted to know if I was going to go to the dance or not. I said no. I guess I didn't feel like dancing. I wasn't very good at it anyway. The next after-noon my same buddy came into the Quonset and said, "Your girlfriend is outside." I went out to meet her and we decided to walk along the beauti-ful hedgerows. It was a warm afternoon in early April. We crawled into a hiding place behind the hedgerows on the side of the road. We kissed and made love. We were exhilarated and happy.

On April 9, 1945, our group was briefed to bomb the Reims Airfield in Munich, Germany. The Austrian border is about 35 miles south of Munich. Innsbruck, Austria, is about 65 miles southwest of Munich. Eighth Air Force Intelligence sources reported the Munich airfield to have a large number of German jet aircraft on the ramps and in hangars. Our trip to Munich coincided with the Allied ground troop breakthrough over the Remagen bridge and crossing over the Rhine river at that point. We arrived at the bomb run over the Munich airfield without incident and then the fireworks began. The Jerries defended the airfield with heavy anti-aircraft fire. We received a number of shrapnel hits, but none was serious.

We lost one of the B-17 crews in our formation right over the target. I saw five parachutes leave the stricken plane. They floated down right over the center of the airfield. A large number of B-17s in our Group had yet to drop their bombs on the target. I have often thought over the years since that mission, how unfortunate this crew was to be shot down right over the target and then to have hundreds of bombs rain down on top of them. We never heard whether any of the crew from that plane survived.

On our way back to England we were able to briefly observe the beauty of the snow-packed mountain ranges of the German and Swiss Alps.

**Mission 13:** On April 10, 1945, we were briefed to bomb an airfield near Zerbst. We dropped six 500-pound bombs on the airfield from 24,000 feet. The flak was light, but there were many German fighter planes in the area; about 60 jets and a few FW-190s were encountered. They shot down 16 of our B-17s.

Two B-17s in our squadron were shot down. One blew up and one spiraled down. Ed Schoch saw seven chutes. Our fighter planes shot down 20 Jerries and destroyed 335 parked German planes on eight airfields in the Zerbst area. We were lucky, but disappointed, that no German fighters came close enough for us to fire on them. Zerbst is about 20 miles southeast of Magdeberg in NE Germany and about 70 miles southeast of Berlin.

**Mission 14:** On April 11, 1945, more than 1,250 heavy bombers attacked six marshalling yards, two airfields, two ordnance depots and an ammunition factory in southern Germany. Our target was railyards in and around Donauworth, which is located 20 miles northwest of Augsburg and 50 miles south of Nuremberg. This was our 14th combat mission. We shacked the target from 25,500 feet where the temperature was –37c. Flak was moderate but accurate. We sustained a few holes in the right wing and left horizontal stabilizer but no damage to any vital parts. We saw no fighters until we left the target and were on our way back. There was a flight of six jets that flew parallel to us but decided not to attack. They were just out of range of our .50-caliber guns. We completed the seven-hour mission about noon, just in time for some good old Army chow.

**Mission 15:** On April 14, 1945, 1,161 bombers hit 22 defensive installations consisting of anti-aircraft and artillery positions and strong-points covering the Gironde estuary. Other Allied Air Forces and French Naval units attacked similar targets. The air attacks preceded a ground assault by French detachments of a 6th Army Group on the German defense pockets which denied Allies use of port facilities in the Bordeaux area. Our bomber group dropped incendiaries on anti-aircraft positions in Royan, a town at the mouth of the Gironde estuary (bay) that leads downstream to the city of Bordeaux, population of about 250,000. We shacked the target but were buffeted around severely by the moderate but accurate anti-aircraft fire. This was a short five-hour mission. We were on oxygen for only two hours. After diving away from the target and leaving the bomb run it was a welcome feeling to know we were flying back to our field over friendly French people.

**Mission 16:** On April 15, 1945, our crew was one of 850 B-17s to bomb Royan, France again. The sole operational employment of napalm jelly bombs by the 8th Air Force in World War II occurred on this mission. It was carried out against German ground installations (pillboxes, gun pits, tank trenches and heavy gun emplacements) in defensive pockets at Royan. Results were negligible and headquarters recommended discontinuance of the use of napalm against this type of target. The mission was in support of assault by French ground troops under the 6th Army Group on German defensive installations in the Gironde estuary. I had a twinge of conscience seeing those black jelly bombs dropping down and exploding upon contact with the ground into large fire balls that spread over large areas. However, they were meant to destroy defensive installations, not civilian targets. Again, we returned safely over friendly France back to our airfield with a minimum of damage to our plane.

**Mission 17:** On April 18, 1945, our crew flew its final combat mission of World War II. We were briefed to bomb railroad yards at Straubing in Bavaria along with 750 other B-17s. Marshalling yards, a rail bridge and two transformer stations were also hit with 500-pound demolition bombs. We didn't see much of the target because of fairly large masses of clouds and only a few openings. We bombed at 25,000 feet and were on oxygen for four hours of an eight-hour mission. We encountered mild anti-air-craft fire and no fighter opposition, whereas the day before about 50 German fighters, mostly jets, were met at the same target areas. Four German jets and nine conventional fighter planes were shot down.

We flew back and landed safely at our base, not knowing that today was our last combat mission. However, we did go on two mercy missions to Amsterdam and The Hague to drop food to the starving Dutch people before the war ended. The flights were made on May 1 and May 3. The war ended on May 8, 1945. We flew over main airports of these two cities at 300 feet and dropped the crated food out of our bomb bay. We were told that we had a secret treaty with Hitler to drop the food. However, we were wary and manned our guns in case the Germans would disobey the treaty and fire on us. The flights were uneventful. There was no interference from the German anti-aircraft batteries pointed at us from the outer perimeters of the airfields. It was an awesome sight to see hundreds of people on bikes racing from all corners of the cities to the airports as our planes approached overhead.

Finally, V-E Day came and we were one of the lucky crews to be chosen to fly over the milling, joyful, hysterical crowds in Paris.

Billy K. put our B-17 on a vertical turn around the Eiffel Tower at an altitude below the height of the famous structure. The tens of thousands of people were so close we could almost see the whites of their eyes. It was an awesome scene that brought tears of happiness and pride to my eyes and to many others, I am sure.

After a few more tight and low turns around the Tower, and an even lower pass over the waving people in the famous street leading to the structure, we headed back to the air base. We flew at a low level over many small French towns. Many of the happy and thankful residents waved at us as we flew overhead on our way back over Normandy and the English Channel to England.

Our next flight was on May 9. Again, we were one of the lucky crews to be sent on a tour of Germany. We took a half-dozen ground crew personnel with us to have them see first-hand what their B-17s and other Allied aircraft had done to Nazi Germany. We flew at low level over such towns as Essen, Hannover and Frankfurt. The buildings in these towns were in shambles. Any structures still standing were just shells—four walls with nothing but debris in the center. In defense of the near total destruction of Nazi Germany from the air by Allied Air Forces, we must remember: Hitler and his cohorts started it. Early in the war they attacked England with bombers, buzz bombs, and later with V-2 rockets. The V-2 rockets were often sent up from German installations right through our B-17 formations as we were dropping bombs on them. I saw three V-2 rockets launched skyward through our formation during three different missions of ours. They rose many thousands of feet above us. They left behind huge vapor trails as they ultimately leveled off and pointed their nose toward an unsuspecting English town.

# THE BOYS WITH THE CLIPPED WINGS

By Homer Bruce Pou, pilot, 560th Squadron

*Homer Pou arrived in England in January, 1944 and was shot down on his fifth mission, the March 8, 1944 raid on Berlin, flying "Return Engagement." His regular plane, "Lucy Poo," was in for repairs. Pou spent the remainder of the war as POW #3735 in Stalag Luft III. Following are excerpts from his diary, kept during the evacuation march from his prison, and presented exactly as he wrote it. The "Bob" mentioned in the narrative was his co-pilot, Robert Laubach. The following forward was written by another POW, Dave Pollak.*

This tale is dedicated to the boys with the clipped wings. The lads who are fighting the war the hard way, waiting...waiting...waiting for some faint spark to light their dreary hours. Perhaps it will be the mail or clothes, or the sound of bombs on Berlin or Leipzig. Theirs is an untold tale of human endurance, of what we Americans call guts, pure and simple. Theirs is a tale of a fight with death; the fight they won. No decorations, glory or promotions await them. Their reward is life itself.

They think of their lucky buddies safe at home, wearing ribbons, wings and covered with glory. But in reality, the men here are the lucky ones. There are some who had been blown out when their planes exploded; some who had gone down unconscious, crashed, and had lived to tell about it; some who had bailed out of flaming planes into the sure, cold death of the North Sea, only to have their pilot-less plane circle them, drop a life raft, and crash, burning, into the sea after them; some who had spent days alone in the sea without food or drink; some who had fought seemingly unending battles against insurmountable odds, and had lived to tell their tale.

310

These are the lucky ones. Though they outwardly bemoan their unhappy existence and envy their friends at home, inwardly they know that they are fortunate—fortunate because God saw fit to pluck them from certain destruction, that they might live.

Dave Pollak, POW

**Evacuation Notes:**

Big evac. flap raged throughout camp for several days previous to actual movement. Everything was in rumor stage. Room 12 feeling was we wouldn't be moved; however, we were all flapping and making preparations. On the day of evac., we had a communal Victrola in the room for our use while ours was being repaired. For one D-bar we had purchased a package of excellent needles and for several days had been playing classical records in the communal collection. They were splendid records and were being enjoyed very much. Got six new symphonies just after lunch and by meal time had played five of them. The last, Beethoven's Sixth, or Pastorale, was just waiting for the table to be cleared.

The British Red Cross Christmas parcels were given out the week before; one for three, and our four boxes of pancake flour. Saturday, we bashed all those off at the rate of four cakes each, with goon honey. Fish dished up a big gash cake for tea time and we had ample coffee. It was the end of our first week on full parcels since Sept. 11, so we were really in. We bashed off eight cans of salmon for supper plus spuds plus a big Klim pie mit raisins and chocolate. We finished eating and were sitting around shooting the breeze as per usual while waiting for the wash water to get hot.

*You Can't Take It With You* opened to a first night audience at 7:30 p.m. At 8:05, Col. Goodrich stopped the play and gave the order for everyone to get to his block and be ready to move out in 30 minutes. Being next to the theater, we got the dope almost immediately and were galvanized into action. Wright, Clausen, Ramsey, McIntosh, Levin and myself used GI blanket rolls ala Civil War. Fisher, Woody, Sereno and Bob used shirts sewn up for packs. Mayer, Epps, and Everts used one-piece longjohns as packs with Red Cross suitcases. Turner had built an Indian pack carrier and sewn up a shirt to use with it. The room was in a complete shambles by the time everyone was ready. We mixed a big jug of Klim and cleaned out the cupboard pretty thoroughly for food to carry. By 9:30 we were all formed and ready to go.

It was a pretty night—fairly clear, no wind and the cold wasn't penetrating. After waiting in line for quite awhile, we began to move and so we took our last look at Stalag Luft III.

Word was passed back that Col. Goodrich ordered that there be no escapes. It was followed by word that the goons said they would shoot two men for every escapee. This later proved to be just a rumor.

Not long after midnight the temperature dropped considerably and a strong cutting wind sprang up. With short intervals for rest and a goon issue of bread and marge we marched thus 'til after daylight. Our first stop was Gross Seltzen. We were put into a barn there around 11 a.m. and given a five-hour rest. We bashed food, lightened our loads and, with hot water kindly provided in small quantities by the farmers, consumed all the coffee possible before trying to catch 40 winks.

The next stage of the journey was undoubtedly the most difficult. The goons issued each man a ½-pound of marge as we started out into the light snowfall. Darkness came soon and with the cessation of the snow there was a drop to subzero temperature with a freezing wind of 25-35 mph cutting us to the bone. Just eating hunks of plain marge and lumps of sugar from time to time managed to keep most of us on our feet. The entire march that night I was aware of the fact, as were several others, that to stop and sit down would mean inability to keep going, so during each rest stop we would remain standing, just moving our feet in an effort to keep circulation up. Nothing would get them warm except brisk walking, and our marching degenerated into a 6-inch sliding stumble-and-stagger combination that would have seemed funny had we been normal.

The guards marching along with us were in no better condition. One guard threw his rifle down and a Kriegie carried it for him for quite a distance before he would consent to take it back. Most of the guards started the night before with enormous field packs which we estimated to weigh at least 75 lbs. On the first night one of them gave us quite a laugh by just walking out of his pack with a contemptuous *"kaput!"* and, not even looking back, he trudged forward.

After remaining 4 km away for hours, we crawled into Muskau, making our night's march 25 km and our total distance from Sagan, 55 km. A tile factory with its cement floor and slight warmth was Seventh Heaven to us that night. We bedded down at 2 a.m. fully dressed except for our wet shoes and socks, and sank into oblivion. The factory proved to be an excellent home. It was comparatively clean and well lighted, and after moving a lot of pipes outside we were not too cramped for space. A hot water faucet at one end of the building remained operational most of the time and a workers' kitchen upstairs gave us assistance with oatmeal, barley, etc. We remained there all Monday and Monday night. In the middle of Monday night, some 250-odd men from the West camp joined us and filled up every inch of remaining space. You could walk all over the building without putting on shoes and never see the floor. We again hit the road Tuesday morning at 9:30 with the column reversed, the sergeants in the lead. Bob remained at Muskau, to come on with the West camp. His side was beginning to show signs of giving trouble.

The march that day was comparatively easy. We covered 18 km and put up for the night in a barn at Graustein. The last day's march was a snap as we only had 7 km to go to Spremberg. We stopped at a large panzer school and went into an empty repair garage for our short stay. The goons issued us hot barley soup, which was declared by all to be damn good. At 3 we started for the train and arrived there to be herded together; 51 men in our tiny European boxcar. For two-and-a-half days and three nights, there we were until we got off Saturday morning at Moosberg. It was a continuous nightmare of being crowded, cramped and exceedingly uncomfortable.

We were short on water, food, time for any natural activity, space, temper, light and any relaxation of tired legs and feet was almost impossible. We got off the train only to go into a barn that was inferior to any other barns we had been in. Nearly 600 men were jammed into one barn. The goons did issue warm tea in the mornings, soup at noon, spuds, bread and a spread in the late afternoon. Air inside was always foul and there was a lot of sickness and dysentery.

> *Pou's son, Bruce, reports the following: "After the war, my father was hospitalized and treated for severe depression and physical wounds he received when he was shot down. Like many other veterans, he didn't talk very much about his wartime experience. The depression he suffered after the war was due primarily to the feeling that he somehow let his country down by not completing his missions. My father died from cancer in 1981."*

# A Prisoner of War

By Raymond Harwood, engineer and top turret gunner
Paul Williams' crew, 562nd Squadron

I was a prisoner of war from Oct. 10, 1943 until May 7, 1945, being held mostly at Stalag 17B at Krems, Austria, by the German Government.

Incidentally, that date, Oct. 10, 1943, was also my 23rd birthday.

But just a little background on myself. I was born Oct. 10, 1920 in the village of South Shaftsbury in the town of Shaftsbury, Vermont, in Bennington County. After a childhood in this small rural community, and completion of the 8th grade at the local grammar school, I went to North Bennington High School, walking (mostly) three miles each way, and graduated in 1938. Like most young men of my age, I then started working at whatever I could find, but in a reasonable time found employment with the Eagle Square Manufacturing Co. owned by Stanley Tools. I made carpenter squares.

Conditions in the world seemed to make a war almost certain, so in 1941 I enlisted in the Vermont National Guard, Co. I, 172nd Infantry Division. Soon, with the bombing of Pearl Harbor, this outfit was alerted for active Federal service. The physical examination then required revealed that I had a hernia, and I was automatically discharged without any recourse. In early 1942 I had an operation to repair this condition, and in July received my draft call, although I had been told that I could not enlist until six months after the operation. From here things moved fast. On Aug. 4, 1942 I had my full physical and on Aug. 18 departed for active duty. First stop, Fort Evens, Massachusetts for initial processing and assignment to the Army Air Force. Next stop, Miami Beach, Florida for more processing, a little basic training and a school assignment to a B-17 specialist Aircraft Mechanic course, lasting four months at Amarillo, Texas. This was followed by six weeks of Aerial Gunnery School at Las Vegas, Nevada, then a move to Salt Lake City for assignment to a bomb group.

I joined the 388th Bomb Group, 562nd Squadron, when it was formed in Boise, Idaho. We completed our so-called phase training there and in Wendover AFB, Utah, and Sioux City, Iowa, and then to England and into the 8th Air Force in May 1943, flying the first mission to Amsterdam around the middle of July. On Oct. 9, we flew a mission to Gydnia, Poland and on the return trip lost about 15 feet of our right wing over Norway or Denmark. We were hit by a group of FW-190s. Our assigned *Little Lass*, #25898, was out for an inspection and we were flying another plane called *Li'l One*, as best as I remember.

Following this mission we were awakened around 3 a.m. the next morning for a briefing for another mission, our 18th, which turned out to be Munster. I don't remember the scheduled take-off time; however, I do remember that this was delayed because, according to Intelligence, the German Air Force was up there waiting for us. Prior to the scheduled take-off, the mission was again delayed. We had another meal and finally took off on a nice, sunny Sunday at about 11 a.m. As I remember, there were no incidents during the climb out and form up, except that we lost our intercom system. Since we were flying Lead ship of the Low Squadron, the pilot had to stay on "command" and the rest of the crew had no communication whatsoever. I suppose we could, and maybe should, have aborted the mission; however, we had never aborted. We were leading the Group in the number of missions, had never stopped for a rest and relaxation period, and I guess we were a little gung ho. At any rate, we started in with no intercom system.

As I remember, we picked up our escort on schedule. They stayed up pretty well to the IP. We encountered some flak, but mostly moderate and not too accurate. The 100th Group was in sight in front of us. At about the IP they picked up very heavy fighter attack from all quarters and of a very persistent nature from the ME-109s, FW-190s, JU-88s, ME-110s and ME-210s. The 100th Bomb Group was literally shot to pieces in a very short time and there were parachutes and B-17s going down, seems like all over. I recall mentally counting up to 100 parachutes. And then it was our turn.

I was flying the top turret and we were suddenly being hit from behind. Our number three engine was hit in the upper aft section of the nacelle with either a 20mm or a small rocket and the engine just stopped without our being able to feather it. Seems like about the same time a JU-88 just seemed to appear off our right wing tip and just a little higher. I gave him a long burst with both .50-caliber machine guns and definitely saw his cockpit turret canopy fly off. However, too many other things were happening to follow him. It seemed that we lost RPMs on our Number 4 engine, but I don't know for sure why it wasn't feathered, or really what was the matter with it. Without intercoms we had no way to find out anything other than what we could see. At about this time we dropped our bombs.

Shortly thereafter, all the .50-caliber ammo left in my ammo cans went sailing up into the turret canopy. For a second this bewildered me and I then realized that we had gone pretty well over on our back and were in a spinning dive out of formation. Again, without our interphone system, we could not receive instructions from Lt. Paul Williams, the pilot. At this point, Lt. Garver, the navigator, tapped me on the leg indicating a bail out. A quick glance into the cockpit revealed the co-pilot, Lt. Rogg, getting out of his seat. Our air speed was up around 350 mph (the aircraft was redlined at 305) and the altimeter was unwinding too fast to read. I immediately put on my chest chute and dropped into the nose section crawlway. Here I found Lt. Macy had tried to bail out without jettisoning the nose hatch door. Consequently, he was hung up with just his head visible, hung by the back straps of his parachute harness on the inside hatch door handle. I lifted him by the chute harness at the shoulder, pushed the door away and released him. I never saw him again. I then closed the hatch door, pulled the release handle, pulled the hinge pins and kicked the door free. Lt. Garver then left. Just as I left the aircraft we took a hit from probably a 20mm in the nose section and I received some small fragments in the top of my head. As best I could figure, we, at that time, were at about 20,000 feet. Our altitude over the target was 27,000 feet. I free-fell until I stabilized on my back and then pulled the ripcord and got a perfect opening at about 15,000 feet.

Things at that point were so very quiet that it seemed like the war had suddenly left us. After awhile I heard a strange noise behind me as I floated down. Turning, I discovered a German fighter coming straight at me and I thought he was firing his machine guns. Actually he had throttled back and it was only the engine noise that I had heard. He banked part-way around me, wobbled his wings and flew away.

My drift in the chute was taking me toward a large canal or river, so I attempted to slip the chute. The first time it was okay but it didn't seem to be doing what I wanted, so I tried again much harder. That time the chute nearly collapsed so I decided to let well enough alone and land wherever I might. I actually landed high in a pine tree and had quite a time getting down. I started removing my heavy flying clothes on the move. Before I could get the flying pants off, I encountered a German soldier who took me into custody. It's a good thing he did, because shortly thereafter some armed civilians appeared and I feel sure they would have shot first.

According to the rest of the crew, the ship had continued earthward, but no one else was able to bail out because of the centrifugal force. The pilot was finally able to pull out of the dive just off the ground. The remaining fighters who initially hit us were still with them. There were still two engines running and the pilot had her headed home with seven men aboard—five gunners, pilot and co-pilot. The pilot thought he and the co-pilot were alone. The gunners kept pecking away at the fighters until they got all of them. By this time they were really shot up and nearly back to the North Sea. Running on two engines, he was unable to gain any altitude and was flying so low that he hit the ball turret and the tail on top of a dike. Shortly after this, he knocked out Number 2 engine on a steel post in the marshes, just before reaching the sea. With only Number 1 engine running, they prepared to ditch the ship, which they did about three miles from the coast. Their hopes were still high as they climbed into two rubber life rafts. They thought for sure that the British Air Sea Rescue would pick them up, but it was the Germans who picked them up about 11 hours later. All of this I was unaware of until I met the rest of the crew at Dulag Luft, Frankfurt on the Mein, Germany. All 10 of us were prisoners of war, unhurt, except for a few scratches and the 20mm fragment in my head, which I really wasn't fully aware of at the time.

Now to go back to the point where I landed by parachute in Germany. After they picked me up, they took me to the city of Greven where I stayed that night under German guard, as I remained until May, 1945. The next day, they moved me to a Luftwaffe field about 30 miles away. Here I joined about 12 other captured airmen who had been shot down the day before. None of us trusted the other for fear each might be a German spy.

A couple of days later they moved us down to the sweat box outside Frankfurt. Here we were held until they interrogated us. I was here 10 days with a daily ration of one piece of bread and one cup of water. Finally, they took me out, questioned me and took me down to Dulag Luft where I met most of the rest of the crew and found out about the remainder. It was sure a relief to see them all alive.

While at Dulag Luft we didn't do much except have our pictures taken and be fingerprinted for the German files. We received small kits of toilet articles sent by the YMCA, and a GI overcoat. After about three days here they loaded us into boxcars for a trip to our permanent camp, Stalag 17B. The boxcars were what they called 40-or-8, meaning they would hold 40 men or eight horses. They put 48 of us in each car for the three-day ride to Krems, Austria, where we were interned.

At Stalag 17B there were 4,300 Americans after the camp was filled in April, 1944, plus Russians, Siberians, French, English and Italian prisoners, bringing the total in the camp to about 15,000. Each of the different nationalities was kept separated, and we Americans lived far better than the rest, but only because we got some Red Cross parcels. Our barracks were overcrowded so that we lived like sardines in a can. Each barrack was split into two parts with a washroom in-between. Each half was about 100 feet long and 40 feet wide, housing 150 men. The camp was split up into compounds of four barracks each. We stood roll call about three times a day and shake downs for prohibited articles two or three times a week. They were apt to be pulled at any time of the day or night.

The food that the Germans gave us was very poor, consisting mostly of dehydrated soup, which had more maggot-like worms in it than anything else. A number of times men were killed trying to escape. Escape from this camp was nearly impossible. The Russians were dying like flies and I had seen as many as 30 being taken out for burial in one day. Their casket was a piece of canvas wrapped around them. They gave the Americans a regular military funeral.

During the summer we had some sports with improvised equipment. The sports were mostly softball, soccer and boxing. During the winters we had no fuel and most of our time was spent bundled in overcoats trying to play cards, read, or something else to keep warm. Both winters I was there I suffered frostbitten (frozen) feet.

Many incidents stand out about the life of a POW. I guess one which I will never forget was the German guards trying to open and later close a small roller-locking-bladed pocket knife that I had when I was captured. By depressing the blade fully-closed and tipping the handle in the proper direction it would cause a roller to engage the blade and lock it closed. Held in the reverse position it would unlock the blade and a spring would partly open the blade. They nearly went crazy trying to figure it out and couldn't get it through their heads when I showed them. I don't guess they ever got it figured out.

When I was interrogated, a German major insisted on more than my name, rank and serial number. When I refused, he called in a guard, speaking in German. The guard pressed a bayoneted rifle against my ribs and then the major said, "You see, I could have you killed with just a word to the guard." Needless to say, I was scared and not at all sure of just what was going to happen, but I replied to him that if he were the prisoner and

I in his place, he would only tell me as much as I had told him; and like him, I was a soldier. At this point he excused me and I was never really interrogated again.

Often during roll call we would move men around while the guards were counting, to confuse their count—sometimes with a man short and other times too many men. I don't think they ever really caught on to this one, but they always had to recount until it came out right, or they thought it did. About once every three months we were sent to a de-lousing chamber where we were given a shower, had our heads clipped, our clothes fumigated and then stood around in the nude for three or four hours waiting to receive our clothes and be marched back into camp. In the shower rooms, the gas jets that they could probably have used to liquidate us were readily evident and we always wondered if they would use them on us, or had used them on others.

In Stalag 17B we were allowed to mingle with the British prisoners, even though they were housed in another compound. There were only a few of them and we enjoyed talking to them. One night, I remember a group of English bombers coming in. The pathfinder marked out our camp, we thought, to insure the bomb-laden craft would know where we were. Then they dropped the so-called "Christmas Tree" flares directly over us and we knew we were the target instead of an airfield a short distance from the camp. I heard men actually pray in fright as we huddled in slit trenches waiting for the bombs. I guess someone found their mistake at the very last minute and the bombers went into a hard bank and the bombs missed us with no damage.

One other time, two P-38 Lightenings eased over camp to start a strafing run on a bridge and river traffic on the Danube River near us. They made two passes and wobbled their wings at us, obviously knowing we were there. On another occasion, a group of 15th AF bombers came in from a direction we had never seen before and with bomb bays open. They bombed Krems, the town outside the camp. These events were good for our morale.

Most times we could tell if things were going badly for the German forces. The poorer they were going, the less water we had. They would only turn it on maybe twice a day for 30 minutes. If they seemed to be doing well, as in early 1944, the water was on all day.

On April 7, 1945, we were marched out of Stalag 17B in the face of oncoming Russian forces. We were put in groups of about 500 men and marched directly across Austria toward the American lines. The following is a word-for-word, untouched copy of the diary that I kept, in pencil, on the forced march:

*April 7, 1945*: For the past few days rumor has it that we evacuate the camp in face of the advancing Russians. We are supposed to go tomorrow, and all that we can't carry is being destroyed. Our march is supposed to take seven days, and we leave here in groups of 500. The way we feel I don't think I can take the 10 miles. Food is really scarce. I really hate to leave under German guard, but I have maps and other essentials for escape, except food. I'll see what the future brings.

*April 8, 1945:* We left camp this morning at about 10:30 and marched 26kms to Naigen, where we slept in a barn, all tired men. The Germans haven't fed us all day and all we have eaten is what we were carrying with us. The country is rough mountain country, and we are using country roads. We are doing much better than I thought men in our physical condition could.

*April 9, 1945:* Traveled 18 kms to Zening, Austria today and again no food. A barn for shelter, as last night. Legs sore, but I'm taking it much better than I thought I would. Maybe the Germans think we don't need to eat. Once in awhile, when the guards will allow it, we are able to buy bread with some soap or cigarettes.

*April 10, 1945:* Eighteen months as a POW today. We remain in Zening all day and tonight. Two meals of barley (dish water) soup, our first since we left camp. Aside from this, five of us (Conners, Gardin, Cornwell, Moore and myself) had a hen we stole. Reported that our old camp, Stalag 17B, was bombed by Russians. Also, four men from my old barracks, 34-A, were killed or wounded trying to escape. There are storm troopers and volkstrom men everywhere.

*April 11, 1945:* We made 16 kms to Bergen, Austria, the last two uphill, to stay in another barn. No chow today. All is going as well as can be expected, but I'm pretty hungry. What little food we had with us when we left camp is about all gone, and our rations are below starvation.

*April 12, 1945:* Made 14 kms to St. Oswald, Austria, and another barn for shelter tonight. Rained nearly all day and all got plenty wet. Hard marching in the mud. Received small bread ration (18 men to a loaf). Good weather for ducks, but pretty cold even for them.

*April 13, 1945:* A hard day today. Twenty-five kms in the rain and mud and over the worst mountains we have hit. Staying in Grevin, Austria, tonight in a barn and, of course, no chow. It's Friday the 13th for sure today. Looks like we are the flying infantry on foot.

*April 14, 1945:* We didn't move today and the weather is fair. Getting our clothes dried out. Two hot meals today. It must have broken their hearts to give us those. Saw our first game yesterday; three deer, and they sure looked swell, so free and beautiful. It must be wonderful to be free. It's been so long since I have been that way that I'm not sure what it is like. I'm sure a lot of people back home don't appreciate the fact that they are free and have enough to eat and a place to stay, to say nothing of not being pushed around with a gun.

*April 15, 1945:* Made 20 kms to Nearn, Austria and sleep. To date we have been moving southwest from Krems toward Linz, Austria. Today has been nice and we have broken out of the hills into the Danube Valley, which makes marching easier. To date, we have received six hot meals from the Germans, such as they were. Also had two bread and biscuit rations. Four potatoes were our grub for today.

*April 16, 1945:* Made 20 kms today and reached Styregg, Austria. Bread and biscuits before we started and after 3 kms we got hot soup.

*April 17, 1945:* Rest today and one meal from Jerry with a small ration of bread. Hot all day. We go through Linz tomorrow. Plenty of bombs and craters around here, and also quite bit of activity. We stole a chicken today.

*April 18, 1945:* We made 31 kms today and our only meal a small dish of soup and a piece of bread. Went through Linz and crossed the Danube to the southern side. Staying in Weifing, Austria in a barn tonight. Linz was pretty well bombed out, and the Americans hit it again today about two hours after we passed through.

*April 19, 1945:* We made 17 kms today with a small food ration (two spoonfuls of pork, 1/5 loaf of bread, three potatoes and margarine). We sleep in a barn tonight in the town of Kaltenton. It's surprising what a man can do on so little to eat. Passed by an air drome with mostly Messerschmitt 109s, all old and Hungarian pilots. We were buzzed by two P-38s and some of the boys hit the ditch in fear of being strafed. All the German guards did too. The Germans fired anti-aircraft guns at them directly overhead.

*April 20, 1945:* Made 25 kms today to Kallham, Austria. Not too bad a day and we lay over tomorrow. Soup for supper, and we sleep under the stars tonight. Rumor has it only three more days on the road.

*April 21, 1945:* A big surprise today. Red Cross parcels came in by truck from Switzerland and we sure needed them. All the trucks were American Chevrolets and GMCs driven by English POWs. Sleeping in a wagon bed under a shed tonight. It looks like rain. Just soup from the Jerries for supper.

*April 22, 1945:* It rained all night last night. Made 23 kms. Aurolmunster, Austria, in a bitter cold rain and wind that lasted all day. Had small ration of bread and soup for dinner.

*April 23, 1945:* We made 23 kms to Althein, Austria. Hail all day. The roads muddy and hard on hiking GIs. We expect a lay-over tomorrow. Only one day left to reach our destination. No food today.

*April 24, 1945:* We layed over today. Cloudy, but no rain. Soup from Jerries and a small ration of bread. All of this bread on the march and also in the prison camp was made out of sawdust.

*April 25, 1945:* We made 30 kms today to end our trip. A hard day. The new camp is a spruce forest and we built a lean-to for tonight and probably will fix it up more tomorrow. We have to walk a mile for drinking water. We passed through Braunau, Hitler's birthplace. Quite a few American P-51s strafing while we were on the march. All we had to build the lean-tos with were small jack knives.

*April 26, 1945:* Improved our shelter, and received parcels today, three to four men. Jerry rationed 18 men to a loaf of bread, one spoonful of salt, one spoonful of barley and a little horsemeat. Gardin has been sick for the past few days. Medical officer Major Beaumont (American) has charge of us. Ordered us not to escape.

*April 27, 1945:* We're still trying to fix up our shelter. It's tough with only two pen knives. Jerry rationed three potatoes today.

*April 28, 1945:* It rained all day and last night. All of us wet to the skin and a wet bed for tonight. This is really roughing it. The Jerries can't feed us. We had a half-cup of barley for four men, and one-half-cracker per man today. Conners and I have GIs coming on. Gardin is still sick.

*April 29, 1945:* The weather is fair today and maybe we can get some clothes dry. We took Gardin to the hospital, which is an old barn. It's a wonder more aren't there. The rumor last night was that the war is over, but I guess it's not true. Sure wish the end would hurry up and come. I don't feel so good today. We received Red Cross parcels—one to two men. The five of us got one English, one American, and a half a French parcel. I saw my first jet propelled plane today. It's starting to rain a little. Probably means another wetting, but I sure hope not.

*April 30, 1945:* Not a bad day today. It has tried to rain all day but nothing to amount to anything. Gunfire not too far away and I sure hope it is the Yanks. They can't come too fast. The Russian prisoners are starving to death, those that the Jerries don't shoot. Sometimes it sounds like first day of deer season here.

*May 1, 1945:* It was damp and cold all day, which made it miserable. A few potatoes and some horsemeat from the Germans. The Yanks are not far away. We can see the tanks and hear the guns just across the Inns River. Got the GIs (gastro-intestinals) worse; not feeling good.

*May 2, 1945:* It snowed last night. Up most of the night with GIs. What a life. Americans within a few miles of us. They can't come too soon.

*6:30 p.m.:* We're free men! Capt. Summers of California from the 13th Armored Division of the 3rd Army came into camp telling us we were no longer prisoners of war. If I wasn't so sick, I'd be the happiest man in the world. Still under German guard tonight.

*May 3, 1945:* A rainy day. Today I saw something I have been waiting a long time to see. U.S. infantrymen came in and disarmed the few German guards left with us. They were plenty rough and we, the ex-POWs, took everything they had except the clothes they had on and personal property. We captured a lot more Germans around this area with guns we took from our former guards plus a few we got from the Yank infantry boys that freed us. Five of our boys ran into 12 Hitler youth kids and had to shoot five before they would surrender. We eat tomorrow from food we have taken from the Germans. It's take what you want off the Jerry; they did it to us and now it's our turn. And they don't like it! Gardin has already been moved, probably back to a base hospital. He is pretty sick. We should move out of here in a day or so. Most of the former guards have seen their last sunshine.

*May 4, 1945:* Fair weather until evening and then the usual rain. Conners is sick. Moore has been gone all day and it now looks like he will stay out tonight. Since re-capture we haven't had anything except one-tenth loaf of bread. A lot of the boys have gone out to towns and farms to get food, against direct orders from the lieutenant colonel in charge of the re-captured forces. It's either go out and find some food or forget your stomach. I never was so hungry. But I'm getting too sick or weak to even go after water. A lot of the boys are getting sick from lack of food or sleeping on the ground. About 75% of the camp has dysentery, or diarrhea, or both. Quite a lot of confiscated German food came into camp but only the so-called big wheels got any of it. They are wonderful camp leaders.

*May 5, 1945:* A little rain this morning. Conners has gone to the hospital. We haven't seen Moore since yesterday morning. Just two of the original five still together (Cornwell and myself). No one seems to know about food or when we move out. Hope one or the other takes place soon. I'm surprised not to be at least fed after being in the United States hands again.

Later same day: Received K-rations and marched 11 kms. in the rain to a factory and shelter. We left the forest camp around 7 p.m. and carried but very little of our clothes or bedding. We left those to the Russians who needed them worse than we did, because they will have to make their own way home.

*May 6, 1945:* We are in a very modern aluminum factory untouched by bombs. Millions of dollars worth of equipment in it and well supplied stock rooms. We start processing tomorrow and moving out. All of us are supposed to be out in five days. We're still sleeping on the floor, but it's dry. Still eating K-rations, but it's a million times better than what we've had the last 19 months. It's been a month since I've had a bath or been undressed. I sure would love a hot bath, clean clothes and a good bed. Nothing could be better at present.

*May 7, 1945: The war is over!*

# Epilogue: Remembering VE-Day

By Bill Rellstab, navigator
Lou Tilley's crew, 562nd Squadron

In a ritual parting salute, our stripped-down Flying Fortress circled the Eiffel Tower and dipped its wing so that our passengers could take one last look at Paris.

They were ground personnel from various stations of the 8th Air Force's Third Air Division, being returned to their home bases after a three-day pass. Our one-plane airline, flying between England and Paris during the spring of 1945, was created by Division to provide non-flying personnel with a little of the Air Force's perks and glamour before we all had to pack up and leave Europe. Everybody knew the European war was all but over, and the unmistakable scent of victory had been in the air since winter and the collapse of the Germans' Ardennes offensive.

May 8, 1945, started out as just another routine return trip for the flight crew, consisting of Capt. Louis N. Tilley, pilot, and myself as navigator. We collected our returning passengers at the airfield at Villacoublay, took off, and after completing our routine circle of Paris, set course for our destination in East Anglia, about an hour's flying time.

The course was always the same, Paris to Le Treport, across the Channel to Eastbourne, then a wide swing west around London before we turned back east to the Third Division bomber bases in East Anglia.

The sweeping course around London was more than important—it was life or death. For six years, London was one of the most heavily defended cities in the world, and the air space above it was a forbidden death zone, not only to enemy planes, but to our own planes as well, undoubtedly a precaution against wolves in sheeps' clothing.

Course set for the routine flight, I next tuned in to the Armed Forces Network radio to hear some dance music and the news, and the first thing I heard was the announcement of the German surrender. I immediately switched to intercom and told Tilley the good news. After he had heard it for himself, he called me back and asked for a course to London and informed me we were going to be the first plane to buzz Picadilly Circus.

This did not seem to me to be as good an idea as it apparently seemed to him. We might instead become the first plane to be shot down over London after the war because one lone anti-aircraft gun crew didn't get the word in time, or, instead, did get the word, but after six years of ironclad defense of London, didn't believe it.

I had recently read Erich Maria Remarque's World War I novel, *All Quiet on the Western Front.* I remembered the way that story ended: the young German soldier, at 11 a.m., the moment of armistice, sticks his head above the trench to reach for a butterfly and a French sniper picks him off. Apparently nobody had told the sniper that the war was over, or maybe he was told and didn't believe it. Such things happen. Life is not a scripted event, and armies aren't precision machines. I looked at my watch and my map and was not cheered by my guess that we would be over London at about 11 am. I plotted the course as ordered, and when the Thames came in view, we dropped to a lower altitude and flew up it toward the city. The pilot knew what he wanted to do from that point.

The fact that we had not been shot at yet was encouraging to me, and as the huge, four-engined Flying Fortress thundered over the city, just clearing the building tops at what seemed like mast height, I found myself in the Plexiglas nose viewing the scene of a lifetime.

There were hundreds of thousands of people. It looked like millions. They covered the broad streets and filled the side streets from wall to wall; they were swarming over the statues in Trafalgar Square and Picadilly Circus. Some were waving flags and banners and articles of clothing. It was as if you had kicked off the top of a huge anthill.

I could see their faces. They were all turned up toward us and they were shouting and laughing and waving their arms wildly at us, and I was smiling and waving back. What a way to end the war!

I'd like to think we were the first plane to buzz London. Well, maybe the first bomber, or at least the first B-17.

I wonder if there are still some who were part of that celebrating mass of humanity in Picadilly Circus who remember the lone B-17 that saluted them—and the joy of being alive at about 11 a.m. on May 8, 1945.

# About the Authors

Janet Pack is the daughter of Arthur B. Pack, pilot of *The Princess Pat*, 562nd Squadron, 388th Bombardment Group (H), 45th Combat Wing, 3rd Air Division.

Richard Singer is the son of Bernard E. Singer, field lineman, Battery C, 44th Field Artillery, 4th Infantry Division.

2057102

Made in the USA